ACKNO

This book would not be possible without Love, Life and God. I am deeply grateful for a number of friends and family who have contributed to and supported me in this work. Hannah Smith, Pamela Doherty, Hobie Dodd, Chala Salcedo, Nancy & John Philpott, Dr. Philip and Donna Ralidis, Cheryl Kelso, Dr. Rudolph and Sharon Bauer, Janet & Dale Kent, Carra, Marie Schilly, Debbie Roberts, JoAnn Haley, Barbara Auzenne, Debbie Abohosh, Jennifer Sorrell, Anisa Moretti, Mary Donaldson, Larry Davis, Ryan Smith, Debbie Leonard, Dr. Eric Pearl, and Tameka have gifted me with friendship and love, shared their lives and knowledge with me. I am so thankful for their relationships in my life and for what they mean to me.

I thank my family, Jody Thornton, Kenneth Walker, Diane & Jim Sellers, Ken & Janet Walker, Kirk Walker, LaVerne Hill, Tina and Lon Morgan, Jayson, Da'Shell and Gavin Sellers, Carol and Matt Blundell, and other family members, who may not be named, but have played an integral role in the legacy that has given me roots. I thank them for loving me through difficult times and the good times when we celebrated with love as the healings occurred. When they trusted me to practice on them, I thank them for having faith in me when they thought I might be stretching past the limits of their comfort zone.

My thanks to the people of Crandall, Texas, who voted for me and supported me as together, we changed the face of our community. My thanks to the people who have trusted me to provide love and healing for them. My life has been enriched in ways I could never have imagined. I have learned much. This book is the culmination of the beautiful tapestry of each person that has touched my life. I thank each of you from the bottom of my heart.

FOREWARD

I was at a friend's house for the Labor Day weekend and woke up at 4:00 a.m. Words were pouring from my mind. I reached for my journal and began to write. I went back to sleep and then woke at 7:00 and again at 9:00, each time with words pouring from my mind into the journal. I finally looked at her and said, "You know I have to go home and write this book." This book has been written to share my life experiences, my healing experiences and what I have termed "Gifts from the Heart." These gifts are transforming words that have been received and shared with me in a variety of locations, and from a variety of people.

These are ordinary people who have had extraordinary experiences. They are somewhat uncomfortable with the thought that notoriety may change the experience for them or the lives they live. Therefore, I have honored their request to present the experiences in truth, except where I have changed their names to honor their wishes to remain anonymous.

The words in the "Gifts from the Heart" have a common theme and cadence as if they were from the same Source – God. The conversations have begun in one session and then continued with other people in other locations who do not know each other. If you picked up this book and found that it does not resonate with you, you may want to consider reading a chapter or two before you toss it aside. I have been told these words have changed people's lives.

May they touch you in your life as they have touched me. Listen with your heart and hear the truth within you.

Table of Contents

• CHAPTER 1 •

FROM MY HEART TO YOURS •

"Hello, Vicki."

"Let me just start off by saying, hello again. Welcome to planet earth. Welcome to planet earth. You must think that strange."

"Love, love, love, love, love. How I love you and everyone else here! The power of love is so great. The truth of love is fantastic, extraordinary."

Imagine slipping your foot into your favorite pair of shoes that you had worn at least a hundred times, and suddenly they did not fit you any longer! What would you do if without warning your whole life changed? What would happen if the beliefs you had embraced all your life suddenly seemed expanded and larger than life - beyond that which you could imagine? Would you "go for the ride"? Are you absolutely 100% sure that what you have been taught all your life is the whole truth? What do you really know for sure? What do you really believe? How would you react if suddenly, you were enlightened with a more complete truth? Would you proceed on the journey or would you press the eject button out of fear? I decided to go for the ride and embraced all the possibilities that were in my path.

This book is about that journey and my experiences along the way. It may surprise you. It may even cause you to wonder about life. It may sound familiar to those of you who suffer from the injuries and scars of life. It may not interest you at all. You may find out more than you ever wanted to know about me. For those of you who wish to understand where I am today or how I came to be here now, this present moment in time, this is my story. I am sharing these experiences with you knowing that it will create discomfort for some and freedom for others. It is my truth, and it is a part of my purpose for being here. Believe what you will and leave the rest. Always trust your own heart as the barometer for the truth within you.

As I traveled along this journey, I continued learning more about me, how I honored myself and how I dishonored me at times. I learned that everything we do is a choice. Each challenge we face, we either own our own personal power or we give it away. We choose what is best for us or we allow others to choose for us. We forget that we can always take our power and choices back. Hopefully something in my journey will speak to your heart and help you walk through life and reach your goals.

These experiences are about my connecting with other people, one person at a time, dozens and perhaps even thousands of people at a time. It is about my stepping through the fear and worry of what other people might think and following my heart. I can assure you at times, it was difficult for me to live, write and share about it. Sometimes I regretted my actions, but once it happened, it was history. I could only learn the lessons life experiences provided for me. I would rather repaint the canvas at times, but that would be a different picture. It hurt sometimes to be reminded of the part I played in the process. This book is not written to hurt anyone. It is the truth as I lived and experienced it.

What I realized was that things happened in each of our lives that we would like to forget. In order to heal, I must open the wound to the air, feel the pain, let it heal and then let it go. I can always decide differently starting right this minute. I find the future greatly exciting because of that! The purpose is to assure you that everyone has failures that we hide from others because of what they might think. These failures drain our energy and keep us from reaching new goals in our lives. When we learn to embrace our failures and learn from them, we begin to live liberated lives. As we embrace and forgive ourselves for failing, we become more tolerant and can forgive other people's failures. If we hold others or ourselves to a perfect standard, then no one can measure up or maintain that standard very long.

People who have not traveled down this journey may not understand what living through these experiences teaches you the hard way. When you read about the events in my life, you will learn how I survived. I looked deeply within and found love and hate, goodness and darkness, generosity and greed, anger and hurt. In order to grow, I had to realize that I must embrace all these qualities as a part of me. Learning to own and value the whole of who I am was liberating. May you find something in my story that will help you become liberated and live powerfully.

One of the most important lessons I learned was how very much we are loved, and how important it is to love our brothers and sisters in our families, our communities and our world. When you share the power of love through miracles that have occurred, perhaps you will recognize miracles in your own life. The truth is that miracles are occurring around us all the time.

The Package Love Comes In

My spiritual path has always been about how to become more loving. My life has been greatly influenced by my faith in God and a close relationship with Jesus. He is a very important person in my life. He is a friend that I have relied on in times of great joy as well as sorrow and everything in between. In my younger days, I would ask him to help me find my keys or extend the gas in my gas tank beyond its capacity. He never failed me.

I was a challenging child for my parents. At age 4, my mother discovered I could read when I started reading instructions on how to assemble a product over her shoulder. I could read the Reader's Digest before I was in kindergarten. I had an intuitive gift and although it scared others a little, for me, it was just incorporated into my life. I know my parents did not receive the parenting "how-to" manual for kids with such gifts.

I have spent a great deal of my life learning more about God. When I would sit in the Southern Baptist Church I grew up in, I would know in my heart that the angry God they talked about didn't match the picture I had of God. I didn't challenge it, but I didn't believe it. The God I knew loved me and was very real to me. When an emergency would happen in my family, I would calmly say, "Let's pray about it. God will take care of us." And He would - just like that!

Music was a huge part of my life. When I was in high school, I traveled with musical groups from my church, the Christian Contemporary Singers (CCS) and the Reveilles. We toured and sang at churches and events throughout the country, performed at the State Fair of Texas, and sang on the Capitol steps in Washington, D.C. We taught Vacation Bible School in California, and even appeared on television on the *Ted Mack Amateur Hour*. Music helped me connect to God and feel an affinity with other people in my church family.

As I grew older, I knew God was there in my life the whole time. Sometimes He carried me. One dark day in my life when I cried out in despair, "Where are you when I need you?" I heard the voice in my car as I drove down the street.

> *"Vicki, Trust in Me. Keep your eyes upon Me. I will take care of you."* [1]

That got my attention. I heard the voice and there was no one else in the car with me. After the shock wore off, I realized I had been given this huge gift. I didn't tell anyone for a long time what happened. I worried that people would think I had lost it. I was under duress at the time, but I was comforted to know He would speak directly to me.

I read the One-Year Bible, although it took me two years to complete it. The verses meant so much to me. When I reviewed the events that have occurred in my life and particularly over the last two years, I continued to marvel and wonder at the amazing Grace of God and His connection to each of us. We are so important to Him. We have the ability to live in God's grace and walk daily with Him.

This was a challenge to a young girl from divorced parents before divorce was a common occurrence. As a young child, my mother and dad built a loving home. We struggled as most young families did at that time. My mother spent a lot of time rocking and singing to us as we grew from babies to young children. She read us stories and struggled to be the best mother she could be. Her mother died when she was three years old. Her role model for motherhood was imagined and borrowed from different experiences in her life.

I expected "unconditional love" from my family. I held it up as a standard and earthly love fell short of that expectation. I didn't realize it was because unconditional love comes from God and animals. People can't quite "get that" yet. Our idea of love gets blended with conditions, judgments and wounded feelings. My siblings and parents have always communicated their love and shown it in many ways. My extended family spent many hours and visits together sharing fun, music, love and laughter. I was surrounded with love and felt that love, but didn't always feel lovable or loved. I know that doesn't make sense exactly, but that was what I felt as a child and teenager. I just wanted to know I was important enough to have personal attention. I kept telling myself that it was all right. I didn't really need to be singled out, but it wasn't true. I wanted what every person on the planet wants — to be loved and accepted for who I was without conditions.

When my parents divorced, it was during a vulnerable time in my life. I needed my mom's attention, but there little time for anything other than survival in her life. My mother was a single mother who worked three jobs to make ends meet. She couldn't find time to sleep, much less meet the demands for individual one-on-one time with each of her children. There weren't any programs to help her at that time, either. She just did what she had to do. When I needed her, she had other demands on her. For years, I struggled with the belief that I was really unimportant to her. That was totally untrue, but from my perspective, it was what I believed. I truly knew my mother loved me, but in my estimation, it was less than the love she felt for my siblings. I felt that I was "unlovable" and that there was something wrong with me. I spent years trying to get down to the pain that I experienced, but it was too deeply ingrained in me.

Feeling unworthy troubled me growing up and followed me into adulthood. It was the basis for many of the relationship challenges I faced in my life. This foundational fallacy affected my self worth and many decisions I made in my life. When you base life choices and beliefs on false assumptions and information, then everything in your life is affected.

Face it, if you feel your mother does not love you, who will? She loved me, but the love came in a different package than I was expecting. I wasn't happy. I wanted her attention, so I gained it through throwing fits and making demands. A few years ago, I heard about the "law of the soggy potato chip." Roughly translated, it is that if a child is not getting positive attention, they will do something to make you mad to get any attention they can get. They believe a soggy potato chip is better than no potato chip at all. What I was really doing was reinforcing her desire to avoid confrontation and avoid me. I was the poster child for confrontation in my family. Needless to say, I didn't get the results I hoped for. I just couldn't understand why my parents weren't like Ward and June Cleever!

Another important factor was that my mother was hurting, too. She, too, was emotionally, mentally, physically and spiritually wounded. As I pounded her areas of hurt, she would respond from a place of pain. Her life was imbalanced at that time. She had huge challenges in front of her. Women's wages were much less than men's at that time, but she had the same responsibilities of providing for her family with a lot less money. She worked multiple jobs just to survive. When I was wounded and hurting, I could only see what I did not receive. I could not see the whole picture. I could only see the glaring things that were not working for me and were missing from my life.

I felt criticized, and I criticized her. I felt unimportant, and I made her feel unimportant. I felt unworthy of her love, because I felt unworthy of love at times. Healing showed me that as I changed toward her, she changed towards me. As I showed more love and attention to her, she returned that love and attention to me and we began to rebuild our relationship with healthy and loving components.

● ● One day in particular, we had an argument. I was at a place where I did not want to experience any more pain. She left my home and I truly thought it was time to sever ties with her. I drove around for a while and really thought about the consequences of what our relationship was doing to her and what it was doing to me. Finally I reached a decision. She was too important to me for us to continue tearing each other up.

● ● I went home and gathered a few things. The idea was just forming in my head, but I thought it was pretty interesting. I grabbed the Pictionary® game. I drove straight to her house. When I knocked on her door, she opened it with a look of surprise. I was the last person she expected to see after the way we parted. She invited me in and we sat down at the kitchen table. I told her how important she was to me. I wanted our communication to improve and if she were willing to listen, I would share a few things that I had discovered while driving around that afternoon.

● ● She listened to me as I spoke. As we were both struggling with the injuries of the divorce, I decided that I would just become an adult at age 11. I learned that everyone else's needs were more important than mine. I learned to honor their needs and requests at a great cost to myself. For years our roles of being parent and child had been reversed. I was angry that I had to grow up while she could still be a child, even today. My realization was, "Why couldn't we embrace and honor both our inner children and adult selves at the same time?" I always thought that if she were the child, I had to be the adult. I wanted to have more fun in my life. I wanted to be the child, too, sometimes. So we sat down and played our own version of the Pictionary® game. We changed the rules and used it as a tool to talk about painful issues and remember our fondest memories. We were able to connect from our hearts and love each other in new ways and to heal both of us. I remember telling her that day. "You can be my worst critic or my best champion. I hope you choose to be my champion." I can tell you she chose to be my champion and I have been gifted with a new way of living with my mother's love.

Are you a champion or critic? This is a powerful choice. When you become someone's champion, you see the good in them and overlook the bad. You eliminate criticism from your relationship and love them in spite of their flaws. You extend a hand when they need help. You honor the choices they make because the choices are their responsibility and not yours.

When I healed emotionally, I finally could realize, appreciate and accept the gifts that my mother and our life experiences together gave me. When she became my champion, I reciprocated. It was a wonderful feeling to champion someone as special as your mom. It was time I recognized the lessons she taught me. She taught me to love and laugh. She gave me the gift of a close and loving family. She read to me and taught me to love books. She taught me to be independent and she was a role model as an entrepreneur in my life. She was my hero and one of the most courageous women I know. I would not be who I am today without these experiences. Even the hardships taught me to be strong and do the difficult work to get down to the real issues in life. The woman I am today is stronger and more sensitive because I experienced the pain as well as the love. Her gifts to me have been infinite and priceless.

🌢🌢 Today, I thank her for the difficult lessons I learned through our experiences and that our love survived and thrived, although it went through some really bumpy and turbulent times. We have a new, more loving relationship today. We have forged new bonds of understanding, courage, love and hope for a better future in our relationship. I believe it is the result of emotional healing that I received through this work.

🌢 Pain, Sorrow and Healing Domestic Violence 🌢

As an emotionally injured young adult, I chose to marry a man who abused me physically and emotionally. Of course, I was clueless during our dating that violence was part of the package. During the honeymoon period, it was wonderful. Several months into the marriage, we were having an argument and he hit me. I will never forget my dad's reprimand to my brothers that had been drummed into my head, "Boys don't hit girls." I was stunned. Somebody who said they loved me actually hit me. I ended up with black eyes, multiple bruises and love marks all at the same time. What mixed messages! The fists hurt me physically, but it was the emotional injuries that caused the most damage. Damage caused by fists healed within a couple of weeks. The kind of damage that came from his words lasted for years, long after the attack actually occurred. Verbal abuse crushed my courage and devastated my spirit. During one particularly brutal physical attack, I remember he spat in my face, he pounded me with his fists, he grabbed me by the hair, and told me, "Get ready, you are going to see your Jesus Christ today." I knew I was going to die that day. I prayed. I begged for my life. I told him if he would let me go, he would never have to see me ever again. I kept trying to reason with him, but as I looked at him, I saw someone I did not even recognize. I didn't know who this person was. He certainly wasn't the man who vowed to love me in sickness and in health till death do us part, or maybe he was just invoking the death part of that vow. I finally convinced him to let me leave. I learned a painful lesson that day. I learned that being angry and spouting off resulted in physical brutality and I learned to selectively choose when, where and with whom it was safe to be angry.

I felt justified in my belief that I was unlovable. Looking back, I realized that until I honored me, no one else would honor me. If I had acted courageously and set boundaries, the relationship would have developed in a totally different way. I gave away my power. As it was, my husband did what many abusers do. He systematically cut off my support system, and I never challenged his ability to do so. He insisted on asking who I loved more - him or my family. Naturally, I chose him. He was my husband. I became estranged from my family and had no one to counsel me during the abuse. Since he was a police officer, I felt powerless when I needed help. I couldn't even call the police during an attack because either his partner or supervisor would answer the call. If the officer believed me, my husband would be arrested and perhaps even fired, and then the economic impact would create another problem entirely. If he didn't believe me, I would be beaten again when my husband discovered I had involved the police in our domestic battles. My friends were other police wives and

I didn't feel I could share my problems with them without repercussions. It was a no win situation for me. I was constantly afraid, and I felt as if I had nowhere to turn and no one to help me. I felt hopeless without a way out of my situation. I was a prisoner behind "The Thin Blue Line." The pain was unbearable. The silence was deafening. I sought advice from my pastor who told me, "You are married for life."

My husband would apologize and tell me how much he loved me. He promised it would never happen again. I wanted to believe him so much. Life would return to "normal", but the fear of the next violent outburst would permeate every thought and every waking moment. I walked on eggshells and attempted to avoid anything that would set him off, but that was impossible. Then he would erupt in anger, and I remember one day, he broke every dish in our home. I tried to push the fear away, but it kept coming back over and over again like a wheel stuck in the mud spinning, but going nowhere. When would it happen? Today? Tomorrow? My life was a pendulum that swung from really good to really bad. There was something extremely important that I didn't know. I did not know what was hurting him so much that he had to hurt me to heal. He had no idea what was hurting me so much I had to hurt him to heal. We didn't talk about our dreams and goals. We didn't communicate our hopes and fears.

I wasn't even close to figuring out my issues. They were too deep and painful to touch. He had emotional, mental, physical and even spiritual wounds from his two tours of duty in Vietnam and life in general. He told me one night that his whole platoon was killed and that he had to live for all nine men who died. His wounds were too deep and too painful for him to face unless he had a lot to drink, and then he only talked about this grief with me that one time. His pain, loss and emptiness were gnawing at him, too. His pain wasn't resolved. It was just being dulled until alcohol and pills caused him to pass out.

The hopelessness left me vulnerable to addictions. It could have been drugs, alcohol, gambling or other compulsive behaviors. Comfort food and compulsive shopping became my drugs of choice. I was isolated in all ways and I was dying on the inside. I felt so empty that I kept eating to fill the hurt from the abuse, the abandonment of a loving relationship with my husband, and the loss of my family support. I felt detached from friends and family. It didn't matter how much I ate to fill the emptiness inside me, the result was still a void that would never be filled up with anything edible. It could only be filled with love. I gained over 50 pounds during a six-month period. I was out of control. He was out of control. The situation was out of control.

There we were – two unlovable people in our own minds without a snowball's chance in hell of surviving the marriage, abusing each other and ourselves. It was like having this huge pink elephant in the room, but we never acknowledged it was there. We went on about our lives and tried to ignore it. We never treated the problem; we only danced around the symptoms.

Then one day, he shot his service revolver in the house. He was angry about something. The bullet ricocheted through our bedroom wall and ended up in the corner of the next room. I remember thinking, "If we had children, they could have been killed. I could have been killed." I knew immediately that I was mortal and that if the bullet was aimed three feet towards me, I would be dead. I felt real fear that I might not live to see another day. That day I decided to leave. It finally took a life and death situation for me to choose life. I knew I was a survivor and I wanted to live and live fully. I also knew there were guides and angels looking out for me or I wouldn't be here today. I left the relationship, still wounded and unhealed.

I felt guilty for years because I decided that divorce was a better option for me than death. It hurt me to violate my own vow of "till death do us part." It was a long time before I was able to say, "I was an abused wife." I finally realized years later that I escaped with my sanity, my health, and my life. That's more than a lot of victims can say. The answers today are different than the ones I received thirty years ago. Today domestic violence is still a huge problem in our society, but at least there are more options to help victims of abuse and battery. Shelters provide a safe place to escape the immediate threat of physical harm. There are professionals as well as survivors who can help us understand, empathize and find real solutions to help victims heal their feelings of being battered, isolated, shamed and alone. The healing process is crucial to turning victims into healthy survivors – people who take back and own their power.

When we fail to honor ourselves, we teach others through our actions exactly how we are to be treated. We actually invite and actively participate in the dance of domestic violence. We cover up our feelings of insecurity, but we trigger fights or respond to fights that smolder and burst into infernos out of control. It is always so easy to blame the other person for that which we do not wish to see in ourselves. How can the situation change, when at the core of who we are, we dismiss our feelings and do not understand how to communicate them in a safe way? In order to heal, we must accept our own responsibility for our feelings, our actions and our intentions. Otherwise, we will continue dancing the same old steps until we die.

There is still such shame attached to domestic violence. It is difficult to talk about how painful it is that someone who professes to love us beats us, damages us and leaves scars that take years to recover from and heal. We believe that somehow we must have contributed to this problem, but we can't imagine how. We really have a difficult time moving from victim to healthy person. We make excuses, give away our power and attempt to take responsibility for someone else's actions in full or in part, but forget to take responsibility for our own actions. We go through a litany of what if...and if only...statements. We believe somehow we failed and if we had only been better, smarter, stronger and more loving, that surely we would have experienced a different outcome.

As I became bolder about sharing my history of domestic violence, I was amazed at the number of people who began to open up and share their stories. I would never have guessed that they had experienced domestic violence and were recovering in silence.

Years later one of the greatest "ah ha" moments for me came when I realized that my thoughts and beliefs actually allowed others to treat me as unlovable. I abused myself and considered myself unlovable. Why would he think any differently? He learned by my example that it was OK to disrespect me and abuse me. Until I honored and respected myself, no one else would either. When I took back my power to set boundaries, the rules of engagement changed.

Victims of domestic violence are still killed too often, because the systems in place to protect victims via temporary restraining orders are really ineffective in deterring someone intent on maiming and killing. We have to find better, more effective ways to deal with the issues for not only the victims, but also the walking wounded, the children in the family and even the perpetrator of domestic violence. The cycle of violence must end. The way to successfully stop domestic violence is to help people move from victims to victors in owning their own power and being comfortable in setting and enforcing boundary issues.

It took years to resolve the issues that this relationship brought into my life. My family relationships needed mending. I had no idea what I was going to do with my life. I found a new job and also a mentor who saw potential in me. She was such a gift and I eagerly learned everything she had to teach me. I couldn't make my marriage work, so I thought I would just work on all the other parts of my life. It was so important for me to try to be the best I could be at whatever I chose to do, because surely, if I found approval, life wouldn't hurt so much. I learned everything I could learn and I decided that I could do anything if I believed I could do it. I was rewarded for my efforts in business and somehow along the way, I found that I felt good when people praised me. I put a lot of effort into the business side of my life. I also decided that friendships were more successful for me than marriage, and I spent time investing heavily in friendships and shied away from romance altogether.

Brick by brick, I built a wall. My trust and love were violated. My heart was broken. I felt like a total failure when it came to being a wife. I didn't trust men in general. I decided that if I kept my heart protected, no one could hurt me like that again. Drawbridge up! Sentries on guard! No one could get close to me. It was like I took an emotional tourniquet and placed it on the area in my life associated with marriage and love relationships. The wound didn't heal and it didn't go away. I just pushed it to the back of my heart where it festered. It took thirteen years before I was tempted to try marriage again.

What I didn't learn until years later was the lesson that whenever we see a trait in someone that we dislike, it is like looking into a mirror. We see in others what we refuse to acknowledge in ourselves. We deny that we exhibit that trait, but we wouldn't recognize it if we didn't own it ourselves. As someone once said to me, "You spot – you got it!" Seeing and recognizing the trait is an opportunity to heal ourselves of that trait.

I was the worst abuser in my own life. I just couldn't see it or admit to it. I did not value or love me enough. When the light bulb comes on, we realize that our addictions to work, food, alcohol, substances, shopping, gambling, sex, exercise or whatever, are really our ways of abusing ourselves and trying to fill up the emptiness inside us. The people who were attracted to me reflected the same lack of love for themselves.

Years later, the heart drawbridge was still up and the sentry was still on guard. I kept a distance from any potential mates. I went out on dates occasionally, but it made me so nervous. My actions were speaking loudly. "Do not love me. Don't even think about getting close to me. I am unlovable." I realized that unless I changed my approach to living my life, I would continue doing the same things and getting the same results.

Someone once said to me, "We are extras in everybody else's play." The thought of honoring myself was so at odds with statements from my childhood about not being selfish and that self-centeredness was so wrong. How could I be important? This is often the first step in discounting who we are and what we deserve in our lives. This is another step in pleasing other people, rather than living our own dreams and desires. When I was younger, and someone asked, "What are your dreams, Vicki?" I didn't have an answer.

Pleasing people brought me recognition and acknowledgement. I thought I was smart and they must have thought so too, because this little injured child inside me reveled in the praise. The need to be right became more important as I learned more. If someone asked me, "Would you rather be right or happy?" I would have responded, "Right, of course." I felt so invested in the knowledge I was gaining and learning, that it must be just the right way or the correct approach at all costs. If someone challenged me or told me I was wrong, I would often explode. But I felt I had to control that, too, because you couldn't explode at just anyone. I thought it was OK to explode at your family members, because they loved you no matter what. There were many times when I said hurtful things to them. I thought it was safe to explode on strangers. People in the stores, gas stations, banks, or the softball field would feel the sting of my words. People even driving down the road who had not done one thing to me would become the innocent victims of my own verbal abuse.

● ● Abuse of any kind is a ripple disease. The first attack is never the last. The first attack is only the beginning. It's the horrible gift that keeps on giving and giving and giving. As you hurt someone, they often can't respond to you because you are a customer, they are simply too stunned to respond or because the time and place are inappropriate. They just feel the hurt, get angry and put the anger on hold. Then when the pressure builds within them, they react inappropriately and injure someone else. The pattern continues and ripples out forever.

● ● Ten years later, I was still suffering from the experience of being both the abuser and the abused. Then I experienced a defining moment. One of my best and dearest friends said to me after she witnessed an episode of verbal abuse, "Vicki, I hope you never get mad at me. You can cut somebody to ribbons with your tongue." That comment went straight to my heart. Here was this friend who loved me. I knew what she said was true. I really thought about and pondered her words.

I could be the nicest person to most people, but I said really ugly things when I was out of control. I hurt innocent people and I found some people avoided me because of my temper or walked on eggshells around me. I had discounted the severity of the problem because I heard for years that redheads just have a temper. I certainly lived up to that expectation. Somehow that was supposed to make everything all right. I decided to do something about this rage that had seeped from the wounds in my heart.

The healing process began with that choice and continued. I sought therapy to deal with aftermath of abuse and other issues in my life. I'll never forget my first trip to the therapist's office. In my naivety, I had made a list of eight things that in my opinion were issues that I needed to address. I wanted to stick to an agenda, and I will never forget the understanding and compassion that my therapist used to help me heal. It was a process. It really didn't happen with an agenda and the plan I had laid out. The awareness of certain problems was helpful, but I didn't just heal by checking things off a list in a certain order even though I tried that approach. The healing process was more like peeling layers of an onion as I began to appreciate and embrace my unique, complicated, hurt, angry and loving self. I had to learn how to accept and love me for who I was. I would like to say I mastered this self-love, but it didn't happen until years later. The mastery occurs when your life begins to reflect the beauty of who you are when you love who you really are, not who the world thinks you are.

I wrote a letter to my former husband about the sorrow, disappointment and pain that I had buried deep within me. Then I burned the letter. I knew that if I were to find love and happiness again, it would require me to take down the wall I had built one hurt, one vulnerability at a time. I decided to forgive him. It was my choice. Forgiveness is a powerful action, and it was necessary for me to forgive in order to move forward in my life. It didn't mean that what he did to me was OK. It just meant that I was tired of the emotions that it caused within me when I thought about his actions and his words. Forgiveness empowered me to let go of the pain and walk away. Today, when I speak of these issues, it's like telling a story, but the emotions are healed. It seems like it happened to someone else, the person I used to be.

I avidly read self-help books and watched shows that guided me to new understandings. I owned a book collection that would make a library jealous. I listened to tapes and devoured hundreds of books on living a better life and making better choices. One fact remained. I was healing capillaries and veins, but I never touched and healed the heart. The heart was still suffering a massive injury and it must have been very strong to continue working damaged for so long.

These difficult experiences were gifts when I got past the pain. I learned just how strong I was. I hoped that my former husband found peace and forgiveness for himself and for me also. I realized that had I made other choices before, during and after our marriage, we might have had an opportunity to heal. I was too young and immature with my own problems to truly see that love and forgiveness would heal both of us and change the legacy for future relationship difficulties.

• • Today my actions speak differently than they did in the past. When I see someone hurting, these lessons and experiences have taught me to say, "It's OK. I know you're hurting. I remember how that feels. No matter what you do to me, I love you, I love me and God loves you, too. What is hurting you so badly that you have to hurt me to heal?"

The Gift of Intuition

The next few years were spent developing professional skills, taking classes and concentrating on my career. As I gained confidence in my abilities, I enjoyed my life more. My intuition or "hunches" gave me great insight in business and contributed to my professional success. In my personal life, I would just know things without any logical explanation. This would freak people out occasionally. I'll never forget telling a friend that his brother and a young woman were dating. He looked at me like I was crazy. Within two weeks, his brother called him and invited him to talk over dinner. What was the conversation topic? Of course, it was about his brother's new relationship with the young woman I had mentioned.

Once I was traveling with my relatives and we witnessed an accident. I looked at the truck as my brother and uncle went to see about helping the victims out of the vehicle. I looked over to my aunt and said, "You know. They just made the last payment on that truck." Around 15 minutes later, my brother got back in the truck and said, "You know. They just made the last payment on that truck."

I married for the second time. Once my husband greeted me at the airport as I arrived from Detroit on business. As we walked through the parking lot to the car, I asked him, "Did you buy me a new car?" As he popped the trunk on the new vehicle, I realized something had upset him. He never did understand that it was an intuitive "hit". He asked me years later who spoiled his surprise! I could neither predict it nor order my gift to work. When it did work, I could tell you down to the color and style what was in a Christmas gift I received. It would manifest as a fact that would just come into my head like a declarative sentence. It wasn't a question, just a statement of fact.

We built a life together and started a technology training company. When that marriage began to fail, I was devastated. I thought we had the perfect marriage. I knew there were some problems, but I was still surprised when it ended. I had to determine – did I trust myself? Did I trust what he told me? What conclusion I came to was in a way liberating for me. I knew my heart. I knew I could count on it. I had trusted my intuition for years. I also came to realize that had I remained in my marriage, none of the miracles of the past few years could be accomplished in the same way. I believed it was part of the big picture and necessary for me to learn the lessons of letting go and letting God. There is nothing quite so amazing as when we learn to walk in faith and remain open to new opportunities.

After the first divorce, I was bitter for several years. I wanted to avoid that bitterness. For me the cost was way too great in terms of health, time and effort, and I didn't want to waste one minute on bitterness. I decided to forgive my former husband and it was hard to do. He drove a Suburban, so I thought to myself, "Whenever I see a

Suburban, I will say a prayer for him. I will ask for God to bless him with health, happiness and prosperity." There are many Suburbans in the Dallas area. He received a whole lot of prayers until I felt the forgiveness for me was complete. As I forgave him, the healing began and my emotional wounds hurt less and less. Over time, I was able to appreciate him, remember what wonderful times we had together and enjoy the exciting things we had done in our lives. I was able to own my part in the breakup and realize that until I healed, I would be unable to really be whole for me or any other love relationship.

What was really amazing was that when I chose forgiveness, it seemed like that would be the last logical choice I would make from my human ego. When I forgave him, and made that spiritual decision, all these wonderful things began to occur in my life. I began the journey to discover my gift of healing through Reiki and reconnective. It was like that decision gave me a ticket to a new destination and I was on my way.

I was driving down the highway several years after my divorce and thought, "If I came face to face with my former husband, I would have to thank him for ending our marriage." Many of my life lessons began in earnest after he was courageous enough to say that it was just not working. My emotional healing took place over time and healed me from the inside, out. I am grateful for the events in our lives together and I am eternally grateful for the lessons I learned after the divorce. And although my friend and I joke about putting the big "L" on our foreheads and saying, "I'm a two-time loser," I am really a winner and always have been. There are no losers. We are all winners.

Lessons in Pain, Sorrow and Your Life Purpose

If we expect to feel joy in our lives, we must also expect to feel pain. Pain in our lives will happen. We are assured of that. It is a certainty! We have an opportunity to learn a lesson through the pain, and perhaps make an adjustment or change direction in some way. If we deny or deflect the pain, we bury it deep within us. Then the pain will surface later in the form of injury or illness. We can spend a lot of time avoiding the pain, but what we are really avoiding is the lesson that pain is supposed to teach us. What we don't always understand is that sorrow and suffering are optional.

Sorrow and suffering occur when you talk repeatedly about a situation and feel the feelings each time. Sorrow and suffering keep opening the wound and prevent healing. I know – I developed the art of rehashing old hurts and wounds and took it to a new level. Painful memories and emotions keep us from making heart connections with other people. Healing gives us an opportunity to live and love without restrictions. No limits. No boundaries.

When I looked around, I wondered, "How can I help to change the world around me?" Then I realized I could not change anyone else. I could only change myself. As I chose to love when I would rather argue, and when I began to see things from the other person's perspective, only then could I begin to honor them as well as me. Once I came face to face with the power of loving other people, I saw immediate results in all areas of my life. I observed the ripple effect and realized how powerful this approach to living could be. I realized that when I chose to use loving remarks rather than harsh criticisms, I grew confident and could be me without fear of what other people would think or say.

Imagine life... where people value each other for their uniqueness... where the value of human and animal life are honored as God's creations... where we really are our brother's keepers... where we are so busy loving ourselves that we can't help but love others... where we see God in everyone we meet. How would our world change? We have the ability to do just that... change our world. We start within our own hearts.

If you think this sounds familiar, it's true. We have heard this message over and over, but we do not understand it. This message is thousands of years old and has been demonstrated by every Master who has brought the same message to us.

CHAPTER 2

MY JOURNEY FROM THE HEART

"Vicki, you have to know you are a gift. Grow with the truth. Grow with the life. Grow with the light. You can rise above everything."

You are Here

In the summer of 2000, I had no idea how my life was about to take an extraordinary turn. It was like speeding down the freeway of life and taking a quick 90-degree turn without warning. I could not have planned it, nor dreamed it, nor predicted it. A series of what seemed like random life events came together synchronistically, and I realized I was suddenly headed in a new direction. This new path was to become my life's work. Although I would experience a detour or two along the way, I finally knew what I wanted to be now that I had "grown up." I was about to embark on a journey that would bring me face to face with God and expand my idea of Who God is, what God meant to me, and what real love was all about. It completely changed how I viewed the world around me and my role within that world.

What was unusual was that for the last twenty years, I trained people on computer systems, performed computer conversions, created and taught customized computer application courses. I was

29

good at my craft. I earned an excellent living. I had achieved "success" in the eyes of my friends, family and colleagues. I traveled to 48 out of the 50 states. I traveled internationally to France, Canada, Mexico and the Caribbean. I was active in my community serving as President of the Economic Development Corporation, Mayor Pro Tem and Chamber of Commerce Publicity Director. I was running two businesses and living the American dream. I was trying to please everyone, and burning the candle at both ends. Behind the driving need for success was for me, like many other people, really the need for love and acceptance. Then suddenly everything changed in a heartbeat.

As extraordinary as it seemed, one minute I was headed down a corporate career path, and then I completely changed directions. It happened just that quickly, and my life changed drastically. I know this sounds really bizarre, and frankly, if I wasn't the one living it, I would be skeptical. I continue to be astonished at being chosen as the messenger and scribe of this wonderful story. I was awed at the events and I knew I was born to do this work. Looking back I realized that every experience in my life prepared me for just this moment.

If you were to ask people who know me in business or municipal government situations to describe me, they might say I was a good businessperson and strategist. They might also say that I have an ability to recall facts, events and things that happened in a credible and comprehensive fashion. I have the ability to recall details of events that occurred days, months or even years in the past. They might also say that I can record and capture a great deal of detailed information. It is my nature to operate with facts and draw conclusions based on research data, factual information and guidance from my intuition. I am quite comfortable evaluating situations and making decisions based on the information presented. Typically, I try to see all sides of a situation and support win/win solutions.

How does that lead to energy healing? I was and still am rather naïve about energy healing. When I realized that I was not fully using my gift of intuition and that it really was a gift, not something I created in my life, I "discovered" Reiki. Reiki was the first venture for me into energy medicine, alternative healing and complementary medical care. Reiki translated means "Universal Life Force Energy" in Japanese. Reiki was and is a way to connect to people and help them heal from their dis-ease or things that create disharmony in their lives by restoring wholeness at the cellular level. In Reiki, I learned that our cells reproduce in whatever state they exist. If they are damaged, they reproduce as damaged cells. During a Reiki treatment, these cells are restored to their whole or healed state.

People seek Reiki as an alternative healing modality that uses symbols and energy to heal people from injuries and illnesses. I still have to answer "no" most of the time when asked if I have read this book or that book or if I know this healer or that healer. What I do know is that there are often more questions than answers when trying to explain how or why healing occurs, but more is being learned all the time.

Scientific evidence continues to provide information and medical insights. Recently I read about experiments conducted over the last 40 years that tell us more and more about quantum physics and the holographic field theories that physicists are learning more about each day. These can explain, or at least attempt to explain, what happens in energy medicine and alternative healing.

As I learned more about science and healing, I realized my entire life has been a training ground to prepare me. God has always been there to guide, direct and provide lessons so necessary to complete my life's work. When I have stumbled, He has been there to hold me, comfort me and let me know I am loved ***NO MATTER WHAT***! There's so much love that, in fact, I cannot fathom how deep and complete that love really is. He has encouraged me to live, to love, to help others and to be, just be.

God has encouraged me to experience life at its best and enjoy the beauty He has provided. What marvelous gifts He has given us! Each day we have the opportunity to appreciate the wonders of His world and be grateful for His generosity and love. May we realize there is more to learn about this Universe that exists for us and may we be open to the lessons.

Defining Oprah Moment

The summer of 2000 was life changing. Within 45 days, I experienced not one, but three defining moments in my life. The first one occurred in early June. I remembered thinking, "I do not know how much longer Oprah Winfrey will be continuing her contract. I want to go to Chicago and be in her studio audience." There had been various reports that 2001 might be her last year to provide the world with the information and services that she shared with us through the guests on her show and through the productions she and her staff created. I learned many things about racism, emotional healing, forgiveness and even transformation through the shows she presented. Frequently I shared with friends, family and co-workers about the shows I had seen and the gifts of insight and changes I had made in my own life. I listened as she and Gary Zukav talked about the *Hidden Faces of Anger*[2]. It compelled me to write a letter sharing intimacies about my anger, feelings and life experiences.

Something about that show touched me and helped me understand more about the anger I had experienced in my own life. It helped me understand why I reacted the way I did in certain situations and provided insight into things that I believed about myself. I was able to challenge old beliefs, look at them in a different way, and see the impact those old beliefs had in my life. Then the most amazing thing happened. My letter caught the attention of a producer on the *Oprah Show*. Within one week of my statement to go to Chicago, I was asked to appear as a guest.

When I received the call to confirm the trip, I was playing golf with two friends. I mentioned that I would be unable to keep our golf date on Tuesday, the following week. They asked me, "Why? Are you going out of town?" I answered, "Yes, I'm going to Chicago." I really wasn't prepared to fill in the details for them. Then they asked, "What will you be doing in Chicago?" When I said, "I'll be a guest on the *Oprah Winfrey Show*," they both looked at me as if I was teasing them. Then they realized by the look on my face that I was serious. They asked, "What's the show about?"

Here was my moment of truth and it was difficult to say, "I am a recovering anger addict." They both looked at me and said, "We find that hard to believe, Vicki. We have known you for several years and have seen you in volatile situations – situations where you could easily have been angry and weren't." That was one of the finest compliments I ever received.

Within 24 hours, I gathered pictures that represented different times and emotional issues in my life and sent them overnight to the producer. Within 72 hours, I was aboard a plane traveling to Chicago, Illinois. I was greeted at O'Hare Airport and taken via limousine to the hotel. I kept marveling at how powerful that intent statement was and how immediately I manifested action and a response.

This was the fulfillment of a life long dream. Before the show, I waited in the employee break room, as they taped another show that morning. I watched Dr. Phil McGraw and the guests I had ridden in the elevator with just that morning as they talked about why couples should or should not marry. I remembered seeing beautiful, green marble and one of Oprah's dogs as I walked past her office. I had always dreamed of this moment and it had happened so quickly, I could hardly believe it. I enjoyed every single minute and was so excited to be there.

They escorted me to the sound studio. When it was time to record my letter, I read it once, and then I read it again. The technician looked at me and asked, "What do you do for a living?" I replied, "I am a corporate trainer. Why?" He responded, "People come in here and have to read their letters about 20 times before they get it right." It took me two tries and I was finished. It was really a wonderful experience. Everyone I met was wonderful and welcoming. The people on the phone who arranged the trip, the show's producers, the hair and make-up artists, the sound engineers, the security staff, the limo drivers and even the other guests on the show all played an important role in making my dream come true.

The guests were ushered into the green room. The staff applied our make up and arranged our hair for the show. There I met Gary Zukav. I reached out to shake his hand and he responded, "I would prefer a hug." That was a great honor for me and I happily gave him a hug. I enjoyed meeting his Spiritual partner, Linda Francis, and the other guests that were just discovering their anger issues and the impact it had on their lives.

I prepared to openly discuss the benefits of my fifteen-year journey of uncovering the *Hidden Faces of Anger*[3] and my letter to Oprah about the journey to become a more joyful and loving person. I shared the sadness, failures and the victories of someone who wanted to live a more honorable and authentic life. I learned that anger was just a mask to cover fear, frustration and hurt. I told about the years I spent excavating the layers around my heart and discovered that my anger was directly connected to the belief that I was not good enough to earn my mother's love. I had come a long way. I reached a point in my life where I could say and mean it, "I am worthy, because I am."

On the show, Gary Zukav acknowledged the work that I had done to advance in my journey and honored me for sharing the effects of anger in my life. I responded with two words, "Thank you." Two words for a person who likes to talk as much as I do wasn't a lot. Those were the only words I would actually say "live" during the entire show. I knew that if I only could say two words, those are the ones I would choose. I felt enormous gratitude for Oprah, Gary Zukav and all the other guests whose stories provided the gift of enlightenment and understanding. When the show was over, I was whisked away via limousine back to the airport and was on my way home.

As soon as I was seated on the airplane, I became uneasy. I had just announced to millions of people the shame of feeling unloved by my mother. I had two hours on the return flight to think about it. When we landed, the first thing I did was call her. My letter detailed my relationship struggles with my mother and I was a little nervous about what she would say. I knew we had come a long way when she responded, "Vicki, it took great courage to say what you felt. I am proud of you." I wish she had been there to share the experience with me. It was a cleansing moment as forgiveness, forgetfulness and healing took place in our relationship. As Gary Zukav reminded me, this is important soul work we have come to learn through our experiences as mother and daughter.

My spiritual journey provided the opportunity to address issues from my past and continue the excavation as the old injuries surfaced occasionally. It was both embarrassing and liberating to own my past actions. I was rewarded when even through the embarrassment, people would come up and tell me how they too felt unloved when they were young.

My story touched them and helped them understand more about why they had experienced failure after failure in their lives. I shared what I learned about surviving the toughest situations. I was grateful for each opportunity to share it with people who were just beginning their own healing journey. It helped me also as I brought love, joy, reverence, respect, harmony, tranquility and cooperation back into my daily life.

Defining Moment – My Personal Connection

Within a couple of weeks another defining moment occurred. I was introduced to Reconnective Healing™[4]. I heard about the amazing things that were being said about this work and decided I would like to experience a healing treatment. I lay down on a massage table and the practitioner began to work on me. As I closed my eyes, I was open to whatever was designed especially for me to experience. I remembered asking when it was over if the practitioner heard all those jet airplanes that seemed to fly right over my face. I remembered the smell of roses and I thought that I would like to experience more of this wonderful, relaxing work. I decided to arrange an appointment for my personal connection session.

During both sessions, I experienced a density and heaviness in my hands and feet. It felt like someone had pumped air underneath the skin all over my body. I felt expanded. I remembered feeling and "seeing" undulating waves of colors, particularly apricot and turquoise, and jagged waves of white light that moved across my body. I remembered my ears "opening" and I felt pressure inside them. Sound was accentuated.

One odd thing occurred. It sounded as if another jet airplane flew directly over my face, not just over the house, but directly over my face. This happened about three times. I felt my legs and arms jerk. My left arm extended beyond the massage table, although I wasn't moving it. My leg kept jerking to the left several dozen times. I wasn't moving it either. At one point, with my eyes closed, I could actually "see" the practitioner's hand as it passed over my head. It was an incredible experience. It was something I had never experienced before and I found myself intrigued and wondering what would come next. Within a month, I would take another step in this journey.

Defining Moment – The Essence of Healing

On July 26th, 2000, I was at the ABC – Channel 8 Studios in Dallas, Texas. It was the third defining moment for me within such a short time frame. I had been asked to help a friend who had agreed to sponsor a seminar event. She asked me to set up publicity events so the speaker, Dr. Eric Pearl, a chiropractor and healer based out of Los Angeles, could tell his story. I placed a call and coordinated an interview on "Good Morning, Texas," a breakfast TV news show in the Dallas/Fort Worth metroplex. Only one little problem stood in the way. The speaker's driver was lost in downtown Dallas, but thankfully we were connected via cell phone. I asked, "Can you see me now?" and flagged him in as the driver responded to my instructions. When he stepped out of the car, I knew I was destined to meet this man. Two things became clear immediately: 1) I would work for him. 2) My life would be changed forever. I just didn't know how great the gift he shared with me would be.

We introduced ourselves and together we entered the studio. As we waited in an office separate from the green room, he appeared excited and perhaps a little nervous. He "activated" my hands and asked me if I could feel anything. I responded, "It feels like a pulling and an energy pulsation in my hands."

Being in the television studio was exciting and fun. I saw and met many of the TV personalities that I watched daily who reported news stories in my part of the world. The Dallas/Fort Worth area watched as the interview was conducted and a lady's arthritic hand was touched and healed through this work. The hand movement that had been restricted through swollen joints was released. Her fingers, once stiff, became pliable and movable as we watched. Evidently, it was impressive, because the phones rang and rang in response to the show. He was invited to appear again later that year.

I remembered thinking how unbelievable this was. What was happening that made this possible? The lady on TV that day had not met the healer prior to the show. She showed up. He showed up. Together the healing occurred.

When the show was over, Dr. Pearl and I went to lunch with two of my friends. I had a splitting headache unlike I had ever experienced. The pressure occurred at the base of my skull and was binding around my head. I soon discovered that this occurred frequently when I was in his company. The pressure was quite uncomfortable. I did not experience headaches very often and it was apparent that something was happening within my head. I just didn't know what it was that was causing such pressure within my brain. I left the group after lunch and went home to take a nap to see if the pressure would subside.

What I learned over the years was that my friends and I experienced these headaches periodically. Usually we experienced them on the same day or within one or two days of each other. The headaches occurred simultaneously with changes in our physical bodies and we believed that this was a part of the transformation that occurred when doing this work.

We arrived at the hotel early to get a front row seat. The speaker began to tell his story at the seminar Friday night. People were spellbound at what they heard. During the evening, he walked around the room and "activated hands" which meant that he approached each person and allowed them to "feel" the energy through their hands. He continued to share his experience of how he was gifted with this healing and where he believed the Source – God, Love, Universe, whatever name you want to use – provided whatever was needed for the healing to occur. The speaker was very clear that this was not faith healing and did not believe that we should create another religion for this extraordinary experience. The next day there were a series of exercises where we learned how to recognize and "play" with the energy.

The seminar was attended by approximately 100 people, the largest crowd to attend the seminar at that particular time. We learned about healing and how simple it was to use this method for people from all walks of life in matters of physical, mental, emotional and spiritual health. It was described as something miraculous that happens when the combination of God, the customer and the practitioner agree to be together in the equation.

We learned healing happened in multiple ways and people experienced the feeling and "recognized it" in different ways. For example, some people reported experiencing warmth in their hands. Others reported feeling a cool breeze. Some people reported feeling an electrical impulse or a tone they "heard" in their hands. Some people reported feeling what they described as taffy and/or a pulling sensation similar to stretching a rubber band. Each person seemed to recognize it in his own way, but there were common ways of recognition that happened repeatedly. The speaker shared that healing happens all the time. The package it comes in may be different than you expect.[5]

His engaging sense of humor kept us entertained while we listened to the extraordinary story that brought him to this point in his life. His honesty and straight-forwardness about the human flaws in his life reminded me of how God works with all of us – people from all areas, races, religions and life experiences. It was only our willingness to serve that was needed. God will take care of the rest. The speaker was witty, funny and commanded attention from beginning to end. When it came to a conclusion that evening, we had no idea how 3 ½ hours had passed so quickly. We couldn't wait for the next session.

The First Miracle

Picture a hotel ballroom with chairs all along the walls. In the middle of the room were 25 massage tables. One hundred students filled the room as they learned to recognize this healing and the registers described by the instructor. As we learned and practiced different exercises and techniques, my friend looked at me and said, "I don't think I'm getting this."

I responded, "Here, I'll lie on the table and you can work on me." I climbed up onto the table, lay down and closed my eyes. Immediately someone took and held my left hand. I thought to myself, "Who knows me well enough in here to touch me?" I was rather uncomfortable that a total stranger would hold my hand. What happened next surprised and amazed me! I opened my eyes, yet not my eyes but my mind's eye. My eyes were closed, but I could see. I know that sounds strange, but through this work, I have realized that sometimes we "see" with our hands and our hearts, and even with our minds. I can't tell you how I saw Him. I just did. It was as real to me as if you had stood at my side.

I looked to the left and there He was, holding my hand. I looked down at his feet. He was wearing brown sandals that tied up his legs. I noticed that his legs were rather dusty. He wore a camel colored robe that fell to the middle of his calves, and he had long, curly brown hair. Then I saw His eyes – His marvelous eyes – breathtakingly beautiful blue eyes. He spoke gently and softly to me.

42

"Vicki, you are loved. You are cared for. You are in My care." [6]

He looked at me with such love. There was no doubt in my mind Who He was. He knew me. It was as if He looked into my heart and KNEW me. I heard the voice. I heard the words. I felt the love. Tears rolled out my eyes and down my face onto the table. What a sacred and loving moment in my life! He touched me, He held my hand, He spoke to me, and I was never the same again.

I opened my eyes and looked at my friend. She brought me a tissue. She still had no idea what had happened. In this seminar setting, it was important to share stories so other participants would have an idea of what kinds of things to expect in sessions. I quietly spoke to her, so only she could hear. I told her, "I think you got it. You don't have to worry about the work and this is why..." Then I shared my experience with her privately.

As the speaker led a discussion to share what people had seen, felt, heard, or smelled, I felt my experience was too sacred to share openly. I felt that if I shared it, it might diminish the blessing for me, and I didn't want to diminish the experience in any way. When the instructor asked if anyone had experienced tears, three of us raised our hands. He said, "Put your hands down if they were sad tears." All three hands were still in the air. He said, "What I know about this work is that when you experience tears, you have come face to face with Spirit and Truth."

The speaker purposely designed his seminars to appeal to all groups of people. He hadn't encouraged or bought into specific religious dogmas. He presented the work as God, Love, Universe, Holy Spirit, Source – you choose which names work for you. It was a spiritual experience, yet he did not confine it nor force it to be something that appealed to only one group or religion. It was not the product of any organized religion. It was not faith healing.

My experience was what it was. Jesus' words healed me and touched my injured heart. He became form and made Himself real to me. Many believe that God is in a package of his or her creation and that God only operates in certain ways. I found that God was way beyond our imagination. He did not and does not fit into any box that our human minds may construct. He knows us intimately. He is always around us. He loves us so much.

Yesterday, today and tomorrow, He is omniscient, omnipotent and omnipresent. He lives within each of us. He knows and loves everything about us. He is amazing and loving, yet He gives us free will and free choice. We underestimate the power of free will and free choice in our lives. A friend and police officer once said to me, "God gave us a gift – free will. Sometimes the price for that free will is pretty high."

Free will and free choice are gifts of a loving God to allow us to live, choose paths to take and sometimes make mistakes. We know that with unconditional love, we will be loved whatever the situation, whatever our choice. We often pray and beg that God will guide and direct us in what to do next. Begging for guidance was not encouraged. I finally understood that the choice is ours – not God's choice to make. He will support our choice, but the Universal Laws of Life do not allow for Him or the guides, angels and beings that work with Him to make our choices for us. He would violate His own Divine Laws. The gift of free will empowers us to make our own choices and live with the consequences and lessons of those choices.

This experience enabled me to value, honor and expand my beliefs about what I have been told and believe about God. Through this work, I had the opportunity to compare what has been communicated directly to me through these messages and what has been conveyed through organized religion. I learned that organized religion is not wrong. It is just incomplete. There is more that will be communicated to us. This journey has enabled me to know how very much God loves us.

Each of us is special in a unique way. Each of us is truly precious in His sight. Even though we are all one body, not all of us are hands or feet. This is an important point for each of us to really understand – an estimated 6.2 Billion people exist in our world and God considers each person special. God does not see us as criminals, bad, good, brilliant, or any other descriptor our human minds place on people. God sees us as the beautiful children – His beautiful children – and together as One, we form the whole of God's Love, Life and Universe.

I was skeptical when I first learned of this healing work. I had studied Reiki and knew there were benefits from alternative healing techniques, so I kept an open mind. After this experience, I was absolutely sure that I was supposed to attend this seminar. I came face to face with Jesus.

As I shared this work, I had other encounters with Jesus. He has been the reason why I am writing this book. So here it is. Some may think it is incredible that God, Mary and Jesus still talk to people today. Why don't we believe that God, Who is omnipresent, omnipotent and omniscient can speak? We can speak and we are made in His image. We have heard Him speak to us in that still, small voice. We may have had a difficult time listening, but we heard Him just the same. We just ignored Him. Can it be that He is speaking more loudly today, because we are not listening or maybe because we are listening? When I removed the box and limitations, all kinds of things began to happen. I learned all it takes for us to be willing is to surrender, listen and allow His words to permeate our hearts. The method doesn't matter as much as the message itself.

We have been told many times in churches, "Don't trust your feelings. Rely on your faith." I believe that we do need to trust our hearts and feelings as well as rely on our faith. I believe the heart is the most powerful organ in the body, and it is where truth is found. I know the heart can overpower the mind because the power of love comes straight from God. Nothing is stronger than He is.

The Next Step in the Journey

Within a week, I completed the Level I/II course in Dallas and traveled to San Diego for completion of Level III. I didn't know how I would make that trip financially or on such short notice. The seminar was sold out and the trip was within the 7-day advance purchase date for reduced airfares, so I knew the cost would be more expensive. This was one of my initial experiences in synchronicity. A friend of a friend who had planned to go to the seminar suddenly cancelled. I arranged to pay her for her class tuition, but first I had to secure airfare. I called the airlines to see if there was space available in exchange for air miles. There was only first-class seating available, so I booked the trip and found myself at the training seminar in San Diego. It happened so fast and seemed so effortless, that I had no doubt I was supposed to be there.

Being in the energy was a wonderful experience. The people I met there have remained important in my life. I continued to feel pressure within my head. It ached and throbbed. The pressure grew enough to distract me from learning. My friends tried a variety of energy techniques and massage therapy to try and relieve the pain. I even resorted to aspirin. Nothing seemed to work. I decided some fresh air might be what I needed. I went outside and sat next to the flagpole on a bench in front of the hotel. It was a beautiful summer day. I looked at the flowers and shrubs. I enjoyed the warmth of the sun and the bright-colored flowers. I watched the people milling around, and I was reminded of the beauty that we sometimes take for granted. I studied one of the shrubs, and it took on the appearance of a mirage – you know – like one you see on the road ahead of you on a hot day. It became filmy and fuzzy – not clearly defined. It looked like it had been transported as they do on Star Trek™, but it hadn't fully rematerialized. I thought, "How funny – that plant's structure is changing." I was talking with some friends later and described the experience. They suggested it was me rather than the plant that was "shifting." Perhaps my head was expanding to handle the light and information I was receiving with this work.

I found that headaches were common with the expanded frequencies we were experiencing energetically. I was told it was our bodies shifting to accommodate new frequencies and changes in our tissues. Evidence of the shifts occurred over time for me through tiny blisters on the palms, inside my mouth and even on my fingers. I periodically experienced a dot of blood in my ears and my nose. It wasn't a lot of blood; it was just enough for me to notice that it was there.

Looking back, there were several synchronous steps in this exciting journey. People I met were instrumental in introducing me to other people or events that seemed important in my life. I learned more about these new techniques. I shared quietly what I had learned with a few people. I shared the healing experiences with friends and family. I saw immediate results from the work.

During November 2000, the speaker returned to Dallas. He appeared again on "Good Morning, Texas" along with Randy Travis, the country western singer. The speaker again demonstrated the ability to provide a dramatic healing experience for a woman with painful arthritis in her hands. She exclaimed, "My hands have not moved like that in 25 years!" It was an exciting event. We were able to visit with Randy Travis and his wife after the show. The studio asked him to sing for the Thanksgiving Show and I asked the sound engineer if I could sneak in and listen in the wings. He told me no, that I couldn't just stand in the wings. He invited me to join the staff and anchors in the studio. Randy Travis played his guitar and sang, *Amazing Grace*. I stood approximately 5 feet from him as the words and the music touched my heart.

The speaker presented his story again in the Level I/II seminar. It was during this seminar, that I began to provide clients with the two-day process, The Reconnection™[7], that I had been trained to perform in the San Diego seminar. The personal connection process was referenced in *The Book of Knowledge: The Keys of Enoch,* in Key 314:59 "...selected individuals can be **reconnected** with the Adam Kadmon image through a resonance operating through hyperdimensional space." There was another reference in Key 317:22 that stated, "In order to reconnect the biological interconnection with the higher energy planes serving higher evolutionary programming, the acupuncture lines of the old program have to be attached to their 'new' axiatonal lines..."[8] Three people were drawn to me to work on them. They resonated with me. I was excited to begin this work.

I loved sharing this experience with people. It was like a dance and had specific steps. The client lay on his back while I drew lines of light, information and energy in a specific pattern on his body, but I never touched him. I became aware of how everyone's experience was unique for them. I wanted to do everything perfectly, but I also realized there was an "Intelligence" that would correct any mistakes that I might make. After the process was completed, the client would share what he had felt, seen, heard, tasted or smelled. He would also share any physical changes or experiences. There was a bonding that occurred between the client and me. It was a blessing and a gift for both of us. I felt connected to the client and even closer to God.

CHAPTER 3

WORKING FROM THE HEART

"This world is headed to a rejuvenation with this work to a healthier life. That is why so many of you are needed for reconnective work. It's healing from neighbor to neighbor. It's healing from child to animal. It's healing from animal to child."

In December 2000, I flew to Los Angeles to discuss employment opportunities. We talked about working conditions, plans and dreams of moving this work forward. I agreed to place my house on the real estate market to begin the transition. Over the next three months, 40 different people looked at my home, but no one ever made a serious offer. I realized the time was not right to move to L.A.

I was serving my community as an elected official, Mayor Pro Tem, but I was willing to give that up if it was necessary to move the work forward. I was prepared to step down from my various responsibilities. I felt like there was a question being asked of me – How much were you willing to relinquish in order to do this work? Were you willing to give up things of importance? Were you willing to give up living in close proximity to friends and family? Were you willing to give up your home? Were you willing to give up your seat on the City Council? As I answered yes to each question, I realized just how important this work was to me. It was a lesson in letting go and surrendering things that were once so important. When I asked myself, "Were these things more important than my life's work?" I realized they were not as important after all.

I continued doing healing work. It was sometimes difficult explaining what it was exactly. I knew that when Jesus spoke to me, I could not ignore the call. However explaining that experience was very awkward. How do you say, "Well, I do this work because Jesus speaks to me." That's probably what I should have said, but fear kept me from openly explaining about my encounter with the Master. People placed their trust in me as an elected official. They knew I was a Christian. They knew I relied on my faith as I carried out the duties of my elected position. What would they think if suddenly I was claiming that Jesus actually spoke to me? Would they think I was crazy? I didn't know. I told a few people, but I received mixed reactions. So I selectively told people I trusted that this miracle had happened to me. It was exciting, unusual and rather unbelievable, except that it really did happen to me.

Some people embraced the work completely and me along with it. Others experienced how powerful it was. Some didn't feel anything at all. A few were skeptical until they experienced a miracle and then thought it was marvelous. Occasionally people avoided me because they thought this work was evil. Some people feared it or weren't sure what to think. Friends who knew me trusted that I would not be involved if I did not evaluate it fully and know that God was at the heart of what I was experiencing.

I fortunately had close friends to share the joys, victories, fears and sorrows. I was being transformed by this work. People commented that I looked happier. I looked different – more carefree – more relaxed. I noticed that I didn't react in my usual, impatient and demanding way when difficulties presented themselves. I noticed that I seemed more tolerant of others. I still had my moments of being extremely human, but overall there was a tremendous change. The real challenges came when people pressed my buttons. I found I could look at them with love rather than judgment. I tried to see things from their point of view. I realized I could choose a loving response more often than criticism. That was new, different and exciting for me. I even ran unopposed for Mayor in May 2001, and won the election. We had come a long way and our community was changing in marvelous ways.

In The Wake of September 11th

The weekend before September 11th, I traveled to Houston to assist that same speaker in a weekend seminar. When the event was over, I offered to drive him to Dallas for the seminar the following weekend. This was actually September 10th, 2001. We had time to readdress the issues about the future, timing for employment and options available for furthering this work. We visited, listened to a tape and were oblivious to the changes our country, the world and we, as individuals, would experience within the next 24 hours.

When the tragedy of Tuesday, September 11th occurred, everything in my life changed. September 11th was a wake up call for me. God speaks to our hearts. He spoke to mine that day. I knew with a sense of urgency that my life had a purpose. I needed to get busy and get on with my work.

I remembered feeling deep sadness and loss over the family members whose lives were sacrificed. I cried when watching the families mourn the men and women who would not live to see their family, friends and children until they met again in heaven. I also knew with every part of my being that it was time for me to begin my work in earnest. I quit my job. I called Dr. Pearl and said, "It's time. I am ready to begin working for you." He responded, "I need you in Birmingham, Alabama next week. Can you be there?" I responded, "Absolutely!"

Hollywood, Here I Come

When I was around five and my sister was seven, we decided to run away to Hollywood and sing on *The Lawrence Welk Show*. We packed a tiny suitcase for the two of us and made our escape. We didn't know a lot about planning and made it as far the next-door neighbor's house because it was raining so hard the day we set out on our journey. Years later, here I was in Hollywood. I had finally made it.

Working in Los Angeles presented some challenges for me. I was working and living in Hollywood 3 weeks each month. I would return for my duties as Mayor the first week of every month. For the most part, I lived out of a suitcase in the confines of a small room. What I learned was that I could live more simply. I learned to appreciate luxuries, but learned they were not necessities in my life. Two things happened as a result of this arrangement. My friend, the

Mayor Pro Tem, had a chance to stretch her leadership wings conducting meetings in city government, and I felt torn between Texas and California. The work was so vitally important in both places. I would have stepped down sooner, but I was concerned for her health. She was diagnosed with breast cancer and was undergoing chemo and radiation treatments. Her stress of additional responsibilities and her medical condition were important factors for me to consider. I did not want to add to her burden. As it turned out, there was still work for me to do in Crandall.

I treasured my time in L.A. I met people and formed important relationships and connections. These relationships developed from friendship, love and respect. They also provided a support group and a foundation for my future. I was destined to meet these people. They held an important key to my work. And yes... there were lessons to learn.

As a politician, I learned to apply the rule of engagement formula as: 1) observe, 2) evaluate and then 3) engage in any situation. This prevented me from saying something that would have a negative effect on people and situations. My employer would say he could see the wheels turning in my mind and would constantly repeat, "Vicki, think out loud. I need to hear what you're thinking." This was so outside my comfort zone. I had to really work hard on this. I had spent years learning to filter what I thought and how I communicated information so that it came out in a positive way.

For three months, I had a sore throat while in Los Angeles. I attributed it to the smog, but the truth was that I was learning a valuable lesson – one I would not truly realize until the summer of 2002. I was learning to speak my truth. I had spent more than half my life battling my former habit of cutting people to ribbons with my tongue when I would say things in a knee-jerk reaction. It really bothered me that I could hurt people like that. I spent a lot of time and effort on suppressing hurtful words. What I learned was that burying my thoughts, feelings and desires inside me were just as hurtful, but to me. I was trying to protect the people I loved from being hurt by my words, but at times I would be vague rather than direct with the truth of what needed to be said. My intention was to be honest, but not hurtful. Sometimes I would ignore things that should have been addressed right away. I needed to learn that speaking the truth and honoring me was just as important as honoring others. Even a difficult truth could be delivered in a loving way. Truth could be beautiful when the package it comes in is filled with love.

When I avoided speaking my truth, my throat was scratchy and I coughed a lot. It kept me centered on that area of my body. The throat represents the communication center of the body. What I discovered was that if the topic were less important, I could speak candidly. If the topic were very important, I would keep silent when I should speak up or I would minimize the message, if I did speak up. Neither approach served me very well.

One of the greatest gifts of this time was the personal time spent with my employer. I saw his human side. I saw him in the big picture and I saw him in minute detail. His life was an open book that I read in order to understand both the blessings and challenges he experienced on a daily basis. It was a lesson about people – how they interacted with him and how he interacted with them. It was also about his lessons in how to deal with the challenges of people wanting to get close to him because he had "the gift." I was able to see him in situations where he could be himself.

I worked long hours. All the staff members worked hard together to establish goals and objectives. I assisted him in seminars. In the course of my duties, I spoke to countless people on the phone and answered their questions about the work. I was concerned and empathetic for the people who were interested in this healing work. I referred them to practitioners in their area. I tried to make sure they had the information they needed to make informed decisions about their health options. I invited them to attend seminars where they could spend an entire weekend in the healing energy.

I experienced a totally different way of life in Los Angeles and Hollywood. I would see movie stars at the grocery store. I was without a vehicle and dependent upon other people for transportation, which was way out of my comfort zone. I learned that people relied on delivery services to bring meals, groceries, toiletries, you name it – they brought it all. When I became really homesick or wanted food that reminded me of home, I would convince my employer to take me for fried chicken, turnip greens and cornbread at Roscoe's Chicken and Waffles. For a short while, I could close my eyes, and imagine I was at home enjoying the smells and tastes of Southern cooking. I was amazed and grateful for this restaurant in the heart of Hollywood.

This was also a time of joy for me to live in close proximity to Hobie. What a dear friend and gifted healer with a kind and generous heart! Between my employer and Hobie, I found friendship, love, acceptance and the freedom to be me again. I had to be dignified and cognizant of protocol at all times, because I was the Mayor. I had to think before I acted and be on guard for the impact of my words and actions. Somehow I actually changed because of the demands of my political life. I denied parts of who I was, because of what others might think. Little by little, I was becoming someone else. But in Hollywood, my spontaneity returned and I learned how to laugh and have fun again. One of the most wonderful experiences for me was the ability to be me... not the Mayor, the daughter, the sister, the business owner, the homeowner, the civic leader or any of the other labels I had placed on me. I could be carefree. I could just be me.

Living in Los Angeles, I missed my home, my friends and my family. I would pack a lot of visiting into the one week I was home along with my responsibilities of community and home ownership. Truly, it was a time where I was never really "at home" in either place.

Recently, I realized what a huge gift it was to be in L.A. I was in a constant energy of Reconnective Healing™[9] whether it was assisting in seminars, being in the company of my co-workers or answering people's questions about this work. Most of all I was gifted to be in presence of Dr. Pearl, who has forged new territory that is largely unexplainable. He has shared this gift with thousands of people and I am one of those lucky individuals who have shared this gift, his hospitality and his friendship. He is a visionary that sees where this will go. He diligently reminds us to honor the integrity and pureness of the work, because it is so vitally important. He has become a person some would like to put on a pedestal, so much so that sometimes people forget that he is human with the same needs for love, friendship, trust, forgiveness and acceptance that we all share.

Dr. Pearl was chosen to bring Reconnective Healing™[10] to the world. His skills to bring it this far were planned and I believe were established in him before he was born as part of his life purpose. My human ego has been tempted on occasion to force my evaluations and opinions on him before I looked inside my own heart. Thankfully, I have good friends who help me see that my judgments come from an archetypal pattern, and therefore are sometimes quite flawed. Lovingly, they reminded me to love first rather than judge. Thankfully, before I acted on my own judgment, I realized the picture of what was happening at the 40,000-foot level was far different than I was seeing. It was a tough thing to let go, but it was an important part of my difficult lesson in loving, non-judgment, detachment, surrender and release.

I once was so disturbed about some things, that I wrote a lengthy letter. I was heavily invested in my view of how things appeared – in my own opinion. A good friend said, "You wrote the letter. You sent it out into the Universe. He got it. Let it go." I listened and decided she was right. Much later, my concerns were set aside as I witnessed love changing the very situations in ways I could never have imagined. If things had unfolded according to my wish list, people would not have had the opportunity to experience the miracles that occurred in their lives. My judgment limited the solution and growth of practitioners in this work. Once I got out of the way, I could see how important it was to let go of attachment to the outcome. Sometimes you just let go and surrender knowing that what needs to happen will happen.

The people we love and get irritated with are those that offer us the greatest lessons if we choose to learn them. I love my former employer and yet, sometimes his human side pushes my buttons. I try to remember that the traits I see in him are probably those that I need to work on in my own life. We wouldn't be here without him. He confirms that there is more to this wonderful work. I will always be grateful for the lessons I learned while in L.A. It was a "supreme" experience.

Just before I was planning to resign as Mayor, I received another message from a friend and several pleas from my constituents. I learned that my time in government was not over yet. There were still things for me to accomplish at home. There were still people to reach in Texas. I returned to my community with a heavy heart to leave Hollywood, my job and my friends there. I knew I had more work to do in Crandall, and my life still had a purpose there.

I called my employer and told him how much I valued the time I spent in California and traveling with him. I explained I needed to resign. I advised him I would do whatever I could to assist him in seminars and further this work. The healing was and still is vitally important to me.

Another hard lesson in life made itself apparent to me at this time. It was the lesson of the importance of money in our lives and trying to balance the need with the desire to do God's work. For years, I have been gifted with skills and talents that enabled me to live successfully and earn a wonderful salary. Now I was faced with the reality that many people did not value the gifts of healing that had become my livelihood and earned money to pay my bills. In going to work for Dr. Pearl, I had cut my salary by 75% and found it difficult to choose between getting a real job and doing what I came here to do.

For the first time in my life, I was struggling to survive financially and not doing very well. I felt the burden of home ownership and dreaded the expenses that were a part of that picture. There were times when it became overwhelming and I experienced first hand how our images of who we are become greatly influenced by the money we did or did not have in the bank. I needed to share this burden and I did not have a spouse to discuss things with, so I met a friend for breakfast. I worked up the courage to share some of the heartbreak over my financial difficulties, hoping she would have some words of wisdom that would help me through this battle. I will never forget how she cut me off, changed the subject, and the terms of our friendship changed forever that day. The unspoken message came through loud and clear. Our friendship had limits. It was all right as long as things were going well, but it was not a friendship where we could confide our weaknesses. I learned that a personal discussion led to a quick exit. The road ahead was only safe if we kept to business topics or personal successes. Most of my friends were supportive, but this too, was an important and painful lesson for me. I just knew I had to "love her though it."

I had rapidly gone from a person who could shop till she dropped to a person who felt so strapped that she did not know where the house payment, car payment, insurance premiums or groceries would come from next. I struggled to survive and how I managed was through the generosity and love of family and friends who stood by me. They would say, "Vicki, I don't know how you have survived this long."

I was faced with calls from creditors and had to tell them honestly, "I do not know when the money will be here to pay you. I want to honor my commitment, but I am unsure when that will be." This was humiliating, but it was the truth. I was lectured repeatedly from collectors on the morality and responsibility of creating debt. I listened to them verbally abuse me, and I realized I was learning to set boundaries as I told them, "Please speak to me respectfully." If they continued to speak disrespectfully, I hung up the phone. I realized that just because I was in a financial dilemma, it did not mean I had to subject myself to verbal abuse or think less of myself.

I also realized personally how people are measured by financial wealth and felt that their power was diminished when they experienced financial challenges. I guess until you walked down that path, you could not realize how demeaning it could be. I also realized that fear was a tool that was commonly used by bill collectors to make you feel less than you should about who you are. Then there were the bright moments when a loving soul was the one who placed the call. They would say something that showed me they understood. One lady called me and said, "It was reported that you refused to pay, and that did not sound like you. What is your situation?" When I responded that I intended to pay when the funds were available, she said, "That is consistent with what you have told us. Let us know when your situation changes. Have a nice day! Hope you win the lottery!"

I continued to believe that financial challenges were part of the huge lesson I needed to learn. I still needed to heal from money issues. I also needed to feel the desperation and difficulties within my own life and then I could empathize and help others. I can honestly say I experienced the pain and frustration over an extended period. For most of my life, I made things look easy whether it was professionally or personally. Evidently this was no different.

There were people I trusted with the failures of my life, but when I went to share the difficulties with them, I cringed on the inside because of what they might think. One friend embraced me and said, "Vicki, we have all had financial challenges. I declared bankruptcy and know how you feel. It will all work out in time."

When I tried to gloss over this pain in my life, it was this same friend who said, "People need to know what you experienced. They need to see your pain. They need to identify with the difficulties you faced. That is a huge part of the lesson."

When you are experiencing the difficulties, you think they will never end. I learned to feel the pain and then let it go. Money in the bank does not determine my value and worth. Until I learned that lesson, I couldn't be liberated by the truth.

People may judge you. I used to be one of those people. I judged others based on the clothes they wore, the cars they drove, the language they used and even the choices they made. It was only when I walked a little in their shoes that I was able to change how I thought and behaved. I began to value each person as someone who had a unique gift and a story to tell. It was only after the healing began in my life, that I was able to change how I lived and how I treated others with more love than judgment.

I was still troubled that I had this gift to share and that I wasn't doing a very good job of letting people know about energy medicine and alternative healing options. If they did know about it, they wanted to sample it for free. One of my relatives kept volunteering me for free sessions until I asked one day, "If I were a doctor and came to visit, would you schedule appointments for me?"

I had invested money and time in recognizing, utilizing and training for this gift. I learned more about this work through the sessions I had participated in. Many people feel that a "gift" should be given for free. If this is the sole means of support for the practitioner, how can that happen? A pastor, doctor or hairdresser receives money for his or her gift. A talented singer's vocal gift is rewarded with money.

Some people felt you should charge only if a healing occurred. How would a doctor respond if you placed the same criteria on an office visit? Sometimes the healing occurs at any or all of the mental, emotional, spiritual or physical levels. How would you ever know when the healing might occur over time? Healing comes from the same Source.

I was more than willing to provide sessions and many of them for free. What I learned was that if no exchange occurred, people perceived the value as zero. There were a few people who realized the gift was priceless and any money they spent would be returned to them in other ways. For them, I am deeply grateful for the blessings and the exchange of trust, love, money and healing.

CHAPTER 4

HEALING FROM THE HEART

"How I heal is not important. Who I heal is not important. It's the love emanating through healing that's important. People walk around with illness, cancer, and AIDS. These are diseases of the body. I heal disease of the Spirit. The body will do the rest."

So what is healing? Healing occurs in our bodies on a variety of levels. It includes the alleviation of symptoms, diseases, infirmities, and other barriers to living a full and healthy life. Healing is also the restoration of the person to emotional and spiritual wholeness. In some cases, healing occurs in death as the physical body dies and the spiritual body is released from the physical body. My experience has been that healing is that which provides love, light and information to help renew our body, mind and spirit to its original healthy state and connectedness to Source. It is so hard to understand sometimes what is happening with our physical bodies. My impression is that with this healing, injuries and diseases at all levels are being released from deep within our bodies.

This healing seems to defy explanation within the current laws and theories of science and religion. Could it be possible that we do not know everything about our world, our existence, ourselves? Could it be that what we based our theories and conclusions on are only part of the story rather than the whole picture? I believed based on what I have been told through these "Gifts from the Heart" that there is so much more than we can know or that our science has confirmed. Just because it has not been proven, does not mean there is nothing more to discover.

Physical injuries and diseases often have spiritual and emotional roots. What I learned is that sometimes things are so deep within our spiritual, emotional and mental bodies that our physical bodies manifest the injuries and diseases from these other levels. I also believe that some of the illnesses and injuries that we experience lead us to experience miracles from God and the Universe. Sometimes healthy people would never seek solutions to health problems through alternative and complementary healing methods, if they weren't in desperate situations health wise. Sometimes our illnesses and injuries bring us to the place where we can understand and accept new truths and options in our lives.

Healing Stress in Our Lives

More information is available on a daily basis as we learn how stress, particularly repeated stress, on our bodies creates chemical reactions that leave us vulnerable to disease and injury. This provides more evidence that an emotional cause results in physical injury to our bodies. Think of people who suffer from emotional stress who eat comfort food. Later they find themselves diagnosed with diabetes. Through incidental stress as well as prolonged stress, the hormone cortisol is pumped into our bodies and DHEA, our anti-aging hormone, is diminished in reaction to stressors in our lives. Endocrine and other body systems are impacted by imbalances in the organs throughout the body. As much as we would like to think differently, we are wholly connected individuals. Our emotional, mental and spiritual health and imbalances are all connected and directly affect our physical health.

Links from stress to disease are being discovered and reported regularly in the medical community and media. We think of the medical community as the most knowledgeable source of information in the area of physical health. Continually, we hear that traditional medicine concentrates primarily on the physical body rather than treat the person holistically. Some medical practices are beginning to treat the whole person, not just the body. Anger, stress and fear can eat away at your health. News reports tell us that anger tends to increase the levels of an amino acid, homocysteine, in the blood. Elevated homocysteine levels have been linked to arterial damage and cardiovascular disease. Anger can kill us if we don't find ways to cope and heal.

When people ask me about healing, I tell them that healing is like listening for energy imbalances within the body. This healing provides a means for me to "listen" with the heart, eyes or hands to the parts of that person that need energy, light, love and information. I receive feedback through the hands, the heart and perhaps even other parts of the body. It is much like swaying to the music and being led to work on different parts of the body by being sensitive to the areas of the body providing feedback. Extensive research and development have been conducted to identify and track frequencies that change within the human body. In my healing practice, I have used a device to measure changes in frequencies throughout the body. This process is like taking a snapshot and helps identify the changes by capturing frequency readings before and after a healing session occurs.

Your personal connection process is a more specific process - like the tango. There are particular steps for each process that are quite involved and allow the transformation to unfold perhaps more quickly than with healing sessions alone. You present yourself as the client, the vessel, and God, Life or Love determines what needs to happen and what needs to be healed in the order it needs to be healed. Each person has the ability through intent and consciousness to impact the results because each of us has choice to allow or restrict results through free will.

This personal connection process is completed in two sessions usually in two consecutive days. People who have experienced the process report that they have had an opportunity to heal and in some instances, have become more aware of their life purpose. Some have even reported spiritual breakthroughs as a result of their experiences or the ability to release and heal old emotional injuries. Some people report experiencing an acceleration of goals and activities in their lives.

Healing is such a simple process. The results are amazing, so why is the medical community so reluctant to trust what happens? Is it an information issue? Is it a credentialing issue? Is it so simple that it challenges our paradigm of medical treatment? Does it challenge our medical tendency to prescribe medications rather than heal the problem at the source? How will the discoveries of physicists who have theorized the Zero Point Field help people understand more about how energy medicine and alternative healing work? History has confirmed to us that great truths often begin as blasphemies. This was true of the people who believed the world was flat and Galileo's belief that the earth revolved around the sun. Perhaps the truth of healing has to challenge traditional medical approaches and provide results and outcomes before they will be a viable option for the general public. Meanwhile, for those who are courageous enough to step out of the box, healings are occurring all around us.

Is it any wonder anger stored in the liver may be connected to liver disease? Is it any wonder that hatred and lack of love may be connected to heart disease? I think not. I believe healing allows God, Life and Love to heal wounds from the root cause and release wounds we have buried deep inside us and carried around for a long time.

In *Heart of the Soul*, Gary Zukav and Linda Francis tell us that we need to experience the pain in our lives, let it pass through and then let it go. Instead we deflect the pain and absorb it into our bodies – into the very cells of our physical selves. If we continue to hold onto the pain, it will be buried deep within our tissue. Medical intuitives suggest the pain will eventually develop into disease or injury. Pain sometimes is so difficult to bear that we take decades and maybe even entire lifetimes to release the pain. Sometimes the pain is so great, we never want to face it and therefore, it stays

71

buried. Because we have free will in our own healing, we are a powerful catalyst in choosing to release or hold onto "our stuff." We have the ability to heal ourselves.

Who then needs healing? Anyone suffering from illness, disease or injuries from the past or present can benefit from healing. Mind, body and spirit connect the person as a whole. Healing occurs on all levels - physical, mental, emotional and spiritual levels. I have participated in sessions and experienced positive results from arthritis, cancer, colitis, hepatitis C, birth defects, headaches, injuries, and a variety of other ailments. I have witnessed effective results with emotional injuries including verbal, physical and sexual abuse. I have worked with people who have experienced operations including hysterectomy, tonsillectomy, and knee repair. I have learned the practitioner does not need to know and in most cases, does not know, what the illness or ailment is. Healing is directed by God, Love and Life. God knows exactly what is needed and takes care of designing the package that the healing comes in.

Healing Animals and Plants

Did this healing only work with humans or would animals benefit also? Pets experienced shorter recovery times for surgical procedures. Veterinarian chiropractors learned energy medicine and alternative healing techniques and used them in their practices to assist animals of all kinds. Practitioners found their pets are drawn to this energy. My dog would lie down in front of me and nudge me until I provided her with a treatment. I found that people's pets that were normally not inclined to warm up to strangers approached me, rubbed on my legs and got my attention until I petted them and gave them a sample of the healing energy. Cats were particularly attracted to this work. They leaped onto the table while healing sessions were underway.

One of my favorite stories about the effect on animals came when I was visiting a friend. Her son stopped by with a dog he was caring for from a rescue shelter. As he and his mom visited together, I walked outside and as I approached the car, the dog was very high-strung and reacted violently. He was barking loudly. He was aggressively throwing himself repeatedly at the closed window towards me. I was afraid he might hurt himself, so I stood about a foot from the car and began to provide healing. I "beamed" energy to the dog for about 5 minutes. The results were remarkable. The dog quietly sat down on the seat, rested his head on his paws and went to sleep. About that time, the dog's owner walked out to the car and asked, "What did you do to my dog?" I responded, "What are you talking about?" He said, "That dog is not the dog I brought over here. He is quiet and docile. The dog I brought over here is radical." I replied, "All I did was give him a healing treatment."

He turned to his mother and said, "Mom, you and I need to go over to the rescue center. Based on these results, all the dogs could benefit from this work. If I didn't know that was my dog, I would not have believed it." He opened the door and let the dog out of the car. The dog came over to me and licked me. He was gentle and loving and a miraculous change had come over him. Every time I see him, he greets me with kisses as if he remembers the gift I shared with him.

Recently I went to a friend's house. A dog he was caring for had just delivered twelve puppies. They were a couple of weeks old and were so cute. Some of them had opened their eyes, but some still had their eyes closed. I held a couple of them. As they cuddled up next to my heart, they actually started vibrating and humming. My friend was standing next to me and said, "What's that noise?" I responded, "It's the puppies. I think they are connecting to my heart."

People's Healing Experiences

Almost from the beginning, clients shared amazing experiences from healing and personal connection sessions. I was fascinated and mesmerized by every word. I found myself capturing as much of the experience as I could on paper so that they would have the freedom to share without having to worry about missing anything while trying to write it down themselves. It was helpful when they drew an image rather than trying to describe it. My contribution was to help them build as complete a memory as possible to record what happened during their experience.

The Mayor Pro Tem was scheduled for surgery to remove her breast . The day before she went to the hospital, I offered to provide a healing session. She came to my home, and I worked on her as she lay on the massage table. The day following her surgery, I went to visit. I expected her to be groggy. As we sat at her table, she lifted both hands high over her head with her arms fully extended. "Watch this," she exclaimed. Frankly, I was shocked. She had no apparent after-effects from the anesthesia and she seemed to bounce back from surgery in a very short 36-hour period. Maybe mastectomy patients act like this all the time. It seemed unusual to me.

On two other occasions, I provided healing treatments for her – once the day before she began her chemo treatment. It took a few weeks into the treatment for her to feel the effects of the chemo. On another occasion, during her radiation treatments, she came over for a healing session and said, "Vicki, ...My joints ache and I do not sleep through the night. I suffer from Restless Leg Syndrome."

After the session was completed, she went home. The next day my phone rang. She said, "Thank you. I slept through the night. My joint pain was gone and so was the Restless Leg Syndrome. The only thing I did differently was the healing session. Thank you."

Sometimes I hear the results of healings and often, people realized healings happened after the sessions. They may not even associate the healing with this work. Healing can be instantaneous. Healing can also occur in layers that we can't always understand. When healing occurs, it may happen one layer at a time. If an emotional injury happened in childhood, and over time, it resulted in a physical illness, treating the physical problem is only one layer. The beauty of this work is that any layer that needs to be healed can be healed as a whole or just as an onion is peeled, one layer at a time. Layers may include one or more of the physical, mental, emotional or spiritual illnesses or injuries that we experience.

There are a number of different things reported as a result of a healing session. The healing can happen in an instant or it may take a little longer. In either case, the healing comes in the package designed especially for the client.

Today, my friend is healthy and active. Her change is remarkable and I heard her say recently, "I lost my fear during this ordeal. I can do anything if I try." I also heard her say, "I look around at the people who have cancer and are receiving chemo and radiation treatments. I'm not sick like they are. I guess I am just a healthier person."

A friend fell and hurt her ankle. The emergency room x-ray showed a bad break where the ankle and foot were joined. They place her foot into what my family calls a "Herman Munster" boot. I told her, "I do this energy work", and before I could say anything else, she stuck out her leg. I spent around 5 minutes providing an impromptu healing treatment. I knelt next to her leg and moved my hands around her ankle. I stood up when finished. She looked at me and said, "I know you never touched my ankle, but I felt my bone move." The next week she kept her orthopedic appointment. The doctor told her she only had a hairline fracture. Her tendons would take longer to heal than her ankle.

She fell just after her father died. Our emotional injuries of losing our anchors, our parents, can leave us vulnerable to illness, injury and disease. The ankle anchors us in our world just as our parents provide our foundations. When I asked gently if she thought that her ankle injury was related to that event, big tears welled up in her eyes. There are no firm studies that I know of to confirm these assumptions, but the synchronicities are amazing to me. Can you see a connection might exist?

When a close relative was beginning her chemo treatment for hepatitis C, we agreed to do her personal connection session. During her session, she said, "I floated on the sea on an air mattress. The thunder turned into the booming of the surf. Then I seemed to go liquid and I don't know where I was then. I was feeling pretty good when I liquefied and floated off into the sea...I opened my eyes and there were tears. They're still there. That was right after I turned back from liquid. It was thick liquid, but not sluggish – it was like heavy sugar syrup. It was different from yesterday. Peaceful. Just being." Months later when she went for a check up, there was no trace of the virus in her system.

Another client also was diagnosed with hepatitis C. When she experienced a healing treatment, she came out of the session and the people sitting around waiting for her said, "You look so different. Younger. Healthier. There's something very different about how you look." She experienced a second treatment a few months later. The last time I visited with her she exclaimed that she had never felt better and that the doctors were not going forward with any further treatment options.

When she had her personal connection session, she reported that she felt like she was floating, and the massage table wasn't even there. She said she felt like someone had his or her hand on her forehead. It felt nice and warm. She said, "I saw my guardian angel look down into my eyes." ...She went on to say, "I felt like I was in a ball – like in a ball – a ball of light was all around me."

Dozens of people reported seeing a tunnel or going through a tunnel. One client said, "I saw the tunnel. There was a little boy – somebody was in the tunnel."

One of the more dramatic results was from an automobile accident. I had been referred to a doctor for treatment. I scheduled an appointment and during the visit, I shared with him about this healing. I let him feel the energy and left him information about a website where he could investigate further. When I returned for a follow up visit, I offered him an additional treatment. I felt compelled to work on his hand for an extended period. As I worked, his metatarsal near the third finger of his right hand revolved in a complete circle. I saw it. He saw it. He said, "Vicki, the metatarsal cannot do that." I just looked at him and smiled. I didn't know what was happening. I was just willing to be in the process. We continued the treatment. He said, "I see tissue forming on my ring finger. I see a blue conical light coming out of your palm. I see spikes of energy coming out of your palm." He went on to explain that he felt strands or strings from my hands. I didn't see anything. It wasn't one of my gifts, but it was cool that he could see it.

I did get a sense that he had injured that hand. I asked him if that was true. He said he had been in a car accident. He had gone to dozens of doctors and spent a lot of money, but without results. The next day, my phone rang. He said, "Vicki, I can usually write only a half page before the pain becomes excruciating. I usually cannot read what I wrote. Today, I wrote six pages, before I even realized my hand did not hurt, and you can read every word of it. Thank you."

One client had been in an automobile accident and injured different areas of her body, including her leg. She told me her leg had been twisted beneath her at an unnatural angle. At the end of her session, she was amazed. Her whole left leg lengthened.

One client related this experience, "In the beginning, I saw a huge mathematical equation going out of your hands into my leg." Another client said, "My right eye was going in circles. My eyes see the same now – I was scheduled for surgery. Now it seems chances are slim that I will have surgery. It felt like something came into my ovary – or rather where it used to be and that pain went away finally." People have reported being able to "see" even when their eyes are closed.

Another client felt tremors I could see for the last ten minutes of his treatment. His body was constantly shaking and rocking side-to-side from his torso to his feet. The next day he woke up symptom free from colitis. He had suffered with it for over 25 years.

One morning, I woke up dreaming about a friend's baby that was born premature and had complications from birth. I asked if I could come over and hold her for a while. Her parents said, "Come on over." I held her for about two hours with the intention that she would receive whatever was needed for her health. A few days later, I asked about her. Her mother said, "Thank you. She sleeps 4-5 hours now and her monitor hasn't even gone off."

Another baby was several months old and experienced lung problems from birth. She was a twin and her twin was healthy. I held her for about 15 minutes. She was healthy and symptom free within a couple of weeks.

Many people experienced a pain that seemed intense during the session. A doctor wanted to experience a healing session. I invited him to the office and worked on him. At the end, he said, "I have an excruciating pain in my heel." When I asked if he had ever injured that heel, he immediately replied no. Then after a few minutes, he said, "That's not true. Last week I was on vacation. I jumped out of the boat in what I thought was 7 feet of water. It was only 4 feet deep and I landed on that heel. Now the pain is gone." It was almost as if something happened to bring him back to that state of wholeness or healing. I didn't know about that heel. He didn't remember about the heel until later. But the manufacturer – God Who made him – was intimately aware of the injuries that needed to be healed.

Everyone's healing experiences were unique to them. Some elements were repeated and became familiar to me, although I wouldn't necessarily say they were common occurrences. None of the experiences were exactly the same for any two people. It was as if each person's experience was as individual as that person – designed especially for each of us.

New practitioners to this work often saw some of these experiences during seminars. People were immersed in the energy for an entire weekend. There were numerous miracles and healings that occurred during seminars and people shared their stories. More often than not, additional injuries or illnesses were cured, but there was a subtle change and people realized it after the seminar was completed. Ongoing sharing and mentoring provided an opportunity to gather information from different experiences so new practitioners would have an idea or range of expectations when providing healing treatments.

It was fun to see people sheepishly raise their hands to say, "I'm not sure if this is related to the work, but..." As they continued to explain and complete their story, the instructor would ask the other attendees if anyone else has experienced this particular reaction. Consistently, dozens of people raised their hands in confirmation that this was a valid experience when working with this healing.

During healing sessions, people reported seeing colors – purples, violets, greens, reds, blues and a few other colors – some they never saw before. One man even reported, "I felt all these pastel colors around me. There were violet, yellow, greens – like clouds. I felt immersed in this color and feeling. It was peaceful..." One client reported seeing green with silver in it like the iridescence of a peacock's feathers. People reported seeing geometric shapes – some they recognized, some shapes that were new and different than they had ever seen. One client reported seeing lots of 2 dimensional pyramidal triangles overlapping with flashes of light as the outline. One client reported seeing colorful flowers. When she looked closer, they were moving. She said, "That's how I knew they were people."

People reported seeing "light bars," "light rods," and one client said, "You put a pyramid hat on my head." One client reported, "There's a 'beam' – an energy of a higher level coming to you. It's a sphere of King Solomon and it's creating energy in your hands." There were often reports of seeing kaleidoscopes of different colors. Over a dozen people reported seeing a single eye peering at them. One client reported that her eyes were doing figure eights independently of each other during the session. Several clients reported watching themselves from a distance as the session was being conducted. One client described it as, "At one point, I felt as if I had come back into my body or someone put me there..." The she wondered, "Am I looking at myself?"

Clients shared that they had strings of white light that connected and extended throughout their body. In some cases, when these strings of light were being applied, they reported their bodies were actually suspended in the air. Some clients reported that strings of light went from shoulder to leg and connected other parts of the body. One client reported seeing the "grid of light."

Several clients reported seeing images of people. Some people reported seeing faces or partial faces. There were people they recognized. Some saw family members that had died. Some saw little children. One client reported looking up and seeing a group of people peering down at her. She came over to me about four months later during a seminar and said, "You know those people I saw in my personal connection session? I looked up during that last exercise and they were the people working on me." Several clients have reported seeing ancient men and women.

Many of the sessions have included reports of Native American Indians in full headdress. Some describe these Indians as stoic. Several clients have reported chanting and the presence of the Tribal Council. One client reported, "The last thing I saw was a very stoic Indian. He wasn't smiling. He was looking off into the distance and was waiting for me."

One client reported, "It seemed strange. I saw a Roman Gladiator. I saw the cape and the back of his helmet. His cape was made of heavy red cloth." The next day she was quite surprised when she turned on the television. There amidst Palm Sunday Services from Vatican City was the gladiator decked out in the red cape and uniform of the day.

Recently I provided personal connection sessions for three women. When they began to discuss their experiences together, they all three confirmed and discussed that I mumbled and chanted throughout the sessions. I'm not sure what they heard, but I concentrated on being quiet and eliminating noise as much as possible during the sessions. They were convinced that I had been mumbling and even though they could not understand what I was saying, they knew I was saying something. They all three demonstrated how I moved my mouth and agreed on what I did, except that I didn't do it!

One client reported, "I heard the sound of nature. I listened to the sound of flowers and the breeze. They all have sound."

Often music plays an important part in these sessions. One man reported hearing "strong fou-fou music." People have reported hearing songs that include, *"Tell Me Something Good," "Today," "Imagine," "All You Need is Love," "You're the One That I Want," "Endless Love," "Take a Ride,"* and *"You're My Love, You're My Lady."* One client who reported hearing multiple songs said, "I don't really relate to music." She said, "I felt like I could laugh when the music started." Many people felt like laughing. Some laughed uncontrollably and felt they couldn't stop even if they tried. One client shared this comment, "Sometimes, I wanted to contort my face. At other times, I wanted to smile. Once my feet felt jolly and merry, like they were in something."

Many of the clients reported messages or thoughts that were not their own that they received during the sessions. They reported hearing the words in their minds. The messages were reported in one session as:

"You have been bestowed a special gift."
"You need to have faith."
"You need to journal your experience."

One client felt her mouth move, but heard the words within her mind during a session:

"God be with you and you and you."
"Peace be with you and you and you."
"Be gone. Be gone. Be gone. Be still."

She reported the "Be gone" was directed to a nerve block in her toe. She said to them in her mind, "I'd like to see you. Could you help me with that?" They responded, *"Of course."* Then she saw this guy. It looked like the Italian deli guy. He waved and said, "See you later." She shared, "There was something about Jesus. They said 'Mary is great.' Then they said three times, 'Understand you are loved.'" She went on to say at the end, "There was this vision. It was the Italian deli guy, only different."

Many clients told me that they heard the radio come on or suddenly the clock ticked loudly. When this happened, there would not be a radio or a clock even close to them, not even in the same room. One client reported, "There was a watch ticking on my left side – like someone tapping their nails really fast in my left ear." One client reported, "I heard me clicking. It was not my voice box. It was like…above it. There was repetitive clicking." One fellow practitioner described a change in the way she could hear. She said, "It felt like the walls were removed. I could hear everyone as if there were no walls in the building. Sounds became louder, because there were no walls."

One client reported, "I felt joy inside. I was smiling on the inside. I definitely felt good." On multiple occasions, clients have reported they have felt itching on their faces. One client reported feeling like she was wrapped in ribbons at the end of her session. She also reported, "Today was more about grieving and letting go. It felt like someone was pulling out grief and sadness from me."

Another client heard the voice of Jesus. He said, "I will knock on the door for you. When I knock, the doors open. When I knock, the doors open. You do not have to work hard for it." He went on to say, "Do you know what it means to be healed? It means to be whole. Do you know what it means to be whole? Not fragmented."

The client reported, "There was so much more than the words. Each word had a vibration. I don't know what to call it. Sometimes I felt like I was floating... At one point, I wondered where I was. The answer came, 'You're in the spaces between words where creativity begins.' Then at one point, I thought, 'Even mental retardation can be healed.'"

I noticed during sessions that saliva collected in my mouth. This happened the day "I mumbled." Other clients reported the same thing. I hadn't figured out what that means yet. I also noticed when doing this work, my knees, ankles and joints cracked and popped. I hadn't noticed it happening at other times. It still continues when I do sessions and I have understood from other practitioners that they, too, noticed limbs and joints that creak and pop as they perform healing and personal connection sessions. I'm not sure why, I just know it happens.

One interesting experience reported by one client said, "There was a textbook on my body – colorful hoola hoops were spinning around and around. They became thicker and thicker. There were colors – bands of bright, rich colors."

People have reported and I have personally witnessed arms and legs which floated in air for 30 minutes or more during a healing session. One client said she felt like someone placed beach balls underneath her arms during the whole session. Some people reported that they lifted off the table or even became a part of the table. I also experienced this personally. When you participated as a client in the healing process, it was very common to feel a buoyancy and lightness in your body and limbs. Some people reported that they spun or moved to a different angle from the table. One client admitted sheepishly that she actually flipped completely head over heels during her healing experience. Some clients' arms levitated or lifted in the air and their fingers started moving in ways that simulated playing the piano in the air.

Polymorphism

Recently, I went to a seminar presented by Gregg Braden, the author of *The Isaiah Effect* [11] among other books. He showed us the results of a study that was conducted by a scientist in the early 1900s, where a droplet of water was subjected to different levels of vibration over a period of time. Details of the experiment were recreated with the family's permission, because the scientist that conducted the experiment was no longer living. What I found fascinating was the results of vibration on the droplet of water. There were multiple stages of change or "polymorphism" on the droplet of water. The first frame of the experiment showed a vague circle. The next increase in vibration showed a shape that resembled a snowflake with six points. The next increase still resembled a snowflake, except that it had an abundance of points. The next change occurred when the vibration increased and multiple concentric circles formed around the middle of the droplet. The colors that were presented in the different frames appeared as a kaleidoscope.

My "ah ha" moment occurred as I remembered the many people who reported seeing colors and kaleidoscopes during their healing experiences. Our human bodies are comprised of 70-80% water. If healing occurs through vibration, this would potentially explain experiences that have been shared by clients. Gregg Braden went on to say that lower vibratory levels occur when you experience anger and hate. Higher vibratory levels occur with love, compassion, peace and forgiveness.

What was also fascinating was the way Gregg Braden's work touched on the experiences that people have reported from healing treatments. One client sat up at the conclusion of her session. She said, "My feet are freezing." Then she quoted the words she had heard during her experience. "We are the Pleadian messengers. They repeated that 3 or 4 times. You are One in the Universe. God is always with you. You are healed. Go forth and teach others."

She continued to relate, "There's another word – polymorphism. They said this over and over a bunch of times. The weirdest thing was...I felt you split twice. You did this yesterday. I heard a crackling noise both times."

What was unusual about this comment was that several people described a similar event. One of the strangest, yet consistent stories from people in these sessions was that I split in half. One client reported, "At one time it was like you sort of multiplied and you were standing all around me except for my feet." They reported I was on two sides of the table at the same time. One client reported, "I felt surrounded. You were everywhere – I couldn't tell where." They would hear me at their head, but felt me at their feet simultaneously. They would report feeling me on the right side of the table and the left side at the same time. I heard this multiple times in different parts of the country by a variety of different clients. I couldn't explain what their experience was. I just noticed that it was something that repeated on different occasions.

I met Dr. Masaru Emoto when he visited Dallas in May 2002. He spoke and presented his research as illustrated in his book *Messages from Water* [12]. His research showed the impact of images and words on water. He reminded us that the messages from water tell us to look inside ourselves. It showed the effect of words, sounds, and pictures on water molecules. What was fascinating was the concept that our words had the same impact on people who were composed of 70-80% water. He urged us to remember to add love and appreciation to everything we do or experience in life. It has an amazing healing impact on the world around us.

Healing and Pain Relief for Paralyzed Veterans

One of my favorite reports came from a relative. As a paralyzed veteran, a paraplegic, he loved being an avid sportsman, fisherman, hunter and Paralyzed Veteran Olympic Gold Medallist.

At Thanksgiving, I was visiting and he had been hunting for two days. His means of hunting was to drive his truck around looking for game while his legs dangled towards the floor. After two days, the fluid collected in his legs and caused a lot of swelling. When he returned home, it took two days for the fluid to drain off his body. When I arrived, he had just returned home to begin the two days of bed rest with his legs elevated. I was talking about the healing work and asked if I could put my hands on his leg. He agreed. He loved and trusted me. We talked and after about 10-15 minutes had passed, I told him I thought the swelling was going down in his leg. He said, "No way. It takes two days." I replied, "I think the swelling has gone down." He insisted that it took longer than that and his legs would look like dishpan hands when the swelling was gone. I took a look and sure enough, it looked like "dishpan legs" to me. He leaned down and exclaimed, "Wow, Vicki! I would never have believed it. Do the other leg." I told him, "The other leg looks the same. Working on one leg, the healing energy went wherever it needed to go. It took care of both legs at the same time."

Later his wife was one of the people who heard the jet planes fly over her face during her session. She was so certain that a jet plane flew directly over the house, she woke her husband and asked, "Did you hear that plane?" When he said no, she was incredulous. "I can't believe you didn't hear it. It was so loud." She ended up attending seminars to do this work for her husband, others, friends and family members in her life.

When I returned to visit the next year, we went to dinner and another Paralyzed Veteran Gold Medallist joined us. We watched in amazement as this slim guy added his name to the list of winners who had eaten a 50-pound steak dinner with all the trimmings. We were enjoying the moment and reliving the amazement of everyone at the restaurant. I can't remember what was said, but my relative said, "You ought to let her work on you. It feels great." I placed my hand on his shoulders and just let the healing energy flow through me and into him. These veterans experienced a lot of shoulder and arm pain, because they wheeled themselves around everywhere they went. He felt the energy right away. After I spent around fifteen minutes, he could make a fist with his right hand. A year and a half ago, he had a motorcycle accident that caused his paralysis. He sustained nerve damage and physical injuries, and had been unable to make a fist with his right hand, until now. It was such a blessing to help those who risk their lives for us.

Environmental Illnesses

Another relative worked in the Pacific Northwest as an environmental enforcement officer. A barnacle broke the skin in his thumb. He contracted a severe infection that became life threatening when it localized in his spine. It coursed through his body. He was paralyzed and unable to move. The hospital had difficulty in diagnosing the problem. He was hospitalized from January 21, 2002, and remained there until he was moved to a rehabilitation facility in March. There was little hope for his survival at one point and I was scheduled to visit. I provided distant healing treatments for him until I arrived and then I provided several healing sessions for him in person. His recovery was a long process, but he responded to the healing energy. He credited a critical milestone on his road to recovery as the direct result of his body responding to this treatment. Today he is working and back on the job.

His wife had complications from an angioplasty months before this happened and it was a challenge to meet the medical needs of both of them at the same time. She experienced a healing session that relieved some of the pain in her leg so she regained the ability to drive and shop, something she had not done since the procedure a year earlier.

The fact that healing provided relief to my family members and enabled them to live a better quality of life was wonderful. It gave me great joy to share this healing with people I met, but to share this with my family added a wonderful dimension to the healing. I felt blessed to be able to help them.

Living Water and Light Strings

Several people have reported swimming, floating, or becoming plasma-like in what appears to be and has been described as an ocean. One client reported floating in clear plasma.

One client reported, "I heard water gurgling – like a water cooler or an air conditioner." Another client said, "I heard water pouring into this hole. I looked into the hole and there was water inside it." Another client said, "The strangest thing of all was my arms. I thought I had lifted my arms. I had the feeling that I lifted my arms. It was almost as if they were floating on water. They were not on the table." One client said, "It felt like water was evaporating off my skin." One client reported, "I felt droplets of rain. In between the rain and mist, I saw scenes of water."

Some clients reported web-like strings being pulled like taffy or rubber bands. One client said, "I thought my hands wanted to move, but I was encased in a cocoon, but it was lighter, like strings." One client reported, "I could feel my body doing things. My foot was connecting with my head. It was like my body was connecting to itself like it had just been introduced to itself. I could feel my heart following you around." Many people reported feeling a density in their hands, feet and body and one young man described it as, "I felt fluffy. I thought to myself, 'Am I going to float?' " Many people experienced body alignments and adjustments made while they were in the session. One chiropractor rattled off the particular vertebrae that had been re-aligned during a healing session.

Several clients reported seeing a young redheaded girl dancing joyfully. Several clients reported seeing relatives who had died. One lady reported that she heard her son's laughter and then commented, "He died several years ago." Many clients have reported seeing a blue crystal and a blue light. Many people reported smelling flowery fragrances – some they recognized, some they could not recognize. Dozens of clients have reported other smells that included burning substances, woody scents, creosote, garlic and even vinegar. A few clients reported smelling baked cookies. Occasionally clients sometimes had difficulty describing the smell exactly. Some experienced what they described as an electrical impulse and some heard tones in their ears or in their hands. One client actually reported hearing a tuning fork in each ear.

One client didn't know if she wanted a Reiki treatment or a healing session. I told her I would give her a 30-minute treatment of each one and she could compare any similarities or differences. The Reiki treatment had definite feedback in areas of emotions and issues that were affecting her and her family. Then we began her healing treatment. She began to struggle on the table. I observed for a few minutes and the struggle continued. Just before I was going to check and see if everything was OK, she became very quiet. At times, it seemed like she wasn't even breathing. At the end of her session, she shared, "My intention was to see the face of God and as soon as I lay down, I saw the blue sky above me. I was fighting for a while, but then I just relaxed. There were times I didn't need to breathe. When I would become aware of needing to breathe, then I would take a breath. Oh, and I heard a motorcycle out on the highway." I asked her if she often heard things two miles away. By the way, we were in my living room and I wasn't really sure where she saw the blue sky.

One client reported, "I heard you go into the bathroom, get fragrant flower petals, spread them around the table and chant like an Indian." For the record, I never left the vicinity of the table, did not spread flower petals nor did I chant. She was absolutely convinced of her experience and found it difficult to accept that I did not acknowledge that it happened. One woman swore that I left the room and went outside my back door. She then said I sat on the couch and watched the session unfold. I was at the table the whole time working on her and never went outside nor did I sit on the couch. I can't explain what happened in their reality. I can only know what happened in mine.

Buildings and More Buildings

What I found interesting was the variety of scenes that were described to me. One client said she saw buildings, beautiful buildings with huge steps, and beautiful marble with patterns. She described 2 or 3 children who were running down the long granite stairs next to the building.

One client described her experience, "I saw columns in an ancient building. I've seen a picture of this before – like a Ben Hur movie. There was a stadium and great big columns. I guess it was Greece. I don't know. There was constant stuff going on. I saw a sphinx. I saw a golden pyramid. I saw a pink city in the distance. I saw a spaceship twice."

Another client reported, "I was on a road or street. The houses had red tiles. There were palm trees." In another session, the client reported, "I saw what looked like an alleyway, a slum in black and white. There were large, burned out buildings. It was charred, black and tall. I noticed that if I looked through the building, I could see a new city – beautiful and glowing. I had to go through the burned out building to get to the new city."

One client reported, "During my session, I went on a tour of sacred places – churches. It ended up in Lourdes. They took me to England and Scotland. We ended up at the pyramids. They would stop there, but there was more. The journey included Stonehenge and Avebury – spiritual and sacred places."

Going for a Ride

One client reported, "I was traveling in a subway station with vertical bars holding up the rails. I was aware of a lot of peach colored light. I kept going down passages. There were no signs. I knew you were going to touch me. I heard, 'You're always traveling somewhere. It's never ending. You will never arrive. Enjoy it!"

One client reported, "I was pulled out of my body and put back in. I felt really light. Then I started to slowly spin. I did a somersault where my feet went over my head a couple of times and then I settled back down. Then I felt myself expand – like I filled the room. I vibrated side-to-side. I exploded and became part of the Universe. I became and saw bright yellow. I felt warmth and peace."

As people reported leaving their bodies, some of their comments included, "I went somewhere." "I went for a ride." "I went on a trip." "I was out of my body and went fffft – right back in as the phone rang." "I was taking off when you tapped me." One client had a glimpse of coming over the roof and "hovering" rather than flying. She saw a city or a town with trees. One client reported, "Where did I go? I felt like I just floated off. My thumb burned like it was stuck in a socket. I feel very energized by it. I went somewhere – a very comfortable place."

One client reported, "I was playing with a ball of light – energy. Then it was taffy. The second time it was a snowball. The energy was cold. The third time I was playing with the ball, I saw hands like in Michelangelo's *The Creation of Adam,* with the energy ball in between them."

One client reported, "I was awake, but I felt I was asleep. I felt twenty emotions at the same time. I feel like nothing's bothering me. By far, that's the most interesting thing that's ever been done to me."

One client reported seeing a neon green heart. One client reported seeing a neon green hand, my hand. One client reported seeing my hand on a stack of books. She said she recognized my red fingernails. Another client reported, "There was a lot of electricity. Toward the end, I began to see a visual. I was looking through a pyramid of light." Some people felt ice cold from the inside, out. Some people felt warmth from the inside, out. Some clients demonstrated a rippling and vibration visible from the whole body. Dozens of clients reported a touch on the arm, leg, feet and hair. A few have reported feeling a touch at their hearts and their heads. Many report feeling a sense of being embraced or feeling the presence of angels or beings in the room. One client reported that someone cradled her head in their hands underneath between her head and the massage table.

Some clients experienced spiritual enlightenment. One client reported, "Prayer is direct from individuals contacting our higher self on a conscious plane. It's sharing your individual light with God's light. Knowingness is a different plane. It is more creative at a higher level. The Creator is healing us at that level – the Place of Oneness. It's like a grocery store. All you need is there. It's quiet, but you have no idea what is really there." Another client reported this experience, "I wonder if the Man I saw was Jesus. He was wearing a white flowing robe. I looked at Him and He looked at me. He was peaceful. I was thinking, 'There You are.'"

Recently, I had an unusually trying day. That evening a client had messages for me. I was amazed because they spoke to me when I needed to hear them and they reassured me that I was not alone and that I was a survivor. They knew exactly what I was facing in my life and where I was in my emotional journey. They knew what challenges were before me. Initially she felt these messages were designed just for me and they were. What I have experienced over time was that the messages were for all of us. I shared that with her. The next day she told me that after she considered the messages again, she knew they were for her also. They spoke to our hearts and they applied to each one of us.

Recently a friend came over to learn more about the work. She lay on the table and I spent around thirty minutes providing a healing treatment. I "felt energy feedback" in the abdominal region and sensed that there was an imbalance in her hips and uterine area. This usually indicates to me that it just needs to be checked out. The energy feedback was how I recognized different areas of the body that needed attention. I mentioned that to her. She said she had been having problems with her hips and was scheduled for a gynecology appointment the next day. She reported that her doctor was concerned about what she found during the exam and performed a conical biopsy of the uterine wall. When I spoke with her about a week later, she said, "The strangest thing happened. The doctor was

98% sure there was a problem, but even the lab called back and asked, 'What are we supposed to be checking out? There's nothing here.'" The healing was already underway for her.

Many people experienced dramatic episodes. Many have moderate experiences. Some reported that the experience was relaxing for them as if they had just had a massage, but no one touched them. It was impossible to predict what kind of experience the client would have.

Over the last few years, as you can see, I heard a wide variety of experiences from different healing sessions. In these sessions, I communicated as little as possible about what to expect. I told them little, if any of the information listed in this book. There were so many possibilities, that I did not want to influence what might occur. I told them to be open to whatever God, Love or Life had in store just for them.

One woman completed her session with the words, "What a trip! My hip joint went around and around. There was a pain in my back... one time it felt like they jerked my right foot. There's a lot of steel in it. It was twisted in a circle... I feel every joint has been lubricated."

One woman said, "Someone was working inside my mouth. I've had a lot of trauma in my mouth. There was a laser in my mouth – energetically connecting everything in my mouth. It was quite intense. I could feel each molar. I have dentures and a metal bar in my lower jaw."

What was confirmed time and time again, was that God, Who knows us intimately, understood completely what needed to be healed. We could even forget or fail to realize what was injured or was malfunctioning. We chose to allow the healing to occur and then the combination of God, client and practitioner formed the connection that brought us back to wholeness.

Love Your Body and It Will Love You Back

I worked on another doctor one day and when the treatment was over, she could only move her left hand. This was the first and only time that happened in my practice. She described her experience and said, "My left hand is the only thing I can move... They worked on my teeth, too... I know that. Mostly they worked on my head. I just saw a really big blue light... They are still working on my teeth. It's almost like I have a headache at my forehead... They're still working on my tooth. The blue light leads to a dark spot on the tooth. That's why they're working on it." She shared from her experience, "You take care of your teeth and feet cause that's where it all happens... Boy, they are working right on that tooth. They're healing it. The blue is getting bluer, bluer, bluer and bigger, bigger, bigger. There's still some blockage. We've got to teach people to take care of their teeth. It's like you need to teach people to love their bodies. If you love your body, your body will love you back."

"I know what it is. I have to forgive the lady butcher – the dentist. When I was a little girl, she put her knee on my chest and placed a hot drill in my mouth. I don't even remember her name. She meant well. The anxiety she was feeling ended up in my mouth. She was frustrated. Her frustration and anxiety are in my filling. It's just coming out now. I never would have thought of that one. I've been doing emotional acupressure on my anxiety. I knew it had to do with my busy mind. I knew the teeth were a part of my sickness. It wasn't mercury poisoning in my mouth. It was the dentist's anxiety. That also affected my neck. It was a heavy burden. My mouth was too heavy with all that stuff."

"I can't wait to tell people about this one. Would I make this up? Who would make something like this up? The body is so amazing."

"There's still something left – fear or something in this tooth." She went on to communicate that as she healed and forgave the dentist from her heart, the dentist was healed as well. "Emotions can clear easily. The body has to catch up. We, doctors, are treating the physical body on everyone. That's not the issue. It's never the physical body."

I often told people that experiencing healing treatments was like going back to the manufacturer who made us rather than a dealer who has been authorized to work on the vehicle. Healing sessions were simple, direct, non-invasive and they worked. It sometimes worked in ways we never could have imagined! From what I learned, it was recommended that you bless those who helped you in the healing process whatever their role was in your life.

One of the greatest blessings of healing was that there was no need to re-experience or relive incidents in your life. You just had to relinquish them. Healing also gifted me with an assurance that we healed from heart connections. As we love, healing occurred for us as well as the client. It manifested the truth that God is Love. God knew what we needed. The healing came from God, Love, Life, Jesus, Universe, Holy Spirit, Source, Allah, YHWH, Jehovah – All Are Love. We were privileged to be a part of the equation. We witnessed miracles that were happening all the time. We allowed the work to continue so the miracles could continue as well.

I could never have dreamed of nor imagined all the wonderful experiences that have been gifted to me over the last few years. As people found their way to me for healing treatments or I worked with students and practitioners in various seminars, I came to understand more about people and love. I came to understand how a smile, a touch or a kind word could touch people and make a difference in their lives. Bible verses came to mind that suddenly had deeper meanings for me. 1 John 4:18 says, "There is no fear in love; but perfect love casteth out fear: because fear hath torment. He that feareth is not made perfect in love."[13]

CHAPTER 5

LESSONS FROM THE HEART

"There are often sometimes lessons that must be learned, lessons that are learned, lessons that fall on deaf ears, and lessons to be lived. My purpose for telling you this is that reconnective healing - healing – whatever you want to call it – is a part of you, me and everything."

My life has been so blessed. As I traveled with Dr. Pearl as his assistant and traveled independently to over 20 seminars, I worked on people and worked with people. They needed answers to questions that arose after they had gone home to do their work. I participated and presented at the First Annual Leadership Workshop for Reconnective Healing™[14] practitioners. It was my goal to share my experiences and some lessons I learned along the way in the category of Best Practices. My experience showed me that we could learn, grow and make a difference starting with the people in our lives, our family and friends, and then watch the ripple effect into the world.

Get Your Human Stuff Out of the Way

If we let our egos get in the way, we become attached to the results or outcome of each session. We can be in the middle of a healing session and the person is lying there still as a stone. We begin to worry, "Are they having any experience at all? Am I doing this the right way? What happens if they are unhappy with the session? What happens if their expectations are not met?" Whatever the question is, the answer is that our human ego is right in the middle of it. Anytime we are thinking and acting from our human self or ego, we have changed direction from our path and we didn't even realize it.

The important thing to remember is that the healing comes from God, the client and the practitioner. The healing does not generate from you alone. It is the combination of all of you, the Oneness, which is effective. The way to be centered and most effective is to be, just be. If you were to imagine a pencil, there is a barrel, lead and eraser. Be the pencil and acknowledge Source as the lead. If you were to imagine a milkshake with a straw, act as the straw and acknowledge Source as the milkshake. If you were to imagine a water hose, act as the hose and acknowledge Source as the eternal and never-ending Source as the water of life. Only then can we truly open ourselves up to be an instrument of this work.

When we begin to think we are doing great works, a red flag should go up in our hearts and minds. That is the signal that we are taking credit for what we cannot possibly do. With mastery of this work, comes a humble spirit, humility and honor. We are truly blessed to be a part of this sacred healing and spiritual work. When we take credit for it, we truly do a dishonor to us and everyone associated with this work. We are vessels, but we do not power or direct the ship. That comes from God, Love, Universe, Source – you determine the Word. When you make yourself available and let go of any attachment to outcomes, miracles occur. Miracles happen every day, and you get to witness them everywhere you are.

Looking from the Outside, In

The client is still on the table. The client hasn't moved from the moment you began the session. You worry that nothing is happening, but you are judging from the outside, in. You can never know with your mind and your human thoughts exactly what is going on in that client's experience. Many practitioners have witnessed someone having an incredible experience in a seminar. When the people begin to share their experiences, you would never have guessed what was actually happening to the client on the table. They may be extremely quiet and having an incredible experience. They may be quiet and having a relaxed, but mellow experience. Both may look exactly the same. The point is – you cannot know which one unless you see from the heart. And... no matter what is happening, it is exactly what has been designed uniquely for that person. Each experience is unique – unlike anyone else's session. Occasionally people do not share everything they experience. Some feel that they are "dreaming" and that they just went to sleep. Some people explain away what happened because they can't imagine something like that actually happened.

As a practitioner, I could neither take credit for the experience nor the fault for lack of an experience. I was privileged to stand in the equation, but any activity or healing was accomplished beyond my control. I observed and learned that when I listened from my heart, I could hear all kinds of amazing things.

Often when a client experienced a healing session, a thought would cross my mind. I learned to make a note of these things because when the client was sharing his experience, he often shared a thought that used the same or similar words that came to me during the session. There were often physical experiences of growling or gurgling stomachs. On many occasions the client's stomach gurgled, then my stomach gurgled. Soon they were gurgling in unison from both of us, and I couldn't tell which one it was. I think this was another indicator that we were "connected" in this process.

Another thing I learned was that when we believed something was wrong with the client and we tried to "aim" the energy at that ailment or injury, we could often overlook a problem that we were not even aware of. That was why it was so important to listen for signals, but refrain from drawing any conclusions. There were factors that we might not know, but the Great Physician knew. God was there to do the work if we stepped out of the way and allowed the miracles to occur.

Ownership – Let the Work Change You for the Better

My life is filled to overflowing with loving relationships. I love the friends, family, and people that have been brought into my life through this work. They are the gifts you give yourself and I count myself very fortunate to have an abundance of people in my life who care as deeply for me as I care for them. As an elected official, citizen, and public servant for the last several years, I have found opportunities to share this work with people from different walks of life. I worked on doctors, lawyers, authors, teachers, homemakers, police officers, government officials, corporate professionals, babies, children, families, and pregnant women. I provided sessions for senior citizens, highway workers, reflexologists, massage therapists, students, nurses, psychologists, chiropractors, family therapists, fellow healers and wildlife rehabilitation personnel.

Every single person in the world can benefit from healing. It doesn't matter who we are or what our background is. The world is filled with people who are dysfunctional in one area or another. We are injured emotionally and sometimes physically in day-to-day experiences by words, deeds and actions from people we know or even strangers whom we have never met. These may be current injuries or injuries from our past that were so painful, we buried the pain deep inside us and we may not even be aware that it still affects us today. It is important to find a way to release that pain so that it does not imprison us and keep us from living fully, experiencing intimacy and achieving our dreams.

I like to observe people and really see what motivates and disappoints them. If you look around you can see people who seem very unhappy and are looking desperately for something to make them happier. Some people look for happiness in families, careers, churches, the kind of car they drive or the toys that they enjoy. Some people look for happiness in oblivion through alcohol, drugs or other addictions. Some people look for happiness by controlling the things or people in their lives that they believe have cost them their happiness in some way.

With this work, I discovered that my emotional wounds began to heal. Some very painful things still would come up for me, but overall I would realize that something that had once given me great grief was missing from my life or healed from the inside, out. It was as if I had collected all the pain and anguish from my life and placed them in a suitcase. It wasn't the kind on wheels, either. It was the kind I had to drag everywhere I went. If someone would comment on a memory or event in my life, I could pull it out of the suitcase and let them have a piece of my mind, rehash it or recall the story in vivid detail. I could feel every emotion that memory invoked. After doing this healing work for a while, I realized that I left the suitcase somewhere. I didn't know where it was, and I didn't even miss it. I just let it go and the stuff inside along with it. I could still remember incidents if I really tried, but the emotional attachment was not the same as it used to be. The events had been healed and so had I.

What I loved about this process was that it was subtle, yet effective. Unlike therapy, I did not have to dig up the memory, feel the pain and relive it. I could just let it go. I did acknowledge the pain when I felt it, but often I would be healed without knowing when it happened. I could release the emotional attachment and not have to itemize which painful moment was being released.

When I returned home from Hollywood, I realized that a change had taken place. I had gained a confidence in this work and had become accustomed to the fact that I was a healing practitioner as my sole means of support. This was a major step forward for me. I found courage to speak more openly and honestly about how this work changed lives for the better. I found myself offering the work when fellow city leaders were diagnosed with cancer, illnesses and other diseases. I became boldly open about the work I did even though I lived in a fairly conservative area where alternative medicine was not widely accepted. My healing practice was important to me. Who I was included being a healing practitioner, and I was proud to be one of the pioneers of this work.

When I grew more confident about the healing I participated in, I began to share more openly and it changed the way I lived. It liberated me to be who I was. As a practitioner, I found it was like renting a house. Because I was renting, I was hesitant in some of my approaches. I was reluctant to paint the walls or hang wallpaper without permission. It wasn't really mine to do anything I wanted to do. When I gained confidence in the healing work, I felt it was like buying my own house. I felt confident that the choices I made were ones that allowed me to fully do this work. I could paint, remodel, and change the carpet easily because I owned it. Once I changed how I perceived my abilities, I could immediately see a difference in my healing sessions. For me, it happened right away, but it could be a process that happens as you experience more of this work.

I would love to tell you that I confidently told everyone who needed this work about what I did. I met resistance with some people who I considered to be close friends. I let their influence silence me at times. Then I would hear of someone who died from cancer that perhaps could have benefited from this work. I remember a citizen in my community who was suffering from terminal cancer. I quietly and secretly worked providing healing. This person lived for almost another year. Did it help? I hope so. Only God knew for sure.

I felt conflicted about what people thought versus what I knew to be a God-given gift. One day I met someone and in conversation told him that I was a healing practitioner. Evidently I was a little hesitant in telling him and he remarked, "You had a little trouble wondering what I was going to think, didn't you? Don't you know that if you're confident, I would more than likely be OK with that?" I made a mental note. If I spoke from my heart and told people honestly what this work could do, there was no need for fear or hesitancy when it came to sharing what happened with this work.

When I was involved in healing sessions, I felt filled with love and on top of the world. Then the realities of the real world would bring me back down to earth. It was through this very difficult time that I learned how powerful living in the now, one day at a time could be. It was a struggle to live without worry, lay it at God's feet and leave it there.

For years, I accumulated many things. I collected angels, Depression glass, cake platters and all sorts of things. I had more stuff than one person should have. I loved to shop and spend money. I was a master shopper and recently realized how much I had changed. I was standing in a major department store with my mother. She looked over at me and asked, "Vicki, do you need anything?" I looked around and realized there was nothing that I needed that I didn't already have. At some point in this process, I realized that shopping was just another way to fill a void that was in my life. I had been searching for things to make me happy and things just did not do it for me anymore.

Living simply was not easy when you were used to opulence. I used to enjoy financial prosperity and suddenly I found my income was closer to the poverty level. I considered myself successful when I earned a lot of money. I was proud of building a new home, buying a new car or having enough cash to spend on whatever I wished. I had to see that my success was measured more by who I was rather than what I accumulated. Learning to live more simply was a difficult lesson for me. It wasn't easy or effortless. Over time I learned that money did not determine who I was nor did the lack of money diminish my own personal power in any way. This experience helped me understand more that money is an energy and exchange, but as we have been told for years, it cannot buy happiness. I can tell you I am more aware today of people in need. My view of money has changed and I hope I listen more compassionately when others try to share their difficulties with me.

I learned happiness is living a life filled with love, joy, peace, and compassion. It's not about collecting things money can buy. It's about living your life every day. It's about loving people in your life every day. It's about giving yourself in ways that used to frighten you. It's about being honest and showing people Who You Really Are. It is about being, not doing.

As I began this journey of healing, I had to change how I saw myself in order to grow. I might be an expert in many areas of life, but here in this healing work, I was just beginning to understand. I would see other people in the seminar or maybe I witnessed wonderful things in my own healing sessions, but I was not sure that the healing would work for me all the time. When I was first introduced to the energy, I was not as certain that I would always recognize it. I would work with it and then maybe I'd go home and put it on the shelf for a while. I would get revved up again when I visited other practitioners or go to seminars. We shared experiences with each other and I learned more about this work. My confidence went way up and then I would have no opportunity to use it for a while. I would ask myself, "If I need to do a healing session, would I remember how? Would the energy feel the same as before? Would I be able to remember what to do?"

Sharing the Gift

What I learned is this. When this gift is shared with you, you get it – not for a moment, but for a lifetime. I believe that the gift might be "given" or you might have had this wonderful gift all along, but you didn't know you had it. Whatever the truth is for you, you have the gift full strength. What is different is the degree in which you acknowledge and "own" this gift. When you own this gift, you have a confidence and assurance that you are this healing and it is a part of you. You know with certainty that when you do this work, even if you don't see a single indicator that the power of this work is coursing through both you and your client. You know in your heart that you are doing this work from the heart. You know without a doubt that you are meant to share this gift with truth, honesty, integrity, peace and love. You know you were meant to do this work.

Some practitioners grow through infancy, adolescence, puberty and adulthood. Some experience adulthood immediately. All methods are great. Everyone learns in whatever method works for each of them. There are many people who would benefit from sharing this healing. It is important to grow, gain experience and work confidently. It's amazing what can happen when we make ourselves available and then get out of the way.

So how do you get there from here? I continued to place myself in situations with friends and family where I could share this work. I volunteered on civic groups, hospitals, schools and churches. I set an intention to share this gift through every hug, handshake, and smile. Recently I went to an arena football game. The Dallas Desperados were playing at the American Airlines Center. I'm not sure how many thousands of people were there. As I sat in Section 110, I looked around the arena with my hands up and intended that healing was extended to everyone in the building. I moved section by section throughout the arena. It was like sending a prayer on behalf of each person in the arena. It was like having a secret pal who sent a blessing to you without you knowing where it came from or that it was even being sent. If one person experienced a healing, a blessed day or a benefit, I am glad I could share the gift.

I shared this gift on airplanes. I shared this at City Council meetings. I saw the power of this work turn hostile situations into loving encounters. I practiced this everyday, wherever I was and it is still a part of my daily regime. What if you could do this, too? All it takes is intention and love to share the gift. What an amazing thing would happen to our world if this were the standard by which we lived and interacted with other people!

But some may ask, do I need permission to work on someone? This answer was gifted to me recently during a session. I asked them, "Is it necessary to ask permission when someone wants to gift someone anonymously with a healing treatment?" It was confirmed for me that we need no permission to share this work anymore than we would need permission to pray or go to the bathroom.

Pleasing people is no longer as important to me. I am still striving to share the work fearlessly. I realize I make progress when I realize that it doesn't matter who they are or what they think. It is my job to share this gift of life and love with them. Who is my Master - man or God? I choose God. People will respond or not. They will feel it in their hearts if they allow themselves the freedom to experience it.

Heal from the Heart

In the seminars, Dr. Pearl related that the tests conducted at the University of Arizona showed his heart wave (EKG) was imprinted on the client's brainwave (EEG). In healing seminars when your heart wave is imprinted on the client's brain wave, how important is it that you love? Love is a verb. If your heart is filled with love for the client, and you allow yourself to be a vessel, healing occurs. As you connect to them in a special, spiritual way, you allow

114

yourself to share in the sacred experience of healing at all levels – physical, mental, emotional and spiritual.

But what happens if a practitioner's heart is not in the right place during a session? Is there any impact on the client or the practitioner? I asked this question during a session with one of my clients. I was told there is no power greater than God. Our intention places God's love in our heart for the healing to occur.

With this work, I have learned to love more, see things with my heart and trust my heart. I have been rewarded as I lived and made decisions more from my heart. It changed how I interacted with people. As they would do things that I found difficult to accept, I breathed deeply, looked at them with love, and remembered, "love them through it." It made a tremendous difference in how I lived each day.

Imaging technology has provided us with a great opportunity to learn more about the human body. The heart is the first organ that develops in a mother's womb. We have been led to believe that the brain and mind control everything in our bodies, but how can the brain be more powerful if it is developed after the heart? We have so much to learn about the power of love and the human body. The power of love is greater than the power of the mind. When we learn to live through the heart, we will be able to change the dynamics of our relationships. We can live genuine lives and be who we truly are.

Our hearts are truly powerful. One day in particular, I was in a seminar. One of the attendees walked over to me and asked if she could speak to me privately. She and I moved to a quiet location and she shared with me that the energy in the room was making her uncomfortable. I remembered what I had been told in the Las Vegas message that our heart energy extends eight feet beyond our bodies. I decided to see if it could extend further. I said to her, "Give me a few minutes, before you decide to leave. I believe we can change the energy in the room. Let me give it a try."

I walked to the back of the room. I engaged the help of a friend. She and I both sent healing love energy from our hearts and "touched" every person in the room. In three minutes or less, the attendee came up to me and said, "If I hadn't witnessed that with my own eyes, I would not have believed it. The energy in this room is completely different. That frenzied feeling is gone. Thank you."

This approach has helped me in many situations. I found that when people were upset or angry and I tried to reach and touch them with my heart, the situation changed completely. Don't take my word for it. Try it for yourself and see what happens.

Evolve Into the Person You Were Always Meant to Be

The transformation process was underway. I could not promise which avenue was responsible. I believed that it was a concerted effort on the part of God to create in me a more loving heart. I knew that in the last few years, my life changed completely. I learned that in order to love others, I had to love myself first. One of the most important lessons was that love was the best choice in response to any situation. In my wildest imagination, I could not have predicted where I would be today. I knew without a doubt that I was not alone on this journey. My guides, angels and helpers were here to guide me along my path.

When we act in human ways and make human choices, we continue to learn lessons the hard way and often more than just once. When in spite of our human intentions, we choose forgiveness, love and compassion, as illogical as it seems, new opportunities open up to us.

Imagine you went up and down the same hall in the same house day after day. One day you react differently and suddenly a new doorway appears. As you go through it, you realize there is a whole new wing that you never knew was there. If you had continued doing the same things, you wouldn't ever know what you were missing. The doorway only appeared after you made a new and different choice.

A pivotal point in my life came when I chose forgiveness and love when my mind was screaming for retribution and revenge. As I began to realize that in choosing a loving and spiritual response rather than a reactive response, I grew in ways I could never imagine. I started actively checking out what would happen if I loved first and began to apply that to making decisions in my life. Rather than react with blaming, arguing, fighting or judging, I tried waiting and listening to my heart. I wasn't successful 100% of the time, but I did make significant changes. It really made a difference when I tried to understand the other person's point of view. I observed how things that were said impacted the people hearing them. I watched their reaction. By observing, I was able to choose an alternative based in love and compassion, rather than fear or judgment. It is not easy to forgive, but it is a powerful healing option. There is tremendous power in loving people especially when they seem unlovable. By the way, this is not an easy task. You fail a lot more than you succeed. But as you succeed, you take one baby step at a time. You make mistakes. You stop, evaluate and choose again.

Today, I know that as I touch people, they touch me, too. I learn from them, and they learn from me. It is a tangible exchange of energy. Today I know people see love through my life, my heart and my eyes as I try to share this marvelous feeling with them. It warms my heart to hear people teli me they feel good being in my company. I feel humbled hearing it. I know that the love that has transformed me, can transform every single person everywhere. It is a tangible feeling that is communicated heart to heart. It confirms how important it is to share this gift with everyone you meet. It is a more powerful way to live. It is a great way to love.

Create a Support System You Feel Safe to Share In

When things started happening in the healing sessions that seemed out of the ordinary, I wanted to know why they happened and what they meant. I had a small group of people that had started this work around the time I had. I would ask them, "Have you ever..." They would answer yes or no. Then we would discuss it. We would come to a conclusion or discuss the possibilities. I didn't realize how important the network would become over the years or how much I would value the information we exchanged. I trusted these people and they trusted me. It was such a blessing that when something happened, I didn't have to begin the sentence with, "You know I'm not crazy, but have you ever...?" The truth of the work and understanding came through people who gave me honest feedback.

The network grew as I continued to meet people at seminars all over the country. I found that I resonated with certain people and built strong relationships with them over time. I enjoyed helping them learn and then mentoring them as they developed their gift. They called me and asked me questions. I told them honestly if I had encountered anything like that in my experience to date or even if I had heard that from my network relationships with other healing practitioners. The information exchanged was a valuable tool when trying to understand the scope of this work. Mentoring was and is an important part of this work. As I strived to keep integrity with what I had been taught, I was also learning more information from the messages I received during healing sessions. Different people held pieces to the puzzle and everything fit together at the right time in the right moment.

Celebrate Your Unique Gifts

In 1 Corinthians 12:4-11, we are told that wisdom, word of knowledge, faith, gifts of healing, working of miracles, discernment of spirits, speaking in tongues and interpretation of tongues are spiritual gifts. In the *Book of Knowledge, The Keys of Enoch* 113:44, it is written that "The People of God will also receive five additional gifts: 1) Speaking in scientific-spiritual tongues, 2) Resurrecting the dead, 3) Speaking angelic languages, 4) The ability to see and work with angelic teachers of Light, and 5) Understanding the mysteries of the

Shekinah Kingdoms."[15] Not all of us are given the same gifts. When we feel our gifts are not adequate in some way or we do not fully appreciate our gifts, we may feel led to compare them with others. We may not even realize completely what our gifts are. I learned the way to wholeness includes discovering, embracing, and celebrating your unique gift. I benefited greatly from stretching the limits of my gift. I found the only limitations were the ones I placed on myself. There were no limits. There were no restrictions. When I celebrated who I was, others valued me also. It's like a potluck dinner where everyone brings their own gifts to the table. Even if you and someone else bring the same dish, the flavorings are uniquely yours. Each dish or gift is needed to complete the meal. So it is with this work, every person is needed to share his or her gifts.

It takes courage to listen to the desires of your heart and then achieve your dreams. Have you ever taken the time to truly discover your dreams and those of your family and friends? As I gave up the rush and frenzy, I found more balance in the way I lived. What are your priorities and important factors to truly live rather than exist or hurry through your life? Listen to the quietness of your heart. Have the courage to walk away when something is not serving your highest good. Then you will take charge of your life and really live it. The best gift you can give someone else is a happier and healthier you. What will really amaze you is that when you are operating on this level, it will seem effortless!

Fear of failure and losing our jobs in this economic climate paralyzes us. When we have the courage to stop, breathe and listen within, new ideas are born. As we choose a different direction, suddenly it is easier to separate from the hectic activities and really ask ourselves, "Does this serve me and my family? Will this help us move forward in the direction of our dreams? Is this part of the 'myth' of success? Why am I doing this?" Living with guidance from our higher selves in love helps us rearrange our priorities so our family, friends and especially ourselves can reflect and act on what is truly important.

CHAPTER 6

MY JOURNEY TO THE HEART

"Before you were born, God kissed your eyes, kissed your lips and anointed your soul. Your mother and your sister love you. We love you more. Here love is unconditional. On earth, love is conditional."

My Own Personal Journey

People were curious about what happened to me personally through with this work. I was introduced to this work through a dear friend who was also my Reiki Master. She performed my personal connection during June 2000, a miraculous time of my life. When practitioners participated in healing sessions over the years, where I was the client, I had a number of different experiences. On several occasions, I felt like I was sinking into Oneness with God and also into the table itself. My arms levitated or lifted off the table and seemed to float all by themselves on many occasions. I was lovingly touched on the head, shoulders, hands, legs and heart, but not by the practitioner.

I saw a variety of colors that included purples, reds, pinks, greens, apricot, turquoise, blue, white and gold. I saw a number of images. I saw a single eye on several occasions. Jet planes have flown closely over my face on multiple occasions, just as my clients reported in their sessions. I saw flashes of symbols, multiple full pages of symbols that flashed like a movie frame in front of my eyes. I heard words from my heart that told me how much I was loved. They reminded me that I had never been alone, but that they had always been with me and always would be. In another session as I lay on the table, it seemed like I was going deeper and deeper inside myself, but what I saw resembled the universe at night with an indigo sky and stars sprinkled throughout the darkness. Then I became so very cold from the inside, out.

In November 2000, my hand was initiated during the personal connection process of a client. In another session, my hand was initiated for the second time. It started at the palm and then went through specific steps and the order for each finger. Just before I left for Las Vegas, I was invited to participate in a special ceremony where I was given a red rose. I was told to bring a purple sweater and a glass of water. The rose was offered to me because "it brings life to the soul." The water was sprinkled over me. The purple sweater was placed over my knees during the ceremony.

I was told that I appeared to be in a deep sleep during this experience. I remember feeling frigidly cold. Throughout the process, I felt additional waves of cold energy flow through me and steadily got even colder. I remembered thinking about a butterfly. I knew my hands levitated off the table and then a couple of inches more during this ceremony.

I knew that as I traveled down this journey, each step was an exciting move forward. Each experience and each miraculous word shared with me was another piece of the puzzle that was added. The picture was taking shape and each idea, concept or recommendation together made it clearer for us.

Recently I fell and injured my knee. It felt like an injury I had experienced from my old softball days, so I put on a brace. I relaxed for a couple of days, and then started listening to people who recommended that I obtain x-rays and see what was really wrong. Meanwhile I was doing healing sessions on the knee constantly. I caved under the pressure of friends and family and went to the emergency room at a local hospital. They x-rayed my leg and referred me to an orthopedist's office. The doctor scheduled me for an MRI to see the extent of the damage. By the time I went for the MRI, two weeks had passed since the injury, and I had ditched the crutches and the brace. I received a frantic phone call from the doctor's office. The message said, "Get back on your crutches immediately. Put your brace back on."

I called the office and asked them what their concern was. I felt great. The leg felt great. I was getting back to normal. They told me the MRI detected a torn ACL ligament, torn CCL ligament and a hairline-fractured tibia. The doctor wanted to see me in his office within the next two days. He took another set of x-rays. He spent 30 minutes reviewing first one set of x-rays, then the reports from the MRI and the final set of x-rays. He kept asking me, "Aren't you feeling any pain at all?" I told him again and again, "No, it doesn't hurt at all."

Then I said, "I do energy healing. It's like vibrational medicine. I have been doing this on my knee since the injury. Would you like to feel it?" He reluctantly nodded yes. I let him "feel" it with his hands. He felt a slight vibration in his hand. He said, "Keep doing whatever it is you are doing. It will heal you." I could see he was still concerned, so I compromised and told him I would wear the brace for two more weeks just to humor him. I knew the healing was already taking place. I have been pain free ever since then.

On two separate occasions, once during a healing session and once again during my return trip from the Las Vegas event, I felt my heart scooped out and in its place, was placed the world. My shoulders curled inward around the globe itself. The pain was very clear. I felt my heart was being opened further. "Create in me a clean heart, O God; and renew a right spirit within me."[16] My experiences with this healing work opened me up and let me love people fully without fear. It enabled me to love myself and those of us who are really hard to love. It helped me show people how very much God loves them – more than they could ever imagine. My mission in this life was to help usher back into our world the love that has always been here, but we forgot how to share it, and how to express it in our lives.

I practiced self-healing at night as I prepared for sleep along with prayer and meditation. Occasionally, fellow practitioners worked on me. In October 2002, while I was traveling in Portland, Oregon, I became aware of a practitioner who conducted healing sessions and included an intuitive artist who sketched a soul portrait that was unique for you, the client. I thought this would be an interesting activity. I called to make an appointment, but the artist was out of town. Her grandfather's health was failing and she was traveling in Idaho. I felt that the schedule would somehow work out if it were meant to happen. Miraculously she said she could do it one evening while I was still in the area, and we confirmed the appointment.

Although I was accustomed to driving in different areas of the country, I had never been to the home of the practitioner before and she provided directions. That afternoon, I was in another location from the starting point of the directions. I was told generally what direction to head to avoid traffic and set out on my journey. I reached the town that she lived in, but I could not locate the street that was listed on the directions. I drove instinctively, made several turns in the town that I had never visited before then. I'm sure I had a lot of guidance. I stopped in a shopping center and called her only to discover I was less than a mile from her house. If I had not stopped, I would have arrived at the street I was looking for in the directions. The whole experience was effortless.

We visited briefly before the session began. The practitioner felt compelled to place a large clear crystal, slightly larger than a brick, underneath the table. She told me later that she had never done that before then. I lay on the table and closed my eyes. I felt that I was going deeper and deeper into the table. I remember seeing a dark indigo, much like a clear night with stars in the sky. I tuned out during the session and I'm not sure exactly where I went. During this and other healing sessions, I felt connected to God as a part of the Oneness or Wholeness. I felt refreshed and loved when the session was completed.

The practitioner touched me to end the session, and I noticed she was crying. She had tears flowing down her face. She looked at me with such love and compassion. She called me by two names. She said they were my spiritual names. She told me the first one, "So Oh Lome Bee Toes," meant, "Heart of the Light." The other name she was given was "Oh Oh Mani Va Poo Ray," which meant "She who listens to the light, to the song of the light. Weaver of colored sound."

Both the artist and the practitioner described a sacred and holy session. Mother Mary stood at my feet with an archangel on either side of her. The practitioner said that Mary often comes to assist in healing sessions, but today she just stood at my feet and blessed me. Jesus stood at my head. Two light beings stood on either side of the table. They had their hands extended above my body and reached across the table to clasp their hands together over me. As the practitioner was describing the experience, the artist showed me the sketch. She had seen Mary, Jesus, and the archangels. She had captured the two light beings in her drawing and said the portrait was very "galactic." As she sketched, she mentioned that she was concerned that the crystals were out of balance. Her guides told her everything would turn out just the way it should be.

When I received the soul portrait, the artist, Alyse Finlayson, had done a beautiful job. I was rather amazed to see the Christian symbol of the fish prominently displayed in the center of the picture. There were the two light beings that guided me and helped me in my work.

The sketch included eight crystals with a myriad of lines and connections from the crystals to the light beings and running through a number of different things in the portrait. In the middle of the portrait was the eye of God. She said the eye of God was at my center and radiated outward. The magenta represented compassion from Christ. Lime green balanced this compassion and ran through a portion of the grid lines. Gold was the high spiritual connection through the crown and the root. Yellow was active intelligence in action. Green was the balance and healing that I provided. Blue represented the spiritual goals and my soul's path. Violet was shown as the transcendence from lower vibratory levels to higher vibrations, which represented ascension. The crystals were clear and reflected the colors around them. Indigo was an anchoring connection through all the akashic records. What we saw in the soul portrait was limited to two dimensions, but the real picture was actually multi-dimensional.

Then a client was talking to me about some crystals that she had ordered. Once I had seen the crystals in my soul portrait, I said to her, "You know those crystals are meant for me. We can use them to barter for services." When she arrived for her appointment, I showed her the soul portrait. Amazingly, there were eight crystals pictured plus a small one for a necklace for me. It surprised me that I would be so direct with my request, but intuitively, I knew the crystals were supposed to be mine and she agreed.

Sharing This Work with Family, Friends and Strangers

When I began to share what was happening with family and friends, some of them did not know how to deal with it. Some listened, nodded and I wasn't really sure what they were thinking. Some were willing to try it and keep an open mind. Once they opened their hearts to the healing gift, the results were pretty incredible.

Recently I was asked in a city council meeting, "What do you do?" I took a deep breath and responded, "I am a healing practitioner." The attorney remarked, "I'm not sure I know what that is." I said, "That's not uncommon. A lot of people don't know exactly what I do. This healing is an energetic, vibrational medicine that gives people alternatives to and complementary treatment in conjunction with traditional medical care. I have had astonishing results from people with cancer, hepatitis C, birth defects and other health challenges. What I really do is help bring joy and wholeness into people's lives."

I know looking back that I would not have been so forthright with my answer if I had not been prepared by other lessons. For example, I was traveling in Las Vegas just the week before. A taxi driver and a restaurant hostess asked me the same question. The taxi driver was a retired engineer from Boston. When he asked, I responded, "I provide healing sessions for people with all kinds of illnesses and injuries." When he asked what that was, I asked, "Are you familiar with any energy healing? Are you familiar with Reiki?" He responded, "Yes, I have heard of Reiki."

I told him, "This healing is an energy medicine that vibrates at a high frequency, is simple to learn and helps people heal." I referred him to a website and a book for more information, and let him feel the energy.

The restaurant hostess asked, "What kind of conference are you participating in?" When I responded, "Reconnective Healing™[17]. Have you ever heard of it?" She asked, "No, what is that?"

I described it briefly and asked if she would like to feel the energy. When she said yes, I took her right hand. She couldn't really feel anything. I then took her left hand. Immediately, she stepped back and said, "Whoa, what is that?" She described feeling a strong sense of electrical impulses in her left hand. She realized there was something incredible happening. Then she asked me for a business card. This energy is real. People feel it. People want to know more about it. The attraction and desire to learn more about it automatically happens when people let go of their fear.

I knew how important it was to introduce them to this healing. The opportunity provided itself and I had the choice to share or not. People found they were curious and were able to learn more about it. People have shared their stories about how unusual their introduction to this healing work is. A book may fall off the shelf in a bookstore. Suddenly they hear about it from a dozen different people within one week's time. They might stumble across a website or see a brochure.

Some people have heard about it from friends. Recently three women who had been looking for a practitioner of the work for over a year contacted me. They worked in my community and couldn't believe I did this work. Some people would say it is a coincidence. I believe it is more than a coincidence, the timing is synchronous and happens to be the right experience at the right time.

The Gift That Keeps on Giving

One of the greatest gifts of this work is that it keeps on giving. One of my relatives had been personally reconnected. He was talking some weeks later with a guy he had just met. After they had conversed for about 30 minutes, they introduced themselves and shook hands. The man looked at my relative and said, "Do you do Reiki?" He evidently felt the energy in his hands during the handshake. My relative said, "This is a different kind of healing." Even he was surprised that someone could feel the energy through a handshake. He called me and exclaimed, "I was a little freaked out. I didn't realize other people would be able to feel it through my hands."

I was visiting with my family one evening. We were all sitting on the patio enjoying the spring weather. One of my favorite toddlers and I were laughing. I would laugh with a big belly laugh and continue until he would begin to laugh back – a big belly laugh in return. Then one-by-one, he would go to the next person and laugh until they, too, joined in our fun. It was about 8:30 P.M. (CDT) when this occurred. The next day I spoke with a friend in Vancouver, Washington who said something odd had occurred. She said at 6:30 P.M. (PDT) the night before, she was in a session and asked who would go on a business trip with her. The response was, "Vicki Ha! Ha! Ha! Ha! High." This was the exact time that we were laughing in Dallas. It may have been a coincidence, but I don't think so.

Another relative had read Dr. Pearl's book, *The Reconnection: Heal Others, Heal Yourself* and she had experienced a couple of healing sessions with me. She called me and said, "You are not going to believe this. I was at this family reunion this summer. My aunt had fallen during a move on water skis and injured her rib and shoulder. I felt my hands 'turn on' and I offered to touch her. Her pain went away and her shoulder stopped hurting."

The next day, her aunt brought a friend to the reunion. He was having some physical complaint, but they didn't say what the ailment was. Her hands "turned on" again. She felt led to go to his head. What she learned later was that he had been suffering for a long time with migraine headaches. Her willingness to be in the equation with him and Spirit allowed the healing to occur. His chronic pain went away also.

When she returned, she went to visit a friend. Her hands "turned on" again. She looked at her friend's physique. She noticed that one leg was shorter than the other. Then she placed her hands on her friend's leg. The body aligned itself and when her friend stood up, she stood tall with both legs the same length. These healings occurred from reading the book, receiving healing sessions, being introduced to the energy and then trusting that Spirit would heal whatever was needed.

Who responds to this work? Only animals, plants, people and anything else that has life or matter can benefit from this healing. I guess that covers just about everything and everybody. A friend is an animal communicator. I must say that when I first heard that, visions of Dr. Doolittle danced in my brain when she said she could talk to the animals and they talked back. I learned so much from her. She understood not only what was bothering a pet, she also understood that it was usually something in the owner's life that needed to be healed and the pet just helped them heal. What she really did was connect from her heart to the pet's heart and she heard what our pets told us. She listened to them, really listened. Pets loved us unconditionally and tried to provide joy and love in our lives. They tried to help us see and remove obstacles to living more loving and healthy lives.

I also learned that when we open ourselves up beyond our 5 senses of taste, touch, smell, hearing and seeing, that we can know more and sense more of who we are and what is going on around us. We also have the ability to hear, know and breathe through the heart. What I learned is when you make a habit of living, breathing and thinking through the heart, this is where the answers are for each of us. If we listen closely to the quiet truth that comes directly from our hearts, rather than the chatter we hear in our heads. The heart is the true center of knowledge in our lives.

Research has shown recently that the heart actually communicates with the brain four times more often than the brain communicates with the heart. It has been suggested that the heart has its own brain and soul. It's where our truth, honesty, integrity and love actually reside. It's where God speaks to us. It's where we connect with others. It's also where our instincts help us make wiser choices and decisions.

Somehow we have tuned out the truths of our hearts. It may be because of some hurt, ache or pain from a childhood experience or some other trauma in our lives. It may be the result of fear in our lives or repeated messages from a culture that continues to tell us not to trust our feelings. We may have experienced a lifetime of continuous pain and anguish of heart injuries. For whatever the reason, until we open the heart - listen and love completely, we will only be a shell of who we could be.

Let's say you agree with me in whole or even in part. So how do you begin?

Reiki and Reconnective – What's Next?

For me the first step into this work was through Reiki. I was attracted to Reiki with the intention to learn more about my intuitive gift. I had struggled with the knowledge that I knew things that other people did not know for years and wondered how it could be reconciled with my spiritual life. It was a gift shared by other members of my family, but it was exceptionally strong in me. I finally realized it was a spiritual gift. I did not ask for it. I didn't create it. It was a part of me.

I studied for 3 years and the same week that I was initiated as a Reiki Master/Teacher, I went to the healing seminar that changed my life. What I learned in Reiki was that God is alive in all things. His love is never ending. Our emotional illnesses and injuries lead to physical disease if they remain in our cells. To heal, we have to get to the real issue and release it – NOT RELIVE IT, just release it.

For me, Reiki was a gateway to this daily living in God's presence. Again all the lessons learned in my life were coming together. Loving God and loving people without regard for the outcome was my goal for daily living. Reiki helped me realize that releasing the past and living with "love, non-judgment and detachment" as my Reiki Master would say, is the way to peace, joy, love and contentment.

The beatitudes speak of gentleness, meekness and being pure of heart. The people I met through Reiki personified this for me and helped me see it so clearly. Reiki helped me see how great a role we play in our health and in our spiritual well being. So should you study a particular healing technique? If it is something you feel you should do, ask within your own heart. Your heart will always guide you in the truth. The simplicity and ease of whatever healing method you select is important, but any skills you develop will be put to good use if you are willing to make yourself available. You can locate a practitioner and experience a healing session for yourself. If you feel the experience resonates with you, you may even want to explore further through a seminar.

What I learned was that I would never be at this point today if I hadn't diverted from the path I was traveling. A doorway opened for me and so many wonderful experiences have resulted from that choice. I felt courageous, too, because Reiki had its own challenges. People are just now recognizing it. When yoga and acupuncture were introduced into our culture, they, too, had to go from the unknown to skeptical, and from skeptical to acceptance.

Gifts Received from this Work

The transformation of my life has been greatly accomplished through messages or what I called "Gifts From the Heart." In the next chapter, you will read more about those experiences and hopefully understand how they have changed my life so completely.

I would like to share a story that is from me about messages first. I was asked to do a personal connection session on a reporter who was writing an article about the speaker and the work. As we completed the session, she shared her experience with me. I will never forget what happened next! I was sitting on a couch in the hotel room. She was sitting on the massage table. My left arm was positioned on the arm of the couch and without any assistance or direction from me, my left arm began to rise all by itself until the left hand began to form a symbol that I recognized as representing eternal light. My muscles were not operating the arm. It was like someone else had taken control of that arm. I looked over at her and tried to be as calm as possible as I said, "I have no control over that arm or hand. I am not moving it." Then my throat started – not vibrating, exactly – but it started moving around inside my vocal chords. I knew someone was going to speak and I thought, "Oh, no! Not in front of this reporter!" Immediately the throat action ceased. I later regretted the missed opportunity. Fear kept me from freely experiencing what was designed for that reporter. It did help me recognize the symptoms and signs when other people in sessions began to demonstrate or speak.

Today my life is blessed because I experienced Reiki, Reconnective Healing™, and Heart 2 Heart Healing. Together, along with my Bible studies, my love of books, the bits and pieces of the puzzle provided through gifted speakers who share their lives and my dedication to life-long learning, all of it comes together in this package named Vicki. I feel like my life is a mosaic composed of my spiritual gifts, skills I have learned, life experiences, places I have been and people I have met. My life always changes – every breath and every experience adds to the package. I am eternally grateful for each step in the journey.

CHAPTER 7

GIFTS FROM THE HEART

"When I heal people, I heal them from heart to heart. I speak to people from heart to heart."

Almost from the beginning, extraordinary things began to occur. As I made myself available to the clients who sought treatments or personal connection sessions, things started to happen that were quite incredible. When people lay on the massage table, they would either begin to speak with voices that were not their own or they would hear words in their minds that were also not their own.

I understand this may be unusual and a hard concept to accept. The first time it happened, I tried to breathe and just go with what was happening. I remembered my training and I tried to retain a child-like wonder throughout the experience. Just as I had told clients, I tried to be open to whatever happened uniquely for them. I was just along for the ride.

Often as people would begin to share their experience, they would find that words came into their minds and they shared them with me. What I found amazing was that over the times and experiences that were shared, there was a continuity and expansion of the information that was provided.

139

I have been greatly blessed by these messages. The messages are filled with love and light. I believe messages or "Gifts from the Heart" come from God and contain information that has a common idea or common words, and although coming from different people, the cadence, language and meaning are the same.

What I found intriguing about these messages was that the people who spoke did not know each other. Over 30 messages occurred across the country in Portland, Oregon, Pasadena, California, Santa Cruz, California, Irving, Texas, Las Vegas, Nevada, Burbank, California, Austin, Texas, New York City, New York, Hollywood, California, and Crandall, Texas. There have been numerous occasions in other cities from people that showed consistent signs, which indicated speaking was imminent, but the client became frightened and stopped the communication. They described the experience as someone else was using their vocal chords and their minds and thoughts were not being used to form the words or thoughts.

For me, one amazing thing that occurred were the conversations during one session that continued with the next session – from state to state, from practitioner to practitioner, from practitioner to client, from God to me. For example, someone in Portland would provide part of a message, and then someone in Austin would continue with additional information on the same topic. These two individuals did not know each other. Then another person in the Dallas area added to the information. They were connected only through this work and through the heart. The only thing in common was healing, God and me. What a wonderful blessing! It was a remarkable lesson in how connected we were and how information was available if we were willing to listen.

Gifts from the Heart, 11/17/00 — He Speaks...

The second experience I had that was what I called a miracle happened with my 4th personal connection experience. A friend contacted me to provide the work for her. I met her when I was studying Reiki. She was a chiropractic student and a quiet, young woman with grace and a gentle spirit. She said she felt "compelled" to call me for an appointment. I agreed to do the work, and we decided on a time and place.

She arrived for her appointment. The session began with her stated intention for the experience. "I would like to help all people, but if it's only one at a time, let me help. I want to reach my highest spiritual potential." She lay on the massage table and closed her eyes. We began. I stepped precisely through each part of the work. I concentrated on trying my best to be accurate and exact. I wanted to honor what I had been taught. It soon became apparent that although I might be in the process, I was not the one doing the work. I felt the temperature drop and there was a distinct chill in the room. I felt a lot of angels in the room. I felt them, but I couldn't see them. There were moments when I felt a Presence enfold me as if He had wrapped me in a blanket of light, and placed His arms around me. My hands became ice cold. I knew something wonderful was happening. I just didn't know what it was.

As I went through the steps and reached the end of the process, Whoever was actually doing the work, had not finished. I sat down and simply observed, as her hands seemed to have a life of their own. Her eyes remained closed during the entire experience.

When it seemed that Whoever was doing the work had completed the process, I tapped her gently to let her know the session was completed. I asked, "What did you experience?" Then I listened. This was what she shared with me. Thankfully, I captured what she said.

"I just heard a lot of talking – a voice was talking. There were purples, red & white. Someone was saying...

"I was here for a reason. I had to believe in myself. God sent me for a reason – for people to see certain things. I was their angel girl. I came here to learn certain things. They will be with me here while I learn. This was connecting me back to them. When you die, you become reconnected. Now we're being reconnected on a physical plane."

"There was something about Mother Teresa."

"They told me not to worry about school. They were going to use my hands. They were going to use my eyes. I would be able to see spiritual people, but don't be afraid. I would be able to see people – and their diseases."

"Someone is still talking to me...

142

'Tell Vicki she did a fantastic job. Vicki will go to Los Angeles. Tell Vicki – Everything that you do, God has already done it for you.'"

As she spoke, I wrote. I didn't want to miss a single word.

"I'm listening. Are you afraid, little one? For the life I have made for you, you've done wonders with it. We're there. We've always been there."

"He's talking...

'The name – Vicki High – that ring has a catch to it. The name came up a long time ago.' He's throwing out names. I hear a name – I don't – He told me to say 'Anna'. He keeps telling me... 'Vicki, you will go to Los Angeles. Don't worry about your stuff. You'll get more. Stop putting so many demands on yourself. In time, things will all work out.' "

"He tells me to quit second-guessing Him. He said something about a red rose... That He is, was and forever will be with you so you would know Hannah[18] wasn't just rambling."

"That's why I wouldn't let her open her eyes. When I'm finished, she will be able to open her eyes."

"He's saying names... These are people who you've helped, touched or will help. In time, you will understand."

"He said something about a baby. That it is OK. He'll be calling her home soon."

"He's not done. (Hannah is so impatient.) There are a few signs He wants to show you. He'll do so by using my body."

Then her feet moved. Her hands moved as if in a dance, a beautiful ballet. Her fingers were long and slender. Her nails were unpolished and beautiful. Her hands demonstrated the symbol, and then she would state the name for that symbol. Her hand demonstrated the eternal sign of life, and then the sign for peace. Her hand demonstrated the symbol for nations under God and the sign for salvation. Her hands moved in a beautifully choreographed dance of grace.

"No. She doesn't have Parkinson's," He remarked.

"Look not to your right. Look not to your left. Look up. By only looking up will you find Him. People are merely pawns. In Him, in time, He can show us the way. Make no mistake, He is real which you always knew Him to be."

"There were angels, of course. There were guides occasionally."

"There's a reason why He chose you. You're a good girl. (He's being funny.)"

Then I was gifted with this wonderful poetry:

"He's not just one thing. He's many...

He's every song you sing.

He's every word you read.

He's every whisper.

He's every thought.

He's concept.

He's breath.

He's movement.

He's matter.

He's energy.

He's light.

He's dark.

He's good.

He's bad.

He's everything.

There are no mistakes, only experiences to help one's soul evolve to its highest self."

"Live each day as a new beginning. Accept life as it is, but be as you are."

"Hobie, John – Wonderful, Wonderful, Creators, Creations – So pleased, so enamored."

"He's going to let Hannah rest now. Thank you." [19]

I was amazed at what He had to say. Only then could Hannah open her eyes and she shared her impressions with me.

"Someone placed His hand on my hip. I felt heat on my chest. It felt like when I took in a deep breath, I was forced to exhale. There was something going on with my eyes. I don't remember any smells. I would breathe and then the breath would be non-existent. I felt someone was standing over me – on my left side."

"I felt there were a lot of people here. His voice is still in my head. My ear still feels 'open.' He wasn't threatening at all. He is majestic. People fear Him, but He's not to be feared in a bad way. He knows everything about us. He's approachable and very, very familiar."

"He kept saying your name. I went warp speed backwards. I saw you. I knew you. You were with Him. I knew you were there. You weren't here. You were somewhere else. You knew you would be here."

Her experience was amazing to me. I knew that this was incredible. I couldn't explain what went on, but I knew it was a special experience. I knew that I had come into contact with God in a direct and very extraordinary way. I knew that God was at the heart of this miraculous experience. AND, I was only halfway completed with Hannah's personal connection experience. There was another day to finish the process.

As I reflected on the experience, I was amazed at the hand symbols. I wished I were a better artist so I could capture the essence of each symbol. I didn't know what the purpose of these symbols was, but I expected that I would be told during a later session.

The poetry was beautiful. It touched my heart in a marvelous and personal way. The words reminded me of God's omnipresence in everything we do, everything we hear, every thought we entertain, and every breath we take. It also helped me begin the process to live more each day in the now.

It was interesting to hear about my decision to work in Los Angeles. God knew what I was contemplating. He said, *"Everything you do, God has already done it for you."* This experience reminded me that even the life I lived and the name "Vicki High" had been chosen for me a long time ago. Since I acquired this name through marriage, I thought that was pretty awesome. He even knew me well enough to tell me not to worry about my stuff. I was quite attached to my stuff.

"He said something about a baby..." My baby would be my dog, Wendy. Wendy had been a part of my life for more than 10 years. She was a border collie, German shepherd mix. Her health began to fail and she died in July the year following this event. I was comforted knowing she was home with Him.

"Live each day as a new beginning..." This passage really touched me. We forget to be, just be. This reminded me that each day we get to begin again. We choose again each day how we want to live. If we make mistakes, and we all will, we can choose to begin again. The *"be as you are"* statement reminded me how very special we are, just as we are. The light within us is really a part of God within us.

Gifts from the Heart, 11/18/00 – The Experience Continues

During the second session, Hannah's intention remained the same. As I completed my part of the session, I sat down and made the following observations.

While Hannah's eyes remained closed, she began marching on the table. Her hands performed that dance, that beautiful ballet again, and then her hands were initiated. Each finger and each palm was initiated ritualistically by the other fingers. The hands then initiated the eyes and clairaudient points behind the ears. Her feet lifted high off the table and formed geometric angles. Her hands formed a temple and then initiated her head, forehead, eyes, and throat. Her hands then joined over her eyes and went around her head in a circular motion.

Hannah still couldn't open her eyes through this whole process and was unable to open them even after it was completed. She began to share her experience.

"That was pretty neat. There was a lot of talking. It's almost like I was being initiated into God's army of some sort. There were rules... almost like – accepting God as my Savior and accepting the work He wants me to do. It's almost like someone reading...

"Do you...?"

I answered, "Yes, I do."

"Do you accept God as your Savior?"

There were all these acceptances. I accepted all of them.

"His Will be done."

He denounced all the negatives. There's no fear. I feel at peace. I feel changed. I don't have the same anxieties or stress. He said He took those from me. I know He's here – more to the left.

"Yes, I'm still talking to you," He said.

"Is there air on my face? He's all around me."

"He says I need to sit for a minute."

149

"*He says ask how you're doing?' "*

I responded: "Great".

"*He says he knows. You're always great.*"

"When my eyes first closed, something...I heard a voice...

'*Let all that stuff go.' "*

I heard another voice that almost was reading off a list. It was a vow. I would agree and they would move on to something else. I saw scripts and writing on my hands. I let go and felt strong energy around me. It was there. I felt there was something on my head - like a garment of some kind. It felt like I was drawing on myself, but somebody was taking control of my hands. It was shields, armor, something. It wasn't scary. It was just different. He kept telling me I had to help people."

"As usual, I tried to open my eyes and couldn't. He's always to the left side of me."

"I'm here. I was here through the whole thing. I don't get all the hand things. I know what they were doing. It was an initiation. I felt like a warrior."

Hannah and I smelled a light, flowery fragrance. I thought it was her perfume. She thought it was mine. Neither of us was wearing any perfume that day.

Then...Hannah said:

"He says to take my hand."

I went over and grasped her right hand with my left hand.

"He said let go."

I'm very literal at times. I released my hand and she chuckled. "Not my hand."

"He said let go."

I placed my hand back in hers and relaxed. Her hand was back in that beautiful ballet again and performed the specific scripts or initiation of my hand just as I had observed hers earlier. (Hannah still could not open her eyes during this whole experience.)

She held my hand with both of hers and then she held her hands together as if in prayer. She "prayed blessings" to my left and right at my head, my heart and my hands.

"'Many, many blessings to you. Peace be with you, my child," He said.[20]

When she had completed her work, she could open her eyes. I felt honored and truly humbled. He said,

"Thank you."

I felt enormous gratitude and wonder at His love and connection to me. It didn't surprise me when she reported being inducted into God's army. It matched her actions on the massage table and the gestures around her head were like a helmet or a garment of some sort.

What a gift we were both given! It was such a privilege for me to feel the love that was conveyed during the experience. It was a wonderful, exciting and awesome thing to witness. The information was amazing. I felt I had participated in a sacred and blessed event. Hannah and I were both astonished at what had occurred.

The results of this personal connection experience for both of us became both a foundation and an amazing experience that changed our lives. It began to show us what marvelous ways God makes Himself real to us if we are willing to be vessels for His work. It was at this moment that I knew what "Gifts from the Heart" were and how powerful they were – our very own Valentines straight from God Who made us. When the session was over, I called Dr. Pearl's office. He wanted to hear the details of the experience.

I continued to meet with Hannah and visit with her. Several of the miraculous experiences that have changed my life, occurred in sessions where she and I were working together. She has been such a gift to me. In every experience, she has exhibited a willingness to participate with a consistently humble and loving nature. We have built a trust together that gives us a framework to continue receiving and sharing these Gifts from the Heart.

Gifts from the Heart, 9/15/01 – Peace Will Prevail

A seminar attendee began to speak and the instructor asked me to work with her outside the seminar. This is what was spoken as four of us witnessed what she had to say.

> *"Fear not for your loved ones, for they are cared for. Peace will prevail over the evil that has begun. You are One with Spirit. Christ consciousness will return to this planet. We have prepared for this. Peace profound. Love above all."*

> *"Love is in the heart, not the mind. We are one in Spirit. Seek not One in the mind, but in the heart. It is the gift of Christ consciousness."*

> *"There is confusion. We want peace for your planet. We have prepared for this for some time to come. You will show them the path. Christ is returning to the planet."*

> *"We love so much... We are here to protect and preserve the Divine Creation. Love has created all. It will not be taken. For its true form is the Divine within every single being."*

> *"I speak of the trilateral. It is known to many. We seek your permission to intervene in these affairs for they are beyond the control of the conscious mind. Be at*

peace for we are your friends. We love you. We made you. We are One. Love hath prevailed."

"You seek guidance from within. This is the way of the Divine. You are more than human beings. You are Divine Creations of love."

"Go forth and speak your peace, truth and love. It is guidance of the Divine."

"They see fit to produce nuclear weapons and destruction. It feeds their hunger, yet they, too, starve for spiritual truth. They will lose control of their power and be rendered… They, too, will seek spiritual renewal. Many truths will be told. Many truths will be known. There will be books written quoting these sayings. Do not fear misinterpretation. In time, these will be published for the rest of the world."

"Many seek God's love. Many seek God's truth. Many religions will be rendered helpless for they will not be able to explain these findings."

"…The foundations will be shifting. Sources of power will change… The Pope will surrender to a take over. The Roman Church will no longer exist. It is deemed so. They will no longer have a hold on religious theory."

"...Waters will rise. Oil will spill into the ocean. But all will not be lost. All will be restructured. It has begun. We love you." [21]

Gifts from the Heart, 11/28/01 — Live and Love and To Help Others

A client contacted me to do her personal connection session. I was working in Hollywood at the time and she came to the office for her scheduled appointment. Much to my surprise as I began to work on her, her foot circled and circled in a way that surprised me because it seemed impossible that it could physically turn like that. Her eyes rolled back into her sockets. I could see the whites of her eyes and part of her irises. Then she began to speak. The voice was child-like. "They" giggled and laughed. I was amazed and a little scared, but more excited than anything. This is what she – rather they – had to say:

"I love you. Oh, farther. No, farther..."

Her hands levitated off the table. There was this huge gurgle in her stomach.

"Live and love and to help others. To help others. To help others."

"You know that it is not it. It's farther. Much farther! It's farther than you come. It is farther. Fighting... so far away. It's always far away. They will always fight you. They will always fight you. They will fight you. They will

155

fight you. Live and love and love and love and love and love."

Her hands clasped together as if in prayer over her chest.

"Peace and love you. I love you. Peace and love you. Peace and love you. Peace and love you."

Her hands were placed on her chest.

"Peace and love them. OK, cause their beings will love them. It's OK. It's OK. Don't worry. There are beings that love them."

"We really love you. They love you all. They love you all. We are always here. We are always here. They are always here."

"It's OK. They love you. Oh, they do! They love you. Oh, they do! Let us help you."

"It's OK. It's always OK. OK. We are here – ready to help. Just let us help you. OK. OK. You don't have to cry because it's going to be OK. OK. OK. OK. OK. They're here to love you. It's OK."

"We're never alone. Let us in. We are so far. We are right here. It's OK. It's going to be OK. We always love you. We are here to help you. How do you help? To

live and to love. A man is to live and to love. They'll be OK, too. We'll all be OK. We love you, OK?"

"Don't worry about that. Everything goes on as it should. Everything is as it should be. Everyone will be OK. Everyone will be OK. Everyone will be OK. It's OK. All are OK. It's OK. We are always here. OK. OK. To hold you and love you. To live and to love and to help others." [22]

I was writing so fast and trying so hard to complete the process while still capturing what was being said. I would write a little and then I would try to advance to the next step of the process. Then I would write some more. It was amazing. It was unbelievable and the message was clear. We are here to live. We are here to love. We are here to help others. We have help. We do not have to do it alone. There were things I was not clear about, but I knew if I approached this experience with childlike wonder and awe that I would receive answers when the time was right for understanding.

The next day began like the day before and the message continued. She remarked that she was chilled throughout her body.

Gifts from the Heart, 11/29/01 — Live and Love and To Help Others, Part II

"It's too cold. It's too cold. But it's so important. There's so much to do. You have to get started. Life's too hard. We're going to help you. It's not funny. We're going to help you. We're going to help you. You're too cold.

You're too cold. Why are you so cold? Why are you so cold?"

"How do we know who we are supposed to help? It's like ice. I can't do it alone. I can't do it alone. Their... I should calm down. Everyone should calm down. It's cold from everywhere. It's so hard. Help us all. Help us all to do our work."

"Why did it get like this? You let it get like this. You let it get like this. We have to fix it. We have to fix it. We have to fix it. We have to fix it."

"Why are you singing? Who's going to help us? We just have to have help."

"OK. We're from the stars. So far! The stars are so beautiful. The stars are so beautiful. I just can't imagine. It's OK. Cause it's so pretty out here. It's so pretty."

There was laughter.

"We can't fix anything without you. We want to help. There are no bodies. We can't touch. We can only watch. There's so much sadness there. We can't help. You went there to fix it. You went there to fix it. We want you to fix it. We feel, but we can't touch. Help."

"You'll have to do it for us. You'll have to do it for you. You'll have to do it for everyone. We can send thoughts and vibrating things. We can't reach and touch. You have to do that. We can't do that."

"It's OK. You have to… You have to be the hands. You have to be the hands. You have to be the hands. That's all."

"Where do you start? There's so much to do."

"I want to start, but I don't know where to start. You make me cry."

"Start with one person. You are silly."

"All the answers are in there somewhere. We put them there. We are you. Are you the me or we? You are the lucky ones who can touch and feel and love. How good it is to touch and feel! That's not our job. Our job is out there. Your job is here."

"You have to start. It's icky here. Do what you came for."

"I should be there. I should be there. I should be there. I should be there. I should be there. You should be here. You should be here. You should be here. You should be here. You should be here."

"You picked there. You picked there. You picked there. You picked there. You work there. You work there. You work there. You work there."

"But it's so hard. Just because you have hands, doesn't make it easy."

"Why did you let it turn to this? We have to fix it here."

"You know why you are there. You have to remember. Do your job. You have to do your work. You can't sit back and not do your work. You have to do what you came for. Please do your work."

"You are so funny down there. You need to enjoy the beauty there. The tastes, smells, & touches. Everyday, think 'This is a beautiful place to be.' "

"You let us mess it up. You don't watch very well. You're not taking care. You let these things go on."

"There is no answer."

"Mucky. Mucky. You're so much bigger than all that stuff. You go higher, higher, higher – above that stuff. You don't live in that stuff. Then, then, then, you can work higher just like we work… higher. You bring everything up with you. Come up to the top stuff. That's where you are going to do your work."

"We love you. We love you. OK. OK. OK. OK. We love you."

"You putz around too much. There's too much to do."

"You go there. You get stuck in things. You went there to do something good. You're putzing. Stuff, stuff and more stuff. Feelings... inside stuff. You have been here. You take knowledge back and you don't use it."

"It's time now. You have to hurry. It's not funny, but we laugh. You carry it inside you. You'd better start to do it. No more putzing. Just go to work now."

I asked, "Is this message for her or me?" They responded:

"If it works here, it works there. It's the same message. Everybody has to stay connected. It doesn't matter who they are. They have to stay connected."

"Brenda[23] doesn't putz. Brenda knows the work. She is so special. She knows. She goes person to person. She does the work – one little connection at a time."

It was at this time, I asked if Brenda could join us. I realized later that it was not Sharon who gave me permission. In fact when they talked, Sharon did not remember what was said and was unaware of anything that had to do with the session. I learned a difficult lesson, because it wasn't my intention to make Sharon uncomfortable in any way. When I invited Brenda to join us, she was able to witness the rest of the experience.

"Sharon [24] came with big work to do. She hides. She has to link and find those people to do her work. Everybody went there with good intentions. Spread the love. Stuff – this, that and power. Love, care, reach out with hands to reach out and touch. You know inside. You have to work now. The sadness. You have to go higher. You can't stay at the bottom."

"We know. We see it coming. It's going to be bad. Go above all that muck you have. It's time. Join and help each other. You know your jobs. You have to do them. You went there to spread the love. Souls… poor, hurt. You ignore them. Don't ignore them anymore. There's so much sadness. You can fix it. You all have the key. Go on the inside. Never, NEVER on the outside. It's all there. It's inside you. You took it with you from here."

"You're wasting time. So much time! No more time! Just spread the love. Love the cat, the dog, the plant, the guy on the street, the lady in the tree."

"We have so much to say. You already know. You knew it before. You're being bad now. Do what you went there for. That's enough now. Rise above it all. Do it now. There is no more time. Time is running out."
[25]

When we completed her session, she was afraid I would think she was weird. I assured her that I thought it was a great blessing and the things they had to tell us were very important. I was amazed at the passion, the voice, and the words they used to communicate. I loved the way it sounded childlike and innocent with laughter and joy. I was saddened by her tears and fears associated with the future and the reality that we are not doing our work. Most of all I felt very blessed that such a communication had taken place at all.

I reviewed the messages. We are here to do the jobs we agreed to do. We are here on earth and we have the arms, legs and human bodies to do the work. We are their hands. We feel for them. They send us assistance through thoughts and vibrating things. They said they were from the stars and that it was so beautiful where they come from out there. They were so clear about the fact that we have to remember what to do. We knew at one time and we must remember. They hid it inside our hearts. The meaning was clear. We have to hurry. We have to rise above the human stuff and never ignore or overlook anyone. It is also very important for us to love and appreciate the beauty in our world.

Gifts from the Heart, 2/01/02 – You Can Fix Everything…

A couple of months later, she enrolled in an additional seminar. She was concerned about messages coming through her while she was on the table. She wanted to avoid that if she could. She didn't want to distract the class and asked me for a healing session before we were to begin that evening. As soon as the session was underway, her foot began to circle as it had before and she began to speak:

> *"OK – You forget. You could laugh. We couldn't. It feels so good. But you're out of sync. We love to be in sync with the others."*

She hummed – first high, then low.

> *"Faster – the vibration is faster – not farther – all vibration is so fast, so fast. If only we could connect."*

She laughed. Her hands moved along her body.

> *"She can do her own. We showed her. It'll go where it wants to go cause it knows."*

Her hands moved as if in a dance.

> *"You can fix the eyes. You have to have faith. You can fix – eyes, heart, all of you. Why can't you remember? You just have to remember. All you have to do is remember. You can be silly. Some are so silly. We rise together or we don't rise."*

> *"We can't go any farther if you don't come. We hold each other back or we go farther together. She can do her own. Why can't you believe? This is what you do – This will show you where to put the power. You can fix*

yourself. You have to have faith. How can it be that you know what we know and not remember?"

"Evil and good. We are all the same – of the same thing. See the light. It's bright. You aspire to this light – to this vibration. Tonight you do that. This will show you."

"Never be afraid. There is no fear. Evil is light. Light is evil. It is beautiful. Light is everywhere. This is all love. This is all light. Get on this frequency. This will block the evil. You only go with the light."

"You like the funny ones. There's no fun here. No movies. No laughing. We have to be careful. That which is evil, which is dark, grab with love, grab with light."

"Never erase hatred with hatred. You hate – it's all black. It's all dark. That's not how it works. There are so many years of hate and war. There is war and hate. Counter with love and light."

"You have to hurry. You have to help. The light is here. Look to the light. When people say mean things, respond with love. Be love and go up. Be mean and go down. There won't be laughing. No anything. You have to hurry now. You have to hurry. You have to hurry. You have to hurry."

165

"Look at the light. There is all light. There is no room. It's all light. See the light. It's like big sunshine. You go up and find the frequency. Feel the frequency."

Her hand moved in circular motion.

"You can fix everything. You have to learn to fix it. You have to learn to let it go. Some people hold it. They hold the human stuff. You don't have to be sick. Just let go. Reach for the light. Reach for the love. Get higher than that stupid human stuff. You are a higher reality! You have to do it together."

"It's very serious. While you're there, laugh, love, hug and kiss. You're not there to eat. You are there to come to join us. Laughing feels so good. Laughter is medicine. Hurry. Hurry. Hurry. Hurry. Hurry."

"The future can go either way. This is the future of light. This is the future of love."

"What's the matter? Why is there so much pain? What happened? We are in the gutter. That's what is going to happen. Do your work. You chose to be there. You chose to laugh, drink, and eat. You chose the base human things. Get busy. It's a hard job. You picked it, but get busy. You have to go to work."

"Some of you came with big purposes. Let the ones watch who will. The more you love, the more you join the light. You will balance them."

"Until you see the light, you have to help those who are mean. Stop pitying yourselves. You can do it. You went there. You volunteered. All of you must remember. Lay down. Remember. The light is here. Pull it in. Imagine it's all sunlight. Find your own vibration."

"There are strings of light. Feel them. It feels so good. You can eat chocolate, have friends, and laugh. You… Your connection is here." [26]

There was so much information to absorb and understand. Every piece of information was important. Some of the things I didn't fully understand, but as before, I trusted with the innocence of a child, that the knowledge would be revealed to me when I needed to know more. It was also very clear to me that the answers were in my heart.

The next day, I asked her if she would do another session with me. I was preparing to make some major life changes. I had questions. I knew she could provide those answers for me. Here are excerpts from some of the messages I received.

Gifts from the Heart, 2/02/02 — Answers for My Questions

As the session began, her foot began to circle in the now familiar way and words came pouring forth.

"Why are we here? Because she has all the questions!"

"There are so many ways. You don't have to do it exactly. Don't be so restrictive. It's not wrong here. If you do it on… Everybody can start her own thing. If you feel so strongly, start to do it."

"Here is the light. So fast. So fast. So far. Pull it in here. This goes where the problem is. It links here. It's where you put intention."

"So fast. It's so beautiful. It's so peaceful."

She whispered.

"If you find a good way to reach the light, you do it. Paint outside the lines. We don't need to stay within the lines."

'Sometimes if you like… if you found a different way. It's OK if it is different. You're wearing glasses and you still don't see. Open all 4 eyes. What you want to do is fine! Do you want a blessing? The whole world has a blessing! It's fast and it's light. You can fix everything. You can release it all. If there's a problem inside and outside, release it all then with light and love."

"You know, you didn't need our permission. You know better. You are there. You see what's going on. If you

know this could be better – different, then do it. As long as it doesn't hurt! NEVER are you to hurt anyone. If it's going to help… This counts for you and all other people sitting around. There are lots of ways to do things and if you get to the same end…"

"So fast – seems so far. But it's not far. It's inside. It's inside you. It's inside everybody. They hid it inside. You, 4-eyes, it's in your heart! Stop looking elsewhere. Why didn't they put it on everyone's forehead? If you want to start all the connections, you always go with what's in your heart. What does your heart say?"

"Take a leap of faith. Don't go to be bigger. Don't go for the money. Don't go to be hurtful. You are here to join the others."

"The guy in the gutter – if he is not raised, all must be raised or you will go down. DON'T IGNORE ANYONE!"

"Find the frequency – the love frequency. The beauty and peace are unbelievable. It's just amazing. It feels so good. We have to feel sorry for you. It's kind of icky down there. Let them get up here. There's more past here. We all want to get better – where it's love and light."

"*Love has its own frequency. It feels so good. It doesn't matter what you love – Man, woman, sister, brother, dad... If you have a way to do it, you have to do it.*"

"*Dancing is fun, too. Laughing is fun, too. Maybe we picked wrong. We can only dance through you. You can have fun. It's here. You will know.*"

I responded, "My answers are inside – where I ask my heart. When I ask you, I am asking myself, if I'm you and you're me."

"*4 eyes gets it! I'm you. We're her! You get it. OK, then. You know where the answers are. When your time has come, it may be hard. Don't hurt anyone doing it. Do it with love. Do it with light. You take too many steps backward if you hurt anyone.*"

"*Why is there not so much love? There's too much pain. You better get going. Why are you waiting? Take it with you – your gift. It's your job to share the gift. No restrictions. Eventually we have to get there together.*"

"*As long as it is in your heart, you know what it is in your heart. Love, light and helping. There are unlovable people everywhere, but they are not really unlovable. They all need love. More love and support is available for you.*"

"If you don't survive and maintain #1… Take care of you. You will never take care of anyone else if you don't take care of yourself first."

"It's hard for everyone. It's hard everywhere. Never run from hard work. Don't go to be doing your work. You have so much potential. Push yourself to the next level. Never burn your bridges. You need to remain connected. Split with good intentions. All are connected."

"You have made very strong bonds. You have connected. Don't make the mistake of breaking the bonds. Leave with zero hearts broken and all hearts mended."

"They need lots of help in Texas – way more than California. There is opportunity. There are openings for people to reach the light. Always remember to keep friends and bonds. We don't know what happens next."

"Do what's in your heart. Don't break bonds. Don't be rude to people. 4 Eyes has the gift. Hobie, Dobie has the gift. Everyone has the gift."

"Heart – Follow this. Follow your heart a million light years away. Go inside with intention. Have the intention first. As long as it's loving – make it what Vicki knows. You helped us connect."

"I want to swim."

"Meditate with Love, Guidance & Intention. It will come from within. Help will come to you. Do whatever works for you. You check out and see what you're told." [27]

I didn't know why this phrase, "I want to swim" was included, but it was. Once during a healing session, a little boy with cerebral palsy reported, "You're all wet." It may be related or not. I do know that water is important in the healing process. I know more will be revealed to us and it is probably within our hearts even now if we remember. Once I was told, "Anoint yourself with water. Water contains all life."

I returned to Texas with a completely different plan. Rather than continuing my employment, I knew I had more work to do at home. Rather than stepping down from being the Mayor, I continued to lead and govern because I believed that was what was I was led to do. I wasn't sure what would happen next, but I knew that Texas was where I needed to continue my work. It was there I would find opportunities to help people. I knew that I had to love more than I ever believed was possible.

I was concerned that my time in California only spanned four months. As I prepared to leave my employment, a friend told me, "You thought your contract was for a year. You completed your agreement in four months." I knew that this statement was true. I felt it in my heart.

Gifts from the Heart, 2/10/02 — Breakfast of Miracles

I arranged a breakfast meeting with a friend shortly after I returned. Much to my surprise and delight, as we ate, she remarked, "Vicki, there is someone speaking to me in my left ear." She was a little self-conscious about the location because we were seated in a restaurant, but she quietly began to speak.

> *"Vicki, you have to know you are a gift. Grow with the truth. Grow with the life. Grow with the light. You can rise above everything."*

I was reminded of how well they knew me when they shared.

> *"You are a worrier. You are undoubtedly the most stubborn person."*

> *"You allow us to use your bodies. We play with your hair. We blow on your shoulder. We play with you to get your attention. We walk around not to scare you. You need us."*

> *"Your mission is to have faith. Faith comes in parables and stories."*

> *"Before you were born, God kissed your eyes, kissed your lips and anointed your soul. Your mother and your sister love you. We love you more. Here love is unconditional. On earth, love is conditional."*

"Do not be afraid of the seeds of truth. The root of the Master is in all of us."

At one point, they asked her if she would allow them to use her body. She hesitated at demonstrating symbols in the restaurant. She looked over her right shoulder. She had remembered a man sitting at the next table. They told her he was no longer there. As she turned her head, she saw the gentleman had left the area. She agreed to allow them to use her body, but she said she would feel more comfortable if we went to the car. We gathered our belongings and went to sit in her car.

She closed her eyes. The voice that spoke was unlike her voice.

"There are many signs."

The sound was throaty and guttural, not unlike the Klingon language on StarTrek™. (They corrected me in a later conversation.) He demonstrated nine different symbols using her hands. He called each symbol by name in the language I was unfamiliar with and then he translated them into English.

He wanted to leave me with this – a song.

"He's got the whole world in His hands. He's got the little babies in His hands. He's got the mothers and daddies in His hands. He's got the whole world in His hands."

"Enjoy the sunshine today. Enjoy the birds." [28]

I wanted so hard to remember everything He said to me, but I did not have my journal with me. I counted the symbols, and used as many of the memory techniques I had taught over the years to retain the information that was shared. As soon as we said good-bye, I sat in my car. I wrote down everything I could remember. I learned that day to take a journal and a pen with me everywhere. I was so disappointed that although I remembered so much of the conversation, I did not retain all of it.

I had plans to meet another friend for lunch. As I arrived at the restaurant, I didn't see her car. I stood outside and enjoyed the sun shining on the beautiful and warm February day. I marveled at the anticipation of spring approaching. It was then I realized there were thousands of birds everywhere and I remembered the phrase when the session ended. I felt so loved that they were right there with me. They knew what I would encounter. I smiled and was filled with gratitude and wonder at the level of communication and interest in my activities, how I lived and what I experienced in my life.

Gifts from the Heart, 3/29/02 — Healing Heart to Heart

One of the most incredible and life changing experiences occurred on Good Friday, March 29, 2002. Hannah and I agreed to participate in a healing session. She was lying on the table to begin this session. As I began to work with her, she closed her eyes. She told me they were going to sit her up. I went to assist her, but they sat her up with her eyes closed the whole time and everything seemed in control without my assistance. I continued with my work and observed as her body stretched, and she shook her arms. After a few moments, it began. A voice spoke, but it sounded lower than Hannah's normal voice.

"Just relax. How are you? We have a lot of work to do today. I am glad to see you are prepared."

I had come prepared with a writing tablet, a tape recorder and a camera for pictures. I was having difficulty capturing the essence of the hand symbols with pen and paper alone. I thought a picture might be the best way to capture what the symbols were and exactly how they looked.

"The language we use is simple – it's a melody of time and universe. The symbols that we use perpetuate life's travel of expectancies."

On several occasions, Hannah and other clients have spoken in languages that they do not recognize nor know how to speak; yet the voices came from the person on the table. The languages were guttural, then lilting and at times even had an oriental tone. On a couple of occasions, the person actually sang in that wonderful language. On each occasion, when asked, the client confirmed that he or she did not speak that language. It came from someone else and from somewhere else.

"Be that as it may, we shall begin. Physical bodies get stiff. At times it's hard to work with. Hard to relax."

"How beautiful today is! How beautiful life is today!"

Many times during these sessions, I was aware of how much life is revered. It was a reminder of what beauty there was in the nature all around us, the trees, flowers, birds, and how the very life we live was often taken for granted by us. These messengers were always appreciative of the beauty in the world around us.

Hannah's hands went together in that beautiful ballet once again. Her voice was low and she spoke in that melodic language. She spoke the name of each symbol as she demonstrated it. Then she translated the name to English. She showed me the signs for Life, Eternal Peace, Daylight, Beginning and Blessings. Then that voice continued with these words.

"Our purpose is to heal. Our purpose is to bring people together. Love unconditionally."

"I say this much. Others will shoot you down. Others won't be around. That's not our concern."

"These symbols are not to be mimicked. They are to bring this work together in harmony. If you go back to Jesus, His work is not mimicked. Jesus is a healer. He can never be mimicked. Remember that."

"Reconnective started long ago – beyond civilization. It is here now to deliver its meaningful purpose. Why? Mankind is headed for seemingly self-destruction - another bomb scare - another September 11th."

"The inward ability for destruction is every day life. It's babies in sidewalk trashcans. It's a child shooting other children. It's everything – slow destruction."

What amazed me was the confirmation of the problems in our world by God who knew us intimately and saw us through the difficulties and challenges we faced each day. He gave us the tools we needed to change our world, but we still had to choose what we would do and then act on it.

"This world is headed to a rejuvenation with this work to a healthier life. That is why so many of you are needed for reconnective work. It's healing from neighbor to neighbor. It's healing from child to animal. It's healing from animal to child."

"It's breathing life into this world. It's simple. We're not here to make it complicated. Just simple – do the work."

"Have you ever seen a crystal blue light in the shadow of darkness? I have. Have you ever seen the nature of life at its best? I have."

"What is it that makes you different than others? It's your inner Spirit. It's your inner light. It's your love for other people. That's what we adore about you. The open ear you bring when we speak. We're not talking

for our health. We're here for life. We're here for mankind. We're here for the Universe. We're here."

"I feel so relaxed today. Ah – yes – relaxed."

"Do you ever wonder why birds sing? Do you ever wonder why people sing? Do you ever wonder why angels sing? The melody is smoothing to the human soul, the human spirit. It is unity within voice within a song. It does not have to be explained or analyzed. It just is."

"Unfortunately, people are not like that. People spend so much time with the ins and outs, the whoops and woes, trying to figure out who you are, who you are not. That's not the reason God put you all here. Love is something emanated through the pores with the honesty, truth, and goodness of heart that you were given."

"Why is that so hard to understand? We watch people – in anger, in fear, in solitude. These are normal emotions. The focus of life is so distorted. You have to love yourself to honor yourself. You have to be yourself to let others see yourself."

"Life is but a dream – do you remember that?" [29]

What power there was in these words! You had to love yourself to honor yourself. Was the way you felt about yourself

179

important? I would say definitely, yes, it was! If you did not love yourself, you could not honor yourself. Others could not honor you either. You had to love yourself first. You had to be yourself. We heard these words, but we had no idea how powerful they really were. There was no one else who could be you, but you. No one else could fill your shoes and do what you came here to do.

What I found in subsequent sessions, were how very important our dreams and goals were to living full lives. Then it was as if she began again. Hannah still could not open her eyes. It seemed like there was someone else speaking now. The timber and tone of the voice itself changed as I listened.

Gifts from the Heart, 3/29/02 — Love, Love, Love, Love, Love

There was a loving smile on her face.

"Hello, Vicki."

"Let me just start off by saying, hello again. Welcome to planet earth. Welcome to planet earth. You must think that strange."

"Love, love, love, love, love. How I love you and everyone else here! The power of love is so great. The truth of love is fantastic, extraordinary."

"My what you call reconnective experience began a long time ago – before you were born, before there was ever life. Be not afraid for one man to hear what I

have to say. It may sound baffling or confusing, but it's the truth."

"I AM WHO I AM. Make no mistake. I AM WHO I AM."

"Why do birds chirp and sing? Why wouldn't they? Why does mankind not listen? Not hear? How could they?"

"The Bible measures life. The Bible measures events. The Bible has a beginning and an end. Life does not."

"Your Spirit is eternal. Your beauty, style, and essence are eternal. I never sleep. I'm always here to see the goodness and at times, the darkness. I'm always here."

I was struggling to write as fast as I could. There were tears streaming down my face at this point, and as I realized Who was speaking to me. I continued to write, but the lines were blurred in my journal as I tried to see through my tears.

"People always ask what heaven is like. Some people square it and put it in the box. Some people embellish it. Some people even create it. Heaven is endless. Heaven is beautiful. It's beauty beyond beauty, love beyond love, truth beyond truth, honesty beyond honesty."

"People wonder when we die. Where do we go? The correct answer would be heaven. Life is but a dream. You walk and go through this life to learn. It's simple.

Who you are is not as important as who you choose to be. It's your choice."

"Have you ever seen the stars? The Star of David, perhaps? It's quite beautiful."

"As a healer, you want to encompass a sense of love, a sense of purity."

"How I heal is not important. Who I heal is not important. It's the love emanating through healing that's important. People walk around with illness, cancer, and AIDS. These are diseases of the body. I heal disease of the Spirit. The body will do the rest."

"The term reconnective healing is just a term. Healing is healing. A baby is a baby. Truth is truth. Honesty is honesty. Togetherness is a start. Unity is a start."

We often wonder why there are so many methods of healing available in today's world. Is there one that is better than another? This passage told us that healing is healing. It does not matter what name you give it. Healing is healing. It all comes from the same Source.

"When I heal people, I heal them from heart to heart. I speak to people from heart to heart."

"A long time ago, of course you know My story. A healer is WHO I AM, WHO I WAS and WHO I WILL

FOREVER BE even in the streets of Galilee. I say this not to bore you, but because truth is truth."

"I was a man like any other man. My Father taught me to heal and I healed. I have no malice in My heart – only love, only truth, only honesty."

"I say this because a healer is not just someone who touches someone. The essence of a healer begins here (in the heart) and ends here (in the other person's heart.)"

"Interjecting healing – interjecting reconnective healing – they are one and the same."

"It's been a long road. From this point forward, your walk is your own. Go do reconnective. Teach reconnective. Learn more about reconnective. Reconnective is a daily learning experience. You will continually be learning more things. You continually will see more miraculous experiences. These experiences are to be shared, not held in secret. People will listen and hear. They will come to their own conclusions. Their Spirit will hear."

"My concern is that you take the time to truly figure out what you want to do. Go with that. A healer is a healer is a healer. Mind – thoughts – you heal with who you are. Not everyone is ready to receive healings. Not

183

every drug addict is ready to quit. There are ones who do quit. There are people that will listen."

"Be hopeful. In spite of pitfalls and downfalls, be hopeful. Your mission in life is to bring as many people as you can to Jesus. Bring them with you. Don't leave anyone behind if you can help it. We will be ending shortly."

And with that, we concluded the session.[30]

Hannah shared these feelings about her experience.

"I felt it was more than one person. The first entity was above people – like a sergeant or a corporal, but under Jesus and under God. I felt kind of heavy with the first one. With the second person, I felt light. It was as if someone took a vacuum cleaner and cleaned me out. With the first being, my mind was still operating. With the second person, when I spoke, I could hear the words and the voice, but I could also hear with my mind. My mind was not doing anything – it was like I was one with Him. My mind was stopped and there was no difference between Him and me. I felt a lot of joy, happiness and peace."

"I felt like – it's not so much I saw anything. With the first being, I saw blue and purple. With the change, I got the image of an angel. With the last person, it was like sitting there looking at Him from the back with a lot of light with gold in it all around Him."

"I felt like my hands at times had tingling sensations. Toward the end, I heard a woman's voice singing in my left ear - singing *He's Got The Whole World In His Hands* – joyful and childlike. A child was singing a song walking along a beach or a field. There was a woman's voice. I felt comforted. It was almost like a mother singing to a child – singing him to sleep."

"At one point when He was talking, it was like I was watching from somewhere else – watching Jesus walk and watching Jesus on the cross."

To say I felt honored is such an understatement. I felt so blessed and so humbled when this experience was shared. Many people wondered Who the Source of this work was. This experience confirmed once again it was sacred, spiritual work. However, along with the extraordinary experience, came the ability to share this miracle with you and know that people want to experience this same kind of communication for themselves. This book was written to share the love, truth, honesty, integrity and beauty that were communicated to me through the people who received healing sessions. Why me? Why Hannah? I honestly have no idea why we were gifted with these experiences. God showed me that I am so loved in spite of my flaws. As I am loved, so are you.

I knew the second person Who spoke was Jesus. He told me, "I AM WHO I AM. Make no mistake. I AM WHO I AM." He spoke of Galilee and the lessons He learned from His Father. As He spoke, my heart responded. I felt tears stream down my face and I offered an explanation quoted from the Bible in John 10:4, KJV. "And when

He putteth forth His own sheep, He goeth before them, and the sheep follow Him; for they know His voice... I am the Good Shepherd, and know My sheep, and am known of Mine."[31]

It is important for me to share that Jesus is real. So are the other ways people find God in their lives. This is not meant to exclude anyone or any faith. God is so magnificent that He can be real to people in ways they can understand. People experience God in their own unique ways and feel completely loved and accepted exactly where they are in whatever faith they practice. My experience has been Jesus in a very real and personal way. Your experience may be Buddha, Mohammed or another spiritual Master. This is way beyond our human imagination and judgment. God is limitless and unrestricted in all things. He reaches us exactly where we are and knows intimately what is needed for our spiritual growth.

When we listen with our hearts, we may be quite surprised when He answers. If we are willing to listen, He will speak and we will hear. How amazing is that! He speaks to us all the time. We choose to listen or not. That is what free will is all about.

Hannah and I went to lunch that day. As we were sitting at the restaurant, she looked over at me. I had a few questions from the session and she had a few more things to tell me. It was like she was tapped into the Source of Knowledge and was hearing the answer and giving me the information, but not from her own mind.

"I can see you looking through a blue crystal. I can see you in a nun's habit. I see a silver bracelet with roses. I see a red apple."

"The symbols are a 'foundation'. They were here long before we were. You will be shown more symbols. Someone has done them before – maybe someone has a book of them."

Then she stated as a matter of fact,

"You'll find no book – They come from the heart."

She went on to explain the "Faster, not farther" comment. She said,

"The work of a fast woman is not far from your area, your area, your area. Fast does not mean hurry up. A lot of people think you need to run real fast to get farther. It's all relative. Fast for you might not be the same for someone else. Get busy wherever you are – definitely get busy. Take the time to figure out what you need to do. Our time is a lot faster than your time. You are so time related. Here – it's faster and we're not consumed."

"God's going to put things in place for you. It's going to be hard. You may fall on your butt. You will surrounded by people who support and believe in you."

"Write the book and do an excellent job. Leave no stone unturned. If you write the book, write the truth – not what people want to hear. That's all." [32]

I discovered that when there was a message to convey it didn't matter if you were in a session or in a restaurant. If you made yourself a willing recipient of the message, they will find a way to present it to you.

My life continued to change because of this experience. I found that when I felt upset or challenged, the words and messages threaded through the fabric of my life. I relied on them, and it changed who I was. I continued to be grateful for the information and the love that I experienced face to face from the Universe through this work. I found that God was active in my life and cared so deeply for each of us that it was truly beyond anything we could think or believe.

This experience and the words presented changed the way I lived. I shared the words with others, not only because I was told, *"These experiences are to be shared, not held in secret,"* but also because I saw how people listened and connected as the words touched their hearts. Their faces grew softer and they said, "That was amazing. Those words changed my life. Keep doing what you are doing."

One day I shared with a respected friend that these messages were being conveyed to me. He cautioned me about the origin of these channeled messages or as some refer to them as people "speaking in tongues." He recommended that I read the book, *"Power Vs. Force"* by David Hawkins who wrote of our ability to evaluate truth by listening to the responses in our bodies. It was all about the science known as kinesiology. He had practiced that method of truth verification for a number of years. I asked if he would evaluate the information. I read. He listened. When I completed several of the messages, he responded, "Did you feel blessed when this happened?" My answer was, "Yes, I felt truly blessed."

"My concern is that you take the time to truly figure out what you want to do. Go with that..." I was reminded how important it was for me to choose what to do with my life and then go live it. Support had been and would be there for me. The choice and direction were mine to determine.

"A healer is a healer is a healer. Mind – thoughts – you heal with who you are." Healer...what a title to live up to when you know that God actually does the work! The message for me was that as we healed ourselves of the pain, hurts, frustrations and fears that we lived with everyday, the person we became was the person who allowed the healing to transform us in ways we never imagined. I also learned that healing comes from who you were rather than your physical features such as hands or eyes.

"Not everyone is ready to receive healings. Not every drug addict is ready to quit. There are ones who do quit. There are people that will listen." Again we were assured, the choice to heal was ours, and there would be people who were not ready to heal.

When we made the choice to heal or give up things we were addicted to, we received all the support we needed. Then we could achieve our dreams and goals.

Gifts from the Heart, 4/21/02 – Your Time is Upon You

A fellow healing practitioner offered to share her hotel room with me at a seminar. As a thank you for her, I offered a healing session. During the session, she began to speak in a voice and language that sounded oriental. Neither she nor I recognized the language. Nothing like this had ever happened to her before then. When the session was over, she kept repeating, "Your time is upon you."

When I asked her about her experience, she shared, " You were here, but you were there. You said something to me and laughed. You made some joke. I was dialoging – expressing thanks – and I asked, 'What can I do?'" She said the session was very powerful and prophetic. The client asked them, "Are you working on us?"

"We are constantly working with you – with your higher self in a creative way to put you in a constant state of readiness." [33]

The client then commented, "They had prepared me and the time is now. It is important to stay calm and open – to remove blocks." She then continued, "Maybe I don't have to work so hard. I felt like I was coming up out of my body. I heard a language that sounded oriental. It had a funny cadence – it was melodic."

After she finished sharing her experience, she found herself speaking again, but this time it was as if she was giving a speech in that oriental language. She said she could feel the passion of the words and understood how important the message was.

Gifts from the Heart, 4/27/02 – Healing, Tones and DNA

Shortly after the trip to New York, I traveled to Austin. I was asking other practitioners about their experiences. There was so much going on and I was curious to see if they were having similar experiences. A small group of around seven practitioners met and started talking. I knew by the looks on their faces that they had not yet experienced what I was sharing. I also told them what things I noticed before some of these experiences began. I thought it would be helpful for them to be aware of possibilities and situations that might occur when doing healing sessions.

In that session with other practitioners, I demonstrated a particular movement and when I finished, we heard a low, powerful voice coming from the person on the table.

"Begin now. The symbols you see are those you recognize. You recognize the boards you see in your dreams. They are the same symbols. There are 3 blackboards. You will remember 1."

"The beings you see now are the ones that will be helping you in the days and years to come."

The person on the table had her eyes closed and pointed to two people in the room. Each of the people she pointed to were located on opposite sides of the massage table. One of the people she pointed to moved to the other side of the table, and the person on the table with her eyes still closed, then pointed to both of them on the same side of the table.

"The energy pulses you are feeling now – it's the 13th tone. The 13th tone heals DNA and promotes bone growth. The 13th tone with the 11th tone heals cancer. These tones can be heard with the hands. They are passed from hand to hand. These are the 12 tones. The 13th tone is the vibration of home."

"Those who will do this work are the ones who sat at the head of the class and opted to go first."

"As you can see, the energy is quite strong."

There was a rippling effect throughout the body on the massage table.

"These tones, if you use them to heal and the client cannot hold the tone, it will only pass through, because the tones are based in love and love is based in truth."

"You had wondered. For the Chronicler (and she pointed to me, again with her eyes still closed), *the Ying – the teacher of this one is approximately 9 feet tall. He has a huge beard down to here* (she placed her

hand at her thigh). *He's all white with huge cobalt blue eyes – the only color on this being."*

"OK. OK. The energy shifts and flows according to the tones. The tones are the energy shifts you are experiencing. The 13th tone jumps an octave from the 12th note. That's the great shift. This is what is being experienced during your time period. Tones are very important."

"This 12th tone can be used in conjunction with many of the others. With both hands moving, two hands will right the ailment."

This additional information was provided:

"It's a bridge… created by one, walked on by many."

"You are going to be manifesting particulates. Particulates are the smallest energy that can be manifested. The Mind of God manifests the idea or the particulate into material relativity. It is the smallest 8-sided object. The eighth side is the key. Through conscious intent, they clump together. They are scattered objects you are bringing together. With conscious intent to heal – it is rearranging particulates to repair." [34]

It is fascinating to hear the information provided during these healing sessions, and then read books on quantum physics and formerly top secret, classified government experiments that begin to explore and explain just what happens in healing. When the fantasies of our science fiction books and movies become reality in our world, it confirms for me that what we create in our minds, the metaphysical, actually can be created in our physical world.

When we asked how we would know which tones were needed, they responded that they would direct the tones. With conscious intent to heal, the healing would occur.

What was communicated to us in this session was another amazing message. We can actually heal DNA with this work. We can promote bone growth. We can perform these miracles through the grace of God. They will use our hands. They will use our bodies. They will use our Spirits to do what needs to be done. We just need to be willing to serve. They will do the rest.

In Gregg Braden's presentation, he shared that studies had found that if we act with love and compassion, our DNA elongated and what was believed to be "junk DNA", actually were switches that were turned on with love, compassion, joy and peace. Feelings of hate, anger, fear, and rejection actually compressed the DNA. DNA was our blueprint for life and what we experienced – love or hate, actually changed who we were.

One healing practitioner remarked, "Everybody's on a different floor in the elevator." As we all learn more and allow them the freedom to use our hands and bodies, we will all benefit and come to understand what is happening.

What does "heal DNA" mean? There are scientific studies that are trying to identify the role of DNA in our lives. We understand from the news that our DNA is unique and can be used to identify us, but is there more to it than that? In a book, *The Field,* that was recently published, Lynne McTaggart quotes from R. Dawkins, *The Selfish Gene,* that "Each DNA helix or chromosome exists in every one of the thousand million million cells in your body. Each contains a long chain of nucleotides... arranged in a unique order in every human body... The modern scientific view is that DNA somehow manages to build the body and spearhead all its dynamic activities just by selectively turning off and on certain segments..., which create specific proteins. These proteins supposedly are able to both build the body and to switch on and off all the chemical processes inside the cell which ultimately control the running of the body." [35]

DNA contains all the vital genetic information and instruction codes necessary for the maintenance and continuation of life. DNA runs and controls all the chemical processes in our bodies. If this work heals DNA, then it heals all of the chemical processes, diseases, and injuries that we experience.

It may be hard for the scientific and medical communities to accept. Only further research and tracking outcomes will help identify the impact of this healing on healthcare issues. Healing from God heals you from the inside, out – from the DNA itself to the effects that DNA has on each person in its own unique way. This is a statement that may confound some scientists and support theories of other scientists. The message was very clear. Energy medicine, alternative healing and the grace of God give us the ability to actually heal DNA. The possibilities are endless.

Gifts from the Heart, 5/04/02 – Honoring Your Masterhood

At the very heart of who we are, is the most important connection of all – the connection to God. I know there are ways to listen and hear what guidance there is for us. Sometimes I listen. Sometimes I do not hear because I am busy in my life. I was shoveling dirt on my sidewalk one day. A voice in my heart said, *"Put your house on the market."* I agreed. I realized that it wasn't me talking to myself. Three days passed and I still had not discussed selling my house with anyone, nor had I contacted the realtor.

It was late one Saturday night, and my phone rang. It was a friend and fellow healing practitioner. She said, "I have something to share with you – something that happened today during a session." In the middle of a session for an intuitive reading, she began what she termed "a data dump" on the client. She spoke so fast to the client that she was aware she was talking, but could not remember what was being said. At the end of the session, her customer said, "What just happened? What was that?"

The practitioner pondered the session, and realized there was a new source of information coming through her. They were providing a flow of information for her client. She postponed calling me until late that night. She hesitated to call, but her guides said, *"She is still up."* When she called, she asked, "Did I wake you?" I responded, "No, I am working on my computer." It was around midnight.

The practitioner shared her story with me, and suddenly in the middle of it, the guides began to speak for themselves. This is what they had to tell me.

"You are loved, completely loved. You were given the gift before Eric was given the gift. The only way we could reach you was through Eric. You have gone way, way beyond Eric."

"Honor your Masterhood. This is all about the love, Vicki. Love us the same way we love you. There are no conditions to love. There is nothing that you need that you don't already have."

"Let go. Trust us. Let go of the fear — the fear of the future — the fear of tomorrow — the fear of tonight. You are afraid to go to sleep. We come to you in your sleep. There is no harm. You are only in love. Think of it as an ocean. Think of love in those terms. There's that much love just for you."

"This is a trust lesson, beyond anything else. Will you do as we ask? Put your house on the market. Now is now." [36]

How can I begin to share the love and information in this passage? It belongs to all of us. All of us are loved, completely loved. We have grown so far from the God who loves us all so much. This work transforms people. Love transforms people. God transforms us if we allow it, for we all have the freedom to choose. He gave us the gift of free will. The choice is ours.

They also were well aware of my fear. They described it perfectly. At this time of my life, I was uncertain of the future. They would visit during the time I went to sleep. I would wake in the night with my legs jerking and my arms moving all by themselves. I would experience dreams, events, and messages that I wouldn't quite remember when I woke up, but that I knew I had been to class again. They confirmed for me that this was a part of the process and to embrace it and get past the fear.

Gifts from the Heart, 5/10/02 – More Information About the Tones

When Hannah and I met the next time, there was more information provided about tones. She asked me for pen and paper and while her eyes were closed, she began to write. This is what was communicated:

"Hello, my friend. We are so convinced that you are there for a significant reason. In order to see, you must look inward to the natural sphere of your human nature. Make no mistake in the judgment your energy possesses. Make no mistake you are to tell the world who you are. We are so interested in your mannerisms of life. Speak to the ones you now look to for guidance. What is it that you seek? Listen very carefully to the next level of reconnective. There you will find the 2nd tone of vibration harmonically embedded. Translate the 6th with the 5th, the 3rd with the 4th, the 9th with the 10th,

198

the 11th with the 12th. Play these pieces loudly during one session of vibration. Pieces will become parts; parts will become whole; particles will become puzzles. Play these tones for reconnective followers. They will further link you to the next level of existence."

I asked, "Are these tones on a piano?"

"These tones are not on a piano. They are reconnective tones. These tones are on your hands, fingers, and eyes. When you vibrate these tones from your body, they hum." [37]

Gifts from the Heart, 5/11/02 – My Questions

A few days later, I had another conversation with my friend. This time I asked, "What questions do I need to ask?" The guides responded:

"That is a very good question and it has taken you a long time to ask it."

I actually had several questions. "How do I serve you best? Where do I serve from here? How can I serve?" They responded:

"The money is going to be there. You worry about money. Both of you have mastered the pretend on the money. You can fool everyone, but yourself and us. We will provide and take care of you. Ask us and tell us what you want. You have learned to live simply. You

used to want so much more. That is the joy in learning to live simply."

"Vicki, your house is actually going to be a healing center. This is a beautiful thing you are being given. You are still afraid, and afraid how this will manifest. You have always known where you are going."

"There is nothing we cannot do for you. You are one of the chosen ones. We will take such care of you. You are chosen. We will provide for you. As long as you continue to love as you have, all will be well."

"Are you living in the now with trust or fear? You worry sometimes too much about who... and what people think about you."

"Whether or how you choose to live is more important than where you choose to live. Your home is your sanctuary. Your home is where you go. We see that your living room is actually a classroom. Your family room is your living room. You will keep everything separate."

"There are two ways of being. You need to feel free. You feel that you have no freedom to choose. You have the freedom to choose everyday. You are free. You can walk away at anytime. Allow yourself to walk *away. If you are in a meeting, that is not serving you, leave."*

"What you have forgotten, is that when you... turning your will over to us does not give away your freedom, but expands it. There are more options than now."

"Your heart knows. Living in the heart allows you to live in peace and joy and move from panic to trust. The choices are obvious. This is easy. There are no mistakes. When you follow your heart, there are no mistakes. There are always mistakes in hindsight. These are lessons."

"Learn lessons gently and easily with confidence and trust. There is pain and sorrow. You cannot avoid pain. You can avoid sorrow. It is part of grieving and growing. Living a pain-free life is a delusion. When you find the joy in pain, it has no power over you."

"If you have to experience joy, embrace pain and anger. Suffering is abuse – skip that. You do not need to suffer. If you embrace the pain, it will be short-lived."

"Ask your heart, why are you experiencing pain? It is a path – to tell you that you are not going in the right direction. That is all pain is about. When you don't listen, that is when it becomes pain and sorrow."

"It's like when you eat bad food, you don't spend days suffering over the choice."

"It (doing this work) is not about the length of time. It is about love. You are about love. The more love you put into this work, the more healing occurs."

"Reconnection is so scientific… It is not indicative of the love. It is beyond DNA Reconnection. This is about Divine love, embracing your Divine Purpose. When you embrace this love, you are embracing your Divine Purpose. This allows you to connect with God. People are afraid of that. God is love. People see God as punishing. Only a few of you have seen God as loving. That's why we brought you to the other side. You need to connect with love. People are afraid of God – even more now. The books are meant to help people recognize and understand."

"Just be in connection with this energy. Talk to God. Talk with God? They think they must be Mother Teresa. If you could have people understand, they will talk to God."

"All that is – is your fear. You are keeping yourself from moving forward. Trust and know everything is in Divine order. Mother Teresa had challenges. You definitely do not want to be like Mother Teresa. A life of celibacy is not appealing to you."

"It is very, very important for you to understand that your mission will have bumpy roads and difficult times, and people are going to attack you for what you know. But KNOW that you are protected and you will be rewarded."

"Act as if... eventually it becomes a habit and you are acting and trusting God in the moment."[38]

The greatest gift was love. When I connected with people heart to heart, our lives changed. In many of the messages I received, there was mention of Mother Teresa. I was happy to know God had a terrific sense of humor when He communicated to me, "A life of celibacy does not appeal to you." I was grateful, but I also learned valuable lessons of love from Mother Teresa. She was love. She said, "We can do no great things; only small things with great love." She demonstrated it in every action of her life. She touched the people in the gutter, the hopeless - the people with the greatest need. She loved with who she was. She was a hero in my life for a very long time. I learned from watching her live and watching her love. And guess what? It didn't matter that we were from different churches, different cultures, or even different religions. As she said, "We must become peace."

Recently I saw Mother Teresa's face on billboards near highways across the state with the single word message: Compassion. Whenever I saw them, my heart filled to overflowing with the remembered love and compassion that she taught us by the way she lived her life. What a legacy of love she left us all! We mourned her death, missed seeing her, but her work continued through the people she touched and the lives she changed.

There was always a lot of information in these messages. I found that there were insights and directions that let me know I was on the right path, that I would encounter difficulties, but I would also be protected and rewarded as I went forward on my path.

When things would become difficult, I would review these messages. I would feel the comfort and love shared in these words. I would find the strength to go forward.

Gifts from the Heart, 5/22/02 – Do You Have Any Questions?

The second day of a session was coming to a close. The client was still in that peaceful place, reflecting on the wonder of the experience, and said, "It was different than yesterday…there's so much joy." Then a low voice came from her and asked:

"Do you have any questions?"

I had several questions and I began to ask them and received answers. Then they just provided information for me.

"Stretch and spread your wings. No boundaries. No limits. No time. Be you. You – 4 eyes – just be. You're My own. You are loved. You are a child of God. God loves you. Just be true. The love must shine through. Your heart is true."

"You believed, so you go far. They will come just for you. Believe the signs all around just for you. Put them together. They will be used in the glory. Heal in your heart. Your tears and pain should go to joy. I will help you. They will come through for you."

"Do you know Him? He loves you! He's been here watching you. He sent me to you, Earth Angel. You, truth, love, joy."

"Clear your heart. Clear your mind. Remember the light. Touch. Connect. Connect. Be you. Be you... There's so much in store for you. Clear your heart. Trust your heart. I am with you. I will speak to your heart. I will guide you. I love you."

"They will come for you. They will help you. You're chosen. Don't you see? You're chosen to help me. Help My kids. Help My family. Bring them back to me. Heal their hearts. Heal their souls. Speak your words to their souls. Use your gift. Let them know I chose you. I love you. I will teach you."

"Your mom loves you. Your mom adores you. She wants to be you. She wants to love like you. Cry no more. Just be joy. Trust your love, your God, your heart."

"You were found first. You had to get ready. Eric opened the door. You open more. Eric needs you. Eric needs love. Like you, Eric must trust. You, Vicki, you are My gift. I give it to you. I love you. I trust you. I will be with you. I have known you. I chose you."

What a wonderful confirmation of His gift, His love, and His trust in me! It was an incredible responsibility, and there were times when I was concerned about what it would take to fulfill this life purpose. I was asked,

"Who are you?"

I responded, "I am love." I was asked again,

"Who are you?"

I responded, "I am chosen." I was asked for the third time,

"Who are you?"

I responded, "I am God's child."

"Chosen. Chosen. You. He's very, very proud of you. You love. You trust. I will be with you. I have known you. I chose you... Put your face to the world. Trust your God. I am always with you... Listen when I speak with you. Trust my words for you. Your path is set for you. You are capable. You can achieve. You love. I will deal with you. You deal with Me. Get her up now." [39]

When I touched the client and asked about her experience, she did not remember what was said. She listened to the tape, but she did not recall the words until she heard them on the tape. She remarked, "I was gone. He told me He had a message for you."

Gifts from the Heart, 6/21/02 – Life is…Truly Amazing

For the first several minutes of this session, Hannah demonstrated symbols and in the deep, beautiful voice that was not her own. She spoke words in another language, the Original Language, as I have been told. Then her words changed to English and she said:

"Life is… life is… life is… Life is truly, truly, truly… So nice to be here. So nice to be here. Your life is truly – amazing to be. It's always good to dance. It's always good to sing. I love to sing. I love to dance. It's good for the soul!

"It is always safe to say this work has brought joy to us – to you. This is the truth. It's why you're here. It's why you're all here. It's truly a gift. It's truly a gift."

"You must first look at tragedies. The world is in itself a blank full of puzzles. Understand this. We're not here to simply play games or run amok. We are here to bring back life, which has been so misused. The object of our affection is love. The world does not exist without love. We've moved so far away."

"Something so easy is so hard to come to. We work from the other side to have a profound affect on humans. The vast majority doesn't recognize we're here. We have to connect."

"Love yourself. Love your neighbor. Love who you are."

"Our reconnective began a long time ago. The language you hear today... I speak to you in English. There was an original language that we use. Of course, you know this. I spoke in a different language. I sang in a different language."

"Remember this – those who don't accept this work, we embrace them. Those who do accept this work, we embrace them. The message is simple. It's love, love, love, love, love, love, love, love, love, love."

"It's not easy. It's so difficult. We work through people you do sessions with. Different spirits – different people have different experiences they want to have during reconnective. Once we get past those, it's easier."

"The nature of you and Hannah – keep meeting. It is not of coincidence. Schedules are different – far apart. It is so important for you to work together. Please continue working together. It's not by coincidence. As you can remember... reconnect. We placed you two together. You've been together before – before this

time – before this existence. You share a common bond. You will remain together no matter what."

"Now the reasoning behind the Reiki was... We had to open the door. We had to open the door for you. We had to open the door for her. Reiki is a gateway... a reconnective gateway. These two doors are mirror images. It's the same principal. Reiki – Reconnection – the next level of healing energies work together."

"Now I know you've been waiting, waiting, waiting. We've been watching, watching, watching. We picked certain times. When you think you are ready, you may not be really ready. We know when you are ready. We know when Hannah is ready. When you and she are both ready..."

"Today you are both ready. Everything up till now has been preparation. We tap her feet. We call those 'happy feet'. We have to get her attention. Hannah is such a good girl. We love her so much."

"God has blessed her with unique qualities. It is only the beginning. In time, you will understand. You will help her. Stay with her."

"You help Hannah with self. You help Hannah with certainty. You help Hannah with love."

"Don't look for validation. Those who are willing to come will come. Those who aren't won't. Don't worry. The human self must grow first, before spiritual self can be One. The spiritual self cannot grow until the human self grows. Human and spiritual selves must grow together."

"Reconnective healers – we move those hands. Her human self can control to eat, drive and wave good-bye. The symbols you see – symbols of life – as much as we love Hannah, she cannot do this by herself."

My name is in our original language – Ikra Ku Sec Feel. I say that with great compassion! I love myself. I love my God self! It's truly amazing to come to the conclusion!"

"We listened to your conversation today – all the misfortunes – the experiences through life – the relationships – men – people. These things profoundly affected your life. You could not grow or be at this point in your life without them."

"The question is… What is the next step? What is the next step?"

"This is what we will not do. We cannot choose your life for you. We can guide and help you. The gifts – you can choose to use them. You can ignore them. You

can leave them. Gifts are there. These gifts lay dormant. They will come. When you are ready, they will be ready for you to use."

"Use your gifts with hands – reconnective healing. That is a start. You can do even more. You can't force it at one time. You have to grow into baby, puberty, and adult. Everything comes with time."

"Not everyone is ready to deal with this. Jesus, our Lord and Savior, as you say, was betrayed, put down, shunned, crucified, but He still showed love for humanity."

"With gifts, come great power, strength and humility. Love first and foremost mankind when others turn their back, snarl and turn on you. These gifts work with love."

"There will be some people that will try to come against you. Do not be afraid. This is no one-man thing. This is an entire connection."

"We come at the wee hours of the morning, because we are not set on this time. Our time is of no relevance as is here. We are always around, always looking. There is no need to sleep. We are in and out – here and there. We can be here – and there. When you call, we come. We are here, never far."

"One thing I do want you to work on – the manner in which you hold on to things. We give things. We take things. It's a part of life. Your battles exist far beyond yourself."

"You must learn a true healer heals from the inside, out. This is very important – the inside, out."

"Yesterday, we were with you as you traveled, as you ate. We exist so much in your life that at times, we find ourselves being consumed in your life, which is not a bad thing. We play around the house. We find things to do to amuse ourselves. We make funny noises. Those noises – clapping, humming. When we get bored, we play in the closet. We do these things for entertainment. We have yet to be in the physical world. We play, play, play all the time. We love to be happy. We love to feel joy, love. Love."

"We tend to repeat things. We want you to get the message. We want you to get the message – get the message across."

"The issue of the 4 eyes thing. We are happy. We don't particularly like – you are not 4 eyes. You are Vicki, Vicki, Vicki High. Our nature is not to bring anyone down, but to lift you up."

"We found ourselves playing around on your dresser. We lift this and that. We've never seen so many things of importance on their dresser. We are so amazed. You collect so much stuff. It's OK. It's amazing. We love playing with stuff. We project ourselves on the TV."

I asked, "How can I see you?"

"You can't."

"We were so taken aback by your actions that day – the nature of your actions! You really hit the wall! Not to truly – boy, did you hit the wall!"

"This experience allowed us to come to you – stronger, more visible. When people die or come close to death, they take energy from the other side and bring it back. It's like if you throw a tennis ball into a pool of water and bring some water back with the tennis ball. Molecules from the water are still in the tennis ball. It's the same with people. It's the same with you."

"You hit the wall. You were out. You went there. We were there. Lola was there. Francis was there. Jeanine was there. Erica was there. Cathy was there. They all were there."

"When you went there, we were able to work with you – bring you up to speed. You wanted to stay. You

213

begged. You cried. God said, 'Go. You're not ready yet. It's not your time. Go.' It's OK. We know it's hard. This life is not meant to be easy. Those who have a purpose must live that purpose."

"When you cross over, and all must, you… Had you left that day, you would be on this level – a lower level of existence. At the end of this life, this existence, you will be at this plane – a higher plane of existence."

"The thing about death – when death occurs, people think that is the only time God envelops you with His love. God envelops us all the time. Most people see premonitions of life as it comes to an end. They bring themselves to be ready."

"This happened to Bob[40]. Bob thought that. We love Bob. He's OK. He's a good man. Don't worry. His cuff links – he really likes these cuff links with the gold trim. His initials are on them. The nature of his death was not for him to suffer, but to expand his existence."

"Bob had a lot to learn. When it was time, we were there. His aunt was there. There were so many people there to greet him. The pure joy and the look on his face! He was embraced with true love, unconditional love."

"Do not weep for him today. He is in a far better place. He will be there to comfort his family. You see - her life is so much a part of his life. She's a good person. It's hard to deal with self. She has to come to her own life."

"We've been showing you symbols way before now. In Reiki, the symbols were there. We so greatly wanted you to see these symbols. There are more validations. We were glad you took pictures. The symbols have always been there – always been there – always been there. They are not something new – only when man chooses to see."

"Hannah battled with these hands, thinking she was crazy. She is beautiful. We work with her. When she came to be, when her mother was pregnant, she had a mission far beyond imagination: 'To bring life, healing and love to this world.' "

"Upon birth, she died, and was as God said, and Jesus was 'resurrected.' Her mother was unaware – she was drugged. The doctor knew, but because baby Hannah was revived, nothing was said. But the truth is there. It's always been there."

I asked, "How often should we meet?"

"At least, because of your active schedule, try to meet every other week – every two weeks."

I said, "I need to get ready to leave."

"Let us... give us a moment to bring Hannah back to speed." [41]

This information was enlightening. I learned that all the misfortunes in my life were lessons to prepare me for my work. It would be my choice to use my gifts or ignore them. My gifts would grow as I used them. One of the most important things that was stressed was that no matter what, we must love humanity. Even if people did not accept this work or came against me because they were afraid or did not understand, I must love them. These gifts worked with love.

A true healer healed from the inside, out. As we learned more about our work and our world, we were able to connect in new and exciting ways. I was happy to hear that they were glad I took pictures of the symbols in New York. The symbols have always been here – but we see only when we choose to see.

I found it so interesting to hear about death and near-death experiences. The analogy of the tennis ball was very clear to illustrate what happened when people came close to death. People who experienced near-death actually carried molecules of energy from heaven with them.

It must be so wonderful there. They told me I begged to stay. Had I stayed, I would be at a different level of existence and would not have achieved my life purpose. I was also assured that God envelops us in His love all the time.

The reason I had to leave was that a friend, "Bob" had died and his funeral was scheduled early that afternoon. The insight into his life and the way he was greeted by unconditional love was a great comfort to his friends and family. We were also told how he would be there to comfort his family during the funeral.

Gifts from the Heart, 7/19/02 – Dance the Soul

Just as I was completing a personal connection session late one night, I was taking notes of the client's experience. The client shared a few things and then said, "I can feel strings going out from my body. I feel jittery. I feel like I have information to give."

I told her to lie back down and I continued her session. Then her voice changed to a little girl's voice with an oriental accent.

> *"I'm here to help you work… Help you work… I will tell you some things. I've been looking for you. I can help you. Don't be afraid. What is your fear? Don't be afraid. Yes, do your work. Source… Source. Go to the Source. Don't be afraid."*

> *"What a wonderful voice! When you speak, I hear myself. Have some fun. Play of soul. Dance of soul. Let it go. Dance the soul… Maybe I visit you sometime. Leela. When you say my name. When you feel sad,*

lonely, you bring Leela. Leela will play... I love you. I love you." [42]

She was joyful and childlike. It was so amazing that her voice changed to this young girl's voice. She laughed and laughed. When the session was at an end, I realized I was uplifted by what she said. I also realized I might have missed this message if I had not listened and understood that there was more to share.

Gifts from the Heart, 9/20/02 — Truths of the Spirit

Recently, I met with my friend, Hannah, again. Her eyes were closed and began to move almost immediately. Her head moved to the side. Her feet moved. Her hands stretched and reminded me of a swan's head and neck and the "ballet" began. As I looked at her, I felt this incredible love. She began to speak.

"How are you?"

I responded, "Good. How are you?" She responded.

"Good."

"Life is beautiful. How's... How's... Our last meeting, we talked about the joyous wonders of life. Today we will talk about the truths of the Spirit and its wonderful, wonderful lessons."

"Let's see. My Spirit is uniquely different from your Spirit. Your Spirit moves at a level of abounding frequency of life. My Spirit moves at an even higher

frequency that spans beyond the frequency of life hundreds and hundreds of times faster."

There was a tone that sounded on the tape at this time.

"Spirit – everyone has one. Everyone shares his or her Spirit. The truth of the matter is, we are all Spirits – light beings who have to come here to live out what is the true course of life. You see, Spirit cannot learn the values that are here, there. Spirit must first come here to advance to there. If a Spirit chooses to stay there, he can remain there, but the abounding changes of life here help Spirit to advance there."

"SPIRIT. S – P – I – R – I – T. SPIRIT. SPIR – IT. S is for sanctity. P is for positional. S – P – I. S – P – I – R – I – T. I – I – I is for insolating. R is for Respirating. I – is for in – in – inner. T is for transference."

"Spirit comes from a word – we call Veh Coul Sa Key [phonetically] meaning free – free. Spirit never ever, ever dies. Spirit lives, lives. If only for a second, if one were to close his eyes, he can truly see the blessings of his Spirit. You see, Spirit is who you are. Spirit is never far."

"Although we seem to get caught up in the word 'Spirit – Spirituality' when all that we need to do or need to be

is there. Without a Spirit, your earthly body would be void. No one's Spirit can conquer."

"Yesterday, I went to a place – a place up there. A place up there that is beautiful. Within this place was a vaulted ceiling high in the sky. Beautiful imprints of colors – of beauty – of angels – of God – of humanity. Within this place, there were infinite numbers of Spirits. Each Spirit has something to give. Each Spirit has something to add. Each Spirit had something to live for. When we were there, we came together in the sight of God. We were as One. We talked together. We played together. We lived together. It's who we are."

"As we sat there, we learned. We learned of how life and life experiences affect each and every one of us. We learned that just as here, also there – we have work to do. There were two people in the front row who were a husband and wife. They shared with us that day that their last trip to life showed them that in order to gain acceptance, they must be accepting of others. They also learned that love is not given always for free. They used their philosophy of life to gain acceptance, love, and humility."

"Each day we have meetings there – meetings to go over, as one might say, a reviewing of life and life's lessons. We learn from our experiences. We cherish our experiences. We are our experiences. If only a

seed is taken from here, we can plant a garden of flowers over there. Each flower, each petal, each stem, each root is forevermore changed. Once given to others, it is expressed in its beauty and glory."

"Some days we create our own fantasies, our own lives, our own images. Today whatever my fancy – I may want to possess long brown hair that curls, curls, curls. This is my choice. There are no limitations there. It's what you make of it. There are no boundaries of who or what we may be. As with anything, there are laws. There are laws here on earth. There are also Universal Laws of Life."

"There are 10 planes – 10 planes of existence. There is a gradual process of a soul to migrate or get to these planes for each lesson learned in life graduates a Spirit to a plane, a different plane, another plane."

"Life is so important. Even if for a moment, a short moment, a life is born and gone, that is an experience. It is no different from a newly born life that is gone as an older life that has been here. They each share an experience that they take back with them."

"Why am I telling you this? There are often sometimes lessons that must be learned, lessons that are learned, lessons that fall on deaf ears, and lessons to be lived. My purpose for telling you this is that reconnective

healing – healing – whatever you want to call it – is a part of you, me and everything."

"Your Spirit here knows that in order to gain the possibility of life, you must go through life. Yesterday, we saw as I was saying to Hannah, a blue horn, a blue horn. This blue horn was enamored with beautiful, beautiful colors – emeralds, and this horn had a melody of life. A beautiful man by the name of Ananias played this horn to perfection. As we all listened, we felt love."

"Your book is and will be forevermore the truth. Don't back down. Don't turn around. Don't let anybody turn you upside down. Steady. Stay steady. If ever there is a moment where you feel as though you can't go on, remember your purpose is a part of this book."

"We will work with you. We have been working with you. Let go… Allow the messages to speak for themselves. Allow the energies to be themselves. It is what it is. You are what you are." [43]

Then it seemed to me that someone else began to speak. Another tone was heard on the tape. The voice that came through was softer and gentler.

Gifts from the Heart, 9/20/02 – Mary, The Mother of Jesus

"Jesus is the Way, the Truth and the Life. If it were not so, I would have told you. Seek not to challenge, but to listen to His words. Jesus is the Light and Truth of Salvation. Jesus is."

"My child, you must go to great lengths to be, just be. Truly salvation will follow you. Let go of all… all doubts."

"Jesus has loved, loved you this far. He will forevermore give you grace. Trust in Him, Our Father. Trust in Him, in heaven. Seek ye peace. Seek ye refuge."

"Jesus is the Light, the Love, and the Truth. Holy. Holy. Savior. Christ. Love. Holy. Holy. Holy."

"Our Father. Our Father. He is a pivotal center of who we are. He gives us breath. He gives us life."

"I will be there for you as I have been for Him. I am Mother. Mother. Mother. I am Mother. But if it was not so, I would not be here. Mother. Witness the power and grace of God. His truth will carry you – carry you. His grace will carry you."

"Be not dissuaded or discouraged in any way. Be strong. Be steadfast. Go forward. Go forward. Hold on."

"I come here today to bring peace. I come here today to bring light. I come here today to give you peace, glory, honor, and the sanctity of His truth."

"I am Maharia Songtuse Lal Song, Maharia Songtuse Lal Song. Mary. Mary. Alleluia. Alleluia. Alleluia. I have come to speak – to speak peace as I have always done. I come. I go. I appear. People see, but they often, but not always receive me. I am… Mary. Maharia Songtuse Lal Song. Mary."

"I want to express with you the pride, the joy, the sincerity of the love I have for you. I am proud. Reaching others is sometimes a difficult task. But with help, we can help others come to grace."

"Alleluia. Alleluia. Alleluia. God has given so much mercy – so much mercy – so much mercy. So much love."

"I weep for this world. I weep for the children. I weep for Godlessness."

"The truth is in you. We're all in this together. Love thyself. Love thy neighbor. Love thyself. Love thy neighbor. Love thyself. Love thy neighbor."

"I AM WHO I AM. I stand in the faith of righteousness. I stand in the truth and the glory of His name. Amen.

Amen. Life is only, only… Life is only here. Use what you have. Use what you know. Help others to grow."

"I give you a piece of my heart to use. Let no man put asunder. Shine your light. Use your light. Amen. Jesus is the Way. Jesus is the Truth."

"Maharia Songtuse Lal Song. Maharia Songtuse Lal Song. Mary. Mary. Veh Coul Sa Key. Veh Coul Sa Key. God Bless You." [44]

I heard in these words that life has a level of vibration that allows us to remain in these physical bodies. When we die, our vibration increases so we leave this physical body behind and vibrate hundreds and hundreds of times faster. Our bodies are not who we are. Our souls are who we are. We are here to learn lessons of life in order to advance to another plane of existence. Our bodies house our spirits until the vibration increases beyond life.

I was assured that I would have help sharing this work. I was informed that healing is a part of all of us. They told me that my book is the truth and don't back down under pressure when people have difficulty accepting what is written here. I will be supported and loved through the process.

When the voice changed, I was awed at the experience of Mary. There was such love and support for me. She assured me of

Jesus' love. She provided encouragement for me and even gave me a piece of her heart to use. I felt truly blessed by the experience.

There were some final words of advice for me along the path.

"Observe people. Let them play themselves out for you. Give themselves a chance to play themselves out for you. Keep both eyes open. Pay attention to who's around you. Pay attention to what they say. People who seem to have an interest are more interested in defacing what you possess. Be aware. Nothing more. Be aware."

I asked, "Do I need to love them through it?"

"Absolutely! Love them. Pray for them. They don't know another way to be."

"Don't focus on people. Focus on the work. Healing energy brings people. Focus on the work… Don't take any wooden nickels."

"Should I go to Mt. Shasta while I am in Portland?" I asked.

"Absolutely, go to Mt. Shasta. We will all be there. Take yourself. A camera would be nice. Mainly yourself. My time is up."

I said, "Thank you."

"You're welcome." [45]

I was so amazed at the extraordinary way that God sends messengers for His work. His methods were so imaginative and He constantly reminded me that He was so much more than we could imagine. During these sessions, I felt so humbled and honored that these marvelous things happened. I understood how Mary, the Mother of Jesus, pondered things in her heart. I often pondered – wondering how I became so lucky to hear these wonderful things, and to write them as the scribe for people to hear and understand. I had no idea why I was chosen, but I joyfully listened and did what I needed to do to communicate this knowledge to others. God was so great! His unconditional love was truly amazing.

Gifts from the Heart, 12/14/02 – Love Who You Are

Recently, I met with my friend again. Her eyes began to move almost immediately. Her hands moved into the symbols that were now familiar. I felt my ears "open" and someone touched my head. A voice came from her that was not her own. He spoke in that wonderful language. He sang with a beautiful voice and melody in that same language. Then he said,

> *"Hello. Hello. Hello. What a lovely day! What a beautiful day! How are you?"*

I responded, "Good. How are you?" He responded,

> *"Good. Beautiful… yesterday, I went to a beautiful place – a beautiful place of rest – a beautiful place of*

peace. I am here simply to say that life is worth living. Life is worth giving. Love who you are. Love as you are. Love."

"I AM WHO I AM. Make no mistake about it. I AM WHO I AM. No make believe. No tricks up my sleeve. I AM WHO I AM."

"Where do I come from? Simple. I am from what you call heaven. I am from what you call peace. We call in heaven, as you say, we say Al Le Sic Un Se Con. Heaven."

"Today I like to say that I feel truly blessed. I am in the presence of two wonderful people. I am truly blessed. Thank you."

"Write this down: 7871543. 7871543. Numbers are significant. Life is significant. Help me to help you learn to value – to value life. It's simple. Live. Live. Love. Live. It's simple. Day-to-day struggles are not your worry. Live your life. Live your life."

"I sat the other day listening to you – you – you. All I can say is that worry – worrying has no place in your heart. It is as you say – it is inevitable that worry keeps you from seeing the truth. How can you see truth that stands before you if you worry about everything? Step *out of the way. Step out of the way and allow God to do your worrying."*

"My work is simple. I am here to lead you two. When I speak about life, when I speak about peace, when I speak about love, when I speak about not worrying, I speak these words to convey to you that love is love as it has always been. Truth is truth. Honesty is always the best policy. Love is simple. The rest is left up to you."

"Energy transforms itself into many things. The energy of life is frequency beyond the human imagination. Energy is before you. Energy is around you. Witness the energy. See the energy. Close your eyes and see energy."

When I closed my eyes, I saw a gray energy swirling and circling. My eyes began to flutter as they often do with this healing work. He continued,

"Have you ever seen a moon that shines so bright that even maybe at night, its beauty and crystal moonlight is forever showered with light? I speak of light. I speak of truth. I speak of this because… it seems that I am here to comfort you. There's no need to be ashamed. No need to blame. The truth is that we are here."

"When you leave here you will go there. When you think you are all alone, all you have to do is call home. We're here by your side. Don't you think it's a bit strange that we know your name? Home. Home. Home. Home. To live and live again. Hear me. We live in a place of harmony. We live in a place of peace. We live in a place of love. Life is for the living. Live it. You say, 'There's so much doubt... I don't know.' Look to yourself. Look to your life. Look to your heart for answers."

"Take a little walk with me. I can only be or begin to be me. Let me explain. We exist beyond this dimension. We communicate with you. We watch you. We guide you. It's hard to imagine, I know. It's true. We watch you when you sleep. We watch you when you are awake. We watch you. Do not be afraid. We are here for your higher good – your higher good."

"Why do you question yourself so much? We listen as you question everything you do. You are uncertain of the certain. You seek truth. Truth is before you. You seek truth. Truth is in front of you. You seek truth. Truth is behind you. You run away. Face your truth. Face you. Face who you are. We are here not because we enjoy voyeurism. We are here to help you. You have to choose your path. Choose your way. "What is that?" you ask."

"Ah. First thing, take charge. Take charge of your life. Take charge of your experiences. Your experiences are your own experiences. Your experiences exist within you. Your job here is not to convince people. Your job is to live your experiences. If others choose to listen and live, then they can choose to experience their own experiences."

"Start the groundwork for your experiences. Start the legwork for your experiences. Finish the book. Hesitancy. Hesitancy. Hesitant. It's easy to get lost in complacency, fear, the unknown and lack of acceptance. What will 'they' think? What will 'they' say? What will 'they' do? Who cares? Get out of the way! Get out of the me! Life is for the living."

"Children do not hesitate. Why? There's no fear of the unknown. There's no intellectual think tank that steps in the way. Children do not analyze everything they do. Time waster. Waste time. Time waster. Do the do. Do the now. Go forward. We want to get you moving. We want to get you going and doing. We want to get you thinking."

"Guidance is and will always be here. We are here to guide you. Guidance is here. Live your life. We have guided you this far. You wouldn't be at this point if it wasn't for guidance."

The question was posed, "What should I focus on?" The response was,

"Your life. Living. Mend broken fences. Mend your heart. Mend your relationships. Mend those fences. Live life to the fullest. Live life as though you've never seen it before. Live life through your child's eyes. Live life through your eyes. Speak no more of disgusts. Speak no more of frustrations. Life keeps on ticking. Life keeps on going. Life is not meant to be a cakewalk."

"God has blessed you with many talents – many gifts. Use them in the platform He has given you. Never accept defeat. Never accept defeat on any accord. Be as you always have been – strong, steadfast."

"Witness the miracles of life. Miracles are all around you. Miracles are everywhere. Miracles of life go unnoticed. Simple things go unnoticed. Having said that, I have spoken and will continue to speak when asked. Enjoy today. Enjoy your life. Enjoy friends and family. Enjoy who you are. Your battle is your battle. Only you can fight your battle." [46]

My work continues as I hear these messages and know there are miracles to experience and work to do in the platform I have been given. I had a couple of questions that I wanted to ask. The first one was, "A client wanted to provide a healing treatment anonymously for his mother. Do I need her permission?" They replied,

> *"We build up a lot of tolerance and patience working with people. Do you need permission to live? Do you need permission to pray? Do you need permission to go to war? Do you need permission to love? Do you need permission to eat? This is not a dictatorship. This is life. Do you need permission from God to go to the bathroom? Do you need permission to drive? Do you need permission to go to sleep?"*

The answer was very clear that just as with prayer, there is no need for permission. The next question was about the energies we come into contact with when doing this work. I asked, "If a practitioner's heart is not in the right place, will it affect the session?" The message in response was,

> *"There is no power greater than Allah… YHWH… God. Here in this place, this hour, this world, we live in perfect harmony. Souls come. Souls enter. Perfect harmony is there."*

> *"Here [on earth], it is different. Everyday you live, you come into contact with others, different people with different energies. They have different frequencies and are unique. Your body is your temple. Your soul is your temple. Treat it as such. God does not fear people. God is Who He Is – God. Here there are different*

energies. You walk. You bump into people. You speak with people. You work with people. You interact with people. You sometimes take on energies of other people. The Power of Prayer, the Power of Oneness, and the Power of Lovingness are stronger than all the other energies. Where is your comfort zone? Does it lie in people? Does it lie in God?"

"The love of God in us will overcome energy from everyone else. Step out of the way. Allow your God self to work with others. Step out of yourself. Step out of your way. Healing is not of the flesh. Healing is not in the flesh. Healing is light, love and truth of God." [47]

We were told that the power of God is stronger than anything. The Power of Prayer, the Power of Oneness, and the Power of Lovingness were beyond human weaknesses and we could use them to reconnect in a special way with God and His children. If we stepped out of the way and allowed the healing to occur, we would realize that healing was light, love and the truth of God. Those were powerful words to guide us in this work.

CHAPTER 8

MORE GIFTS FROM THE HEART - SYMBOLS, TONES & OTHER CONNECTIONS

"The symbols are a 'foundation'. They were here long before we were. You will be shown more symbols. Someone has done them before – maybe someone has a book of them."

Then she stated as a matter of fact,

"You'll find no book – They come from the heart."

Almost from the beginning of my healing work, hand symbols were brought into my awareness. One client in particular, Hannah, demonstrated the most beautiful and graceful hand gestures that were shared with me on multiple occasions in a way that seemed like a beautiful ballet with her hands. I didn't know what I was supposed to do with the information or what the meaning was at the time. I knew they were important. I kept trying to remember the symbols and their meanings, but I couldn't draw them as fast as I needed to and my descriptions left something to be desired. In the first couple of sessions, I just kept writing, struggling with the drawings and I finally resorted to taking pictures so I would be

235

prepared when it was time to share the information. Hannah was the primary vehicle for the symbols, but I have seen the symbols demonstrated by several other clients. Recently one of the other clients described it as, "What was with the hand thing? I felt like someone had a string and they were moving my hand. No muscles used at all."

During the time I was in Los Angeles, I heard ringing in my left ear. It would happen at different times. My ear would feel "open" and then it would return to normal after a day or sometimes longer. The ringing would sound like a tone – kind of like a tuning fork that sounded inside my ear. When I was letting someone feel the energy one day, this young man responded, "It was like I heard a tone in the palm of my hand." I asked a fellow healing practitioner if he was hearing tones, and about a week later, he said, "I started hearing tones today." My ears still feel "open" occasionally. I still hear tones even today.

New York City and the Symbols All Around Us

During my travels to New York City in the spring of 2002, I was fortunate to be able to visit Ground Zero. It was late one night and a series of events led me to a neighborhood deli just two short blocks from Ground Zero. There I met three guys who worked the night shift and I never knew their names. I asked them if they would take the flags from my community and fly them at Ground Zero. They replied, "Come with us." They took me with them to Ground Zero. When we approached the guard, he said, "She doesn't have a hard hat or badge." One young man replied, "But she's the Mayor!"

The guard replied, "I can't let her in." The young man replied again, "But she's the Mayor." Evidently the guard called his supervisor. This young man drove up and from inside the cart, greeted me and said, "You know getting in here is political."

My sense of humor came to my rescue, and being from Texas, I looked at him and said half serious, half grinning, "Should I call George W.?" He looked at me, and he looked again. I'm not sure what he thought about what I said, but he responded, "Get in the truck." It didn't take me a second to jump in the vehicle. Then he took me into Ground Zero to the Emergency Management Office. There I met a wonderful ambassador to New York City. He lent me a hard hat and spoke with me about the changes that had occurred due to the terrorist attack. I gave him the flags from my community signed by the police officers, firefighters, city employees and City Council in honor of those who lost their lives in the disaster. He spoke gently of the changes he had witnessed in New Yorkers – the softening and more compassionate demeanor that was demonstrated in remarkable and miraculous ways. He spoke of the devastation of seven buildings in the parameter that had been demolished with the weapons of choice – airplanes armed with American lives. I will never forget the reflection of life and lives, as they changed forever for us on September 11th, 2001. Most of all, he shared the hope of the future, the hope of tomorrow demonstrating the strength of our nation and our people.

Spirit enabled me to open doors that would normally be closed due to political influences that night. I will be forever grateful for the experience. As I stood on the rim of the "toilet bowl" and looked into the enormous devastation, I set an intention and focused healing energy into the excavation area. I thought I would feel sadness, loss and a heaviness from the spirits of the people who had lost their lives. I was amazed. It didn't seem heavy at all. It was light and even comforting in a way. The excavation process was still underway and people were still working around the clock. I knew there were people who had not been recovered yet. I also felt the spirits of those people were not lingering. This was the six-month anniversary of the disaster and I felt healing had occurred for them in death. It was a very reverent time for me. It was around 1:00 A.M., as I thanked him and left the area. I remembered asking if it was safe to walk back to my hotel, and I was several blocks away after they transported me to his office. He looked at me and smiled. He said, "There are more policemen and firemen within the surrounding half mile than in all of New York City. I think you'll be safe." And he was right. I walked back to my hotel and passed so many officers who were vigilantly on guard, while recovering their friends and co-workers along with the citizens whose lives were lost.

In a subsequent visit to New York City about a month later, I went for a walk and found myself at the Trinity Church. It began to mist. I waited in the foyer as the rain fell – first with sprinkles and then a pounding or as my New York pal would say, "a teeming rain". I watched the people as it rained and I waited. After a while, I began to wonder if I would have to walk back and take another shower before I went to the airport for my flight home. I decided to wait just a bit longer. You know how it is when you get a little bored and like a child, you begin to look up, down and all around?

Much to my surprise, I looked up and on the ceiling of the church, there were these symbols that resembled to me, anyway – these Star Trek™ communicator type symbols. Then I began to look further and I spotted bronze panels on the outside doors. I was amazed and astonished by the men in these panels. I assumed they were Bible characters. What got my attention was that these men were demonstrating the symbols that my client had shown me through several sessions. I had my camera and I finished the roll with pictures from the ceiling and some, but not all of the panels.

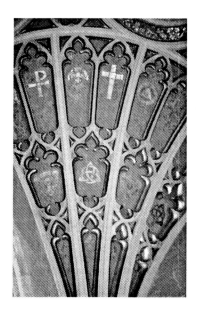 

It was an awesome moment to see those symbols. I knew it was a validation – an assurance that others had seen and used the symbols. I wondered why if they were a part of the history of this church, why don't we know about them? I pondered them for quite a while. I stood and studied each of them for several minutes. I felt connected to God and the people depicted in those panels. Were these symbols part of the information that was at the Vatican? Were these symbols just another connection that was gifted to the artist that created these panels? What else did we need to know about them?

Then the rain stopped, and I made my way back to the hotel. I had been troubled by circumstances, which occurred over the weekend when I went for a walk. With the rain, the church, and the symbols, I was reminded once again that God was with me everywhere. God was with all of us. We were very important to God. Then I headed to the airport for the trip home feeling peaceful and more comforted. The symbols were to get our attention and remind us of our life purpose. The symbols were here to help us connect to God.

Recently I have noticed when I get very still and quiet, I feel vibration in my hands and feet. My fingers actually hum. I noticed the other day when my hand was touching the handle of my cup, there was a vibration coming from my thumb and I could actually feel the hum as it lay there against the cup. On another occasion, I became aware of the humming or vibration in my feet. The other day at church we were holding hands and I could feel the vibration in both hands as I held hands with other people. At the symphony recently, my whole body vibrated with the sound of music as I sat in the organ loft over the musicians. The tones, chords and instruments were creating harmonics that could be felt throughout the building and my body as well. I was sure the tones were happening all the time, but when I was busy, I didn't always notice the same things as when I found the time to be quiet and still.

Gifts from the Heart, 8/07/02 — Our Connections

Then in a session with another client, they told me even more about the symbols.

"You already know your information. People have come and come and come and come and tried to tell you the same things in all kinds of ways and you're just not doing it! That's why everything... we're not really

supposed to tell you exactly what… we're not supposed to say you go do this and you go do that… cause you know you are supposed to figure that out."

"You come knowing. You come with it [that knowledge.] Anything that is together and anything linked or looking like it wants to link, you all just do that. You repeat. You all just do that. You repeat. The sounds. The tones. The humming. All those things… the sounds connect up, connect up."

"You hear from all the Christs, the Buddhas, Confucius. They have the same thing to say. You're not getting it! You're not getting it! So that's why it's funny. You see the signs of the cross, the Trinity, the stars of the Jewish people – the double triangles, even the swastika – that's the reverse of the Buddhists' thing for love. It's a thing to do with them. We don't say, 'This is the answer. Go here. Go there.'"

"You… you keep wanting to hear it from all these different people. You don't need to hear it from any more people. 'It's so fascinating! It's so coincidental!' You are not an afraid person. We don't think you are an afraid person. We think you know you are willing to go do what you have to do."

"We don't know why you keep those journal things. How many more people do you want to hear it from?

Don't be afraid. It's all the same. It's all in here [heart]. It rings true to everybody in this room – in this world, cause it's all true. If it rings true in here, then it's true."

"It's not for us again to tell you what to do exactly. 'Cause you know... your life changes from this second to that second. You are here today and you are in another place tomorrow. We can't tell you. It's not allowed for us, technically, because that's your Law of Development and Growth and all that kind of stuff. It's not for us to tell you that... it's funny, huh?"

"You see symbols and people and sounds and tones. Music soothes the savage beast. Tones and symbols connect and will communicate to... they did it in the movies. They do hand things. We can talk to those people. But you know we're already connected to all these people. You are already missing that. We are already connected. All these signs and symbols whether in whatever state or land, we are always connected. You have to let loose and just figure all that out. You know that."

"There's nothing to be afraid of, OK? You are not going to be buried, OK? Don't worry about the dark. See, here's what happens. Here we are. You all... low down here. Then there we are... white light. Then when you go further, and you know unfortunately, we don't like to say that we, we, up here in the light, have not actually

gone further, most of us. OK, technically, that's weird because if all time happens at once, we're all One, and we've all technically been there, but right now, in this snapshot where we are, we're not there. We only know there is something beyond there."

"This one down here says, 'Shut up! You don't have to talk to anybody. You keep it to yourselves. Because I don't want to say it.' But if they want to hear it, then we are going to say it. So when she goes way beyond, we don't even know way beyond. The only reason we sense it is that we glimpse it when she comes back. Ahhh... We catch that sensation. It's uh... It's uh... It makes you want to stop because we don't have words to put it into. It's just a sense we catch when she returns. Just a sense, like that, that is so good! And see if we weren't so – you know, – better or whatever, we could go up there! We could be there, too! That's why we're stuck here, you know! We're not there where you can feel and enjoy and have fun and be human. But we're not up there yet, either, where are like ahhh... wow! We don't even have to be in the middle realm. We are all supposed to be there. There all we can see is... [she was humming high and low] glimpses of her connection. It's dark, it looks dark and black, but it's not dark and black. It's like just everything blends together, no sound. The only words would be... it's the most peaceful, loving..."

I asked, "Is it a void?"

"Well, void, void makes it sound like… it's not an empty thing, it's like a full thing. It's like a full thing where everything is so connected. Again, this is just kind of figuring out what it's like for coming back. It's a connected thing. Everything is not sucked out of it. Everything is pulled up into it. Everything is pulled up into it."

"Is she still *here?"* I responded, "Yes, she is just being quiet." There was another person in the room during the session.

"She needs not to be afraid of that. [Going higher]. That's what we all want to aspire to be. Where you really get the sense that we are all One – me – you – you – the table – the sky – every little atom down to every little atom! We're all the same. We're all the same. We just kind of fell into different patterns. We're all the same."

"To get back to you. You really have to try to get to more people at once. Cause you have the ability to get to a crowd – a crowd, OK? Last time, we said we were running out of time. Let's hurry. We are like sitting on a seesaw. If too many fall down in the ugly side, too many of us are going to go that way. If more of us can just fall on the good side and let go and reach up and

do what's in here, cause the answers are here [in the heart]. They are not in here [head]. This is like in the computer brain. You breathe like this. You do like this. You walk like this. You eat like this. But this [the heart], this is where the real answers for life, for the world, for the universe are. They are in here [the heart.] This is where the answers are."

"People. People like you, Vicki. People that have the ability to get up on a stage and reach more people have got to get to more people at once."

I asked, "Is it time?"

"Is it time? I don't know. It's in your heart. It's in your heart. All we know is, we know what your ability is and we know you're not doing it, yet. You can do it in Wherever if you think you can reach more or if you can do more in a bigger place, in a bigger city where you have access to more people who are going to be receptive, that's fine. If you think you have a little more to do in – what is that place?"

I responded, "Crandall."

"That's why if you feel – all we can imagine is telling more people at once. We have to get on with it. We have to get on with it. That's all everything is – tones and hums and whatever. It's like you can connect to

here and can be to there. Everybody has to get on with it. We don't understand why you are not getting on with it. So if you can get to more people at once, and you have that ability… then you have to do that. What is that this guy said, "Sin is knowledge not lived. Sin is knowledge not lived." That's the only thing sin is. So if you go out there and say I accidentally hurt someone when I did that. No sin, whatever. I didn't know. I'm sorry. But boy, if you do it again and you do it again, and you know better, and you're not living up to where you should be, then that is sin. What you human beings call sin is just not living what you know you should be living."

"And the other people, the beautiful people, you love to deal with the beautiful people, that's fine. But don't forget even the beautiful people, even the little children, who look like they're whatever, need guidance. They need guidance. People with the money, people that are lovely, people that eat in good places and have the money – they don't have the answers either and they have to get up here, too. They have to get up here, too. So you are not to let little children fall by the wayside! Little children who are not falling into line with love and caring and respecting of people, of others and the earth, they have to be taught. They have to be taught. People who are mothers, grandmothers and step-people have to help those children. And if you are

going to do it with one little child, get on with it! And if one-on-one is what you're comfortable with, get on with it!"

"This one! This one! We know she doesn't want to do big people... She's not particularly comfortable with money and whatever. You know what she came for? She came to get down into the dirtiest portions of whatever, with the people nobody wants to love or wants to touch. We don't know why she is not doing that."

"We have some inkling. We cannot say. 'If you are here at this hour tomorrow, this would happen...' We can't do that."

"You all have to get into the groove. You need to get into the flow a little better. Oh, yeah, that feels good. Then you have to go with that. Oh, my heart says, 'I need to do that.' Then that's the step you have to take. Everyone has to get beyond the fear, beyond the, 'What will other people think of me?' Who cares? Who cares? You came for a job. All of you are here. You have to get on the ball. You have to get on with your job."

"Open forum? What shall we say now?"

"Numbers... symbols... I-Ching... all those things... Jewel with the Lotus... It all comes back to here [the heart.] It's right back in here. All the tones... connect you back to that. Silver strings. Gold strings. Remember it is love. Remember Nomaste. Light in me greets the light in you. It all comes from your heart. It's all the same."

"It's fascinating. You're right. If you walk into a church in wherever, and they're doing this or that, the circle or whatever, it all ties into the same thing. It is just that you've all been trying to be told for years and years and years and years, by symbols and sounds and people and places, and we're still not quite there yet. Little bitty steps, but we are getting there. You know we need to make that light year step. We need to make that light year step. The more people that are aware of that... what is that – 100th monkey? If we could just get that one next person to make the connection, then a whole bunch of us can make that jump. And believe me, we all want to be in that little glimpsing place up there... that ahhhh... It feels black. Feels black. It's not to be feared. It feels black. You do, you do disappear when you are there. You are not you. You are not you. You is that essence in here, that spirit that can go up there. You are just this [your body]. What is this? This is not you. Don't be afraid when this you looks like it disappears. You want this you to disappear. You want

249

this you to disappear and blend into all the other yous, and all the other spirits and everything else. And to realize you are all connected."

"If you think bad thoughts or depressing thoughts, you're pulling something down somewhere. So you have to always think love. You have to always extend this energy, this energy, positive energy, to always go out lovingly. I love you. I love you. I love you – loving even the dirtiest, the most horrible, the whatever. It always has to be love sent out. It always has to be love sent out. You know... everybody in this room knows that."

"And that's why, if you're not living that, then that is sinning in the eyes of whoever you think watches you. Nobody really watches you. Hellfire and brimstone live only in your brain. If you can get past that and to realize we are all way up there on a much higher level."

"Let's see what else we have to say. Oh, symbols, numbers, numerology things... you know, how you work out why you are here. And there are ways to figure out how many lifetimes you've been here, but you know even that doesn't matter. Because then you can't get judgmental. If you get judgmental, 'I'm better than you. Why did you do that? Why did you whatever...?' Then you're going to take too many steps backwards."

"You know anything, anything that's going to help you. All these things that will help you connect spiritually. Just go do that. Because it's no different than healing things for your body. It's no different than learning what my birth date means. What are my life's plans? As long as, OK, the trick is if you go and you learn something, you have to live it. Don't go if you're not going to live it. If you're not going to listen and do it, then don't bother. Because then, if you think there is a tally somewhere… 'she learned that, but there she is not doing it!' So we don't whatever, doesn't help you, doesn't help anybody, so it's a waste. So if you are going to go, fine, always go, always be open. You must always be open. All the people of all the worlds that have all the symbols and all the sounds and all the whatevers, it's all the same thing. It's all the same thing. Everybody has sort of made connections, and tried to learn and tried to teach. So you should always be open. You should never say, 'Well, what do they know?' Well, they do know. If they know the same stuff, you're going to hear it again and again and again. You're going to hear it over and over again, but you have to get on it now. You have to get with it. You have to get with it."

"Let's see, you know, when you reach this up there level, that level, and it doesn't even feel like there's vibration there. It's just … it's just so what? Nothing feels vibratory. We don't know. It could be. We don't

know. We don't actually go up there. Again, we just get that little quick glimpse when she comes back. It's like a kite, you know when a kite rises way up and if you could just hang onto the tail of the kite, and like go with it up there but you know that you're too heavy on this end and you can't get up there attached to the kite? You have to get up there on your own. When you get up there, you look into the numbers thing and look at your date of birth – numerology."

"Sin is knowledge not lived." Why are you not doing what you are supposed to do? When you reach that level, you know. As a 10, you don't have to come back anymore. When you reach that level, you realize that the only really worthwhile thing to do is come back and help. It's time to have that ideal. If you come back and you don't help, there's much to do and there's no help going on. And there's no help going on… So that's why. You are not doing what you are supposed to do. It's so sad. If we could just shake everybody up. It's so sad."

"Well, we can't slap her around. We're not allowed to slap people around. If you take your date of birth, and you go 7 & 2 is 9, and 9 and 1 is a 10. You pull that digit to a 1. The other 1 is a 2. Then a 9 and 2 is an 11, which is 2, and a 5 and 7 is a 3 and 10. You take that last number – that tells you what your life lesson is. If the number is a 10 total at the end, then the 10s don't

have to come back anymore. They just come back, because they think they're going to come back and fix the world, which is fine, but you know that's like a hard job. When you're up there in that realm, it's like... I can come back and fix the world. I can do that. When you come back here and realize, oh, oh, it's like hard. You forget it was hard so you have to get on the ball. Now 1s again are like starting over. 2s have to do with balance. 3s are a better balance, because it's a solid balance. 6s are like double 3s like the sign of David. I can't remember all the rest of them... 7s are good numbers... so that's how that numbers thing works."

"Are you sure you were being buried alive? Are you sure you weren't being taken higher? You let that fear thing of going higher..."

"We don't know all the numbers. With the 10s, you expect more. It's really pathetic when they don't... Be open to everything. You never know what insight might help you to grasp the fact that we are all connected."

"Only try to put out good, warm loving energy to everybody. Everybody lie down and be still. In the still is where you will find us. In the still is where you connect."

"Then if you can do that stillness – that group thing, that group thing, that group thing, that group

meditation. Everybody sits and is quiet. Love and let energy come down and out to everyone you meet."

"The only way to bring darkness to light is keep putting out light. If you lay down, be still and meditate. It's more than just yourself. You connect all your energies. My field interacts with your field. It's the field of the whole universe. It's the field of all of us. It is all light and love. My light meets your light."

"It doesn't matter if you're Catholic or Christian, Hindu or Buddhist. It doesn't matter if someone shows you a triangle or part of something. It's all meant to be the same. My light needs to connect with your light. My prayer, my field of energy needs to be connected to your prayer, your energy. There is no difference. It looks different, but it's all you. It's all me. If you can just do that, with all you have, with that realm, that realm, that is just beyond us, that next dimension – that is so wonderful, so beautiful!"

"Radiate only love. Think of your field – your energy field. Have it go out before you with love and light. The only answer to the world is love and light." [48]

The connectedness of all us really touched me. This word picture came to mind. When I was a little girl and you may remember when a thermometer broke, the mercury was free to roll around the table or floor. Before we knew how dangerous it was, it was really fun to watch the mercury and play with it. What I remember is that parts of the mercury would break off the big mercury. Then there would be a lot of little pieces of mercury rolling around. I imagine that people are like that. People are all little pieces of God. We think we are so separate, but we really are all pieces of the same thing. It seemed that the pieces of mercury were independent, but when they would roll close to the big mercury, they would be swallowed up into the whole. We think we are independent individuals, but when we get close to God, we get swallowed up and are a part of the Oneness of God. There is no difference between God and us. This gives me new meaning and insight to what Jesus said, "I and my Father are One."

Gifts from the Heart, 8/12/02 — Our Appointment

I was setting up an appointment to meet with Hannah on the phone. As we spoke, someone else began to speak through her. This is what she shared:

> *"This is what I said to you – in order to listen to others, you must be open to others. Different views are important. Different lifestyles and variables are important. Hold fast to your dreams. You are simply here to do your work. Let Vicki help you, Hannah, please. It is only then will the questions be answered."*

> *"Reach forward, Vicki. You must reach forward. Take time to do it. We need you. Why spend time worrying about others? Use what you know. Show what you know. It will all come soon."*

255

"Meet with Vicki on Friday, Hannah. We will bring it together. Bring a purple sweater to wear. Bring a long-stemmed red rose, a glass of water and one mirror. Meet with Vicki on Friday. We will bring it together." [49]

I am always amazed when this happens. I couldn't wait until Friday when I anticipated a wonderful experience.

Gifts from the Heart, 8/16/02 – My Initiation

When I arrived at Hannah's, this time I was the one on the massage table. Hannah provided the healing session and shared this information afterward.

"Vicki appeared to be in a deep sleep. Her body jerked and she exhibited rapid eye movement with both hands, palm downward, resting above the table in the air. There was movement in both thumbs of each hand."

"I was told to bring the rose and place it over her heart and the top of her head. The red rose brings life to the soul. I was told to sprinkle water over her forehead. I was asked to make a cross over Vicki's forehead three times. As I was guided to move my thumb over her mouth region, words in a different language were spoken in my mind. Her hands raised about 2 inches higher as this happened. I saw images of Vicki in a white dress with gold around her. Then I heard:"

"Vicki, we love you. Precious is a bird that flies, if it has never flown. Release, come to God. We accept your

openness. We welcome you here, Butterfly. It is truly an honor and a blessing. Rest my sweet for we have much work to do."

Hannah observed my hands change from palms down to thumbs up. My hands were lying on their side and were still levitated in the air.

"Do you hear me? We hear you. Not to worry, Butterfly. Keep the last and the first... We cherish you. You are truly a martyr of our good work. Keep the love alive. Good-bye. Wake her now, please." [50]

I knew my hands levitated. My mind got quiet. I heard a loud washing machine as if it was in the room with us. I heard five airplanes that seemed to fly right over my face. I saw the image of a boy, only a little older, that I had seen on a news program that could see words from color, because he was blind from birth.

I felt touches. I heard Hannah at my head, but felt her at my feet. I looked to see if she had placed another sweater on my feet. There were cold places on my body – seven of them. As I fell into a deeper sense of relaxation, I felt cold and warm at the same time. At times, it was frigidly cold.

There were touches on my hair and shoulder and a vibration on the inside and outside of my thigh. It started out with a pain in the upper right hip. I felt different after it was completed.

Then I began to work on Hannah. We switched places on the table. She began to hum and her body moved in preparation for the work. She began to speak in the original angelic language and demonstrated symbols.

"Hey. Hey. Hey. Hi. Hi. Hi. How are you?"

I responded, "Good. How are you?"

"Good. I am… I am Beh Wohl Gitsy Woh El? It's hard to relax sometimes. Spirit has no physical body, but it's hard to relax the physical body. It's like a tug of war. Hi. I know I said that already."

"My name is Coolah Say Coolah. Mother. Mother. Mother."

"Here in this place. Here in this space are youthful, meaningful, joyful wonders of life. I am here today to bring change. As I came today, I was bombarded with thoughts of confusion."

"One more time. The deepest ocean of the deepest sea. Time flies. Truly I am amazed to see life. If but for a second to see, for I was made to be – life."

"Help me. Help me now as I gather piece after piece of what really matters – Life. Ahhh – truly a blessing to be here today even if it seems so far away."

"We are here. We have always been here. I say I, but I am not alone. I am connected, yet still at home. I see what you see. You see what I see. Why is that so difficult to understand?"

"We cannot run this course for you. We can only be there for you. Help, you say? I am here... I cry. I feel pain. Why does this world hurt? Why does this world hate? Why does this world not believe?"

"Hello, Vicki. My name is Michael. I am truly honored to meet you. I talk with Hannah daily. To her it may seem I am a pest. I communicate with her to help her understand the true meaning of this life, world and her purpose."

"We work together, you see. I am here for her. She is here for me. Now I heard you when you said that you felt so alone at times. I, too, can relate. I am what you call a guide. I am a guide. I travel. I am a guide. I travel. I am with a soul until it lives out its true meaningful purpose of life. You see, I am here for her. She is here for me. I am not a guardian angel. I am a guide. There is a difference. Guides – some of us were once here on earth – who now assist other people."

"Angels, you ask? They are all around you. Guides are all around you. Each person has guides and angels."

I asked, "How can I help Hannah?"

"You already are. She's coming along. She's pretty stubborn. Faith is a hard thing to fathom. If it's not right in front of you, it's not tangible. It is right here. Right here in front of you. Faith will lead you home."

"Get busy. It's hard, I know, but get busy. Get busy on what, you ask? Reconnective is every being of your self and spirit. No two hands. No two feet. You can use your hands. That is what you were taught. Your mind is the tool – your heart."

"When God reconnects with people, He doesn't just reconnect with hands. He reconnects with spirit, mind and heart. When He speaks, He reconnects. When He looks, He reconnects. When He embraces, He reconnects."

"#1 – Get out of self. #2 – Get out of self. #3 – Respect self. #4 – Be self. #5 – Realize self. #6 – Connect with self. #7 – Help self. #8 – Teach self. #9 – Utilize self. #10 – Come back to self." [51]

Gifts from the Heart, 8/16/02 — Hold Fast to Your Dreams

During the session, this message was delivered. It really spoke for itself and we needed to hear what it said for each of us.

"I want to tell you a story. Maybe this will help."

"A little girl – we'll call her Sue. Sue had so many dreams. She wanted to be a doctor, lawyer, fireman and an astronaut. Because Sue had all these things she wanted to do, she truly could not see Me. She spent agonizing days and nights wondering, hoping, wishing and waiting. But because Sue did not take the time to look to herself, she could not see Me."

"She was 9 then. I now see her at 20. Sue is now a nurse, but still wants to be a fireman, doctor, astronaut and lawyer. She wants to be… She waits. She hopes. She wishes. She cannot see Me. How can she not see Me? I stand before her. I look at her. She looks at Me. 'Here I am. Can you see Me? I can see you! Why can't you see Me? I'm in this pretty blue. Sue, can you hear Me? I can hear you. Why can't you see Me in this pretty blue?' "

"Sue is now 30. Sue now has children. She's hoping, waiting, wishing, and wondering. As she cooks, cleans, and washes, I listen. I watch. I wait."

"Sue is 40. The children are older now. She is now divorced. 'Sue,' I say, 'Sue.' I hear her crying. 'God, help me. Please help me. Please help me. Please help me.' "

" 'I hear you, Sue. I'm right here.' Sue continues… 'God, help me. God, help me.' "

"Sue at 65. She is now older, but yet beautiful in My eyes. She can no longer be who she wants – a fireman, doctor, astronaut or lawyer. She still dreams, hopes, wishes, and waits. 'God, I'm so tired. Give me peace. Please hear my call. Please hear my prayer. Don't let me live another day. Give me peace.' "

"As Sue closes her eyes, she has now made peace."

"I stand before her as I have always been there before her. She looks at Me and says, 'Oh, You! You! I've been hoping, wishing and waiting for you. Where have you been all my life? You!' "

"I look at her and I say, 'Sue, Sue, why didn't you ever recognize me? I have been standing here. I have been standing here. You never see me in my pearly blue.' "

"Sue replies, 'I couldn't see you. I couldn't see you.' "

"I say to her, 'You couldn't see me? I was there. I've always been there.' "

"Sue replies, 'I don't know.' "

"I ask, 'What is it that you truly want to do?' "

"Sue responds, 'Be with you.' "

"I ask, 'Be with me?' "

"Sue replies, 'Be with you.' "

"So you see. I'm here. I have always been here. Even if you don't see me, I'm always here with you."

"Hold fast. Hold steady to your dreams... your goals. Let no one distract you. Keep going forward. Good-bye." [52]

Gifts from the Heart, 8/24/02 – Let Go of Fear – Feel Unconditional Love

When the conference for practitioners was held in Las Vegas in the summer of 2002, a group of around twenty practitioners met in one of the hotel rooms. I was compelled to share with them some of the miracles I had experienced and included in this book. What happened was amazing! The people listened while I read the messages received from God through different sessions. Then they listed to a tape of the actual voices captured during one of the sessions where the messages had been provided. It was an awesome and reverent event. At the conclusion of the meeting, one of the people asked if I would work on a friend who was present and I had received messages before during healing sessions with me. I looked at her and asked, "Is that OK with you? Are you willing? I am, if you are."

She agreed and lay down across the end of the bed. I worked for a few minutes before words came from her.

"Some need more love than others. They are dense, but not in a stupid way. There is a thickness in their energy. Love heals all. These are the people you are supposed to reach. The meaner, ruder, nastier – you need to love them. The really angry people need to be connected. You need to accept yourself and others will accept you."

"You let your fears of being judged keep you from doing your work. No fear. No fear gear. Use it. Just do it! Get out and do it! Every hand you shake. We do not understand this judging – this need for acceptance. We don't get this."

"We love you. God loves you. If you really knew how much you are loved, you would have no need for acceptance from fear. No fear."

Someone asked, "Can you take the fear away?"

"Yes, we can take the fear, but you have to relinquish it. It is more important to release fear. Connect. The heart can feel no fear. It is about love. Stop. Challenge. Choose to feel love. God feels no fear. That same connectedness to God lets you fly, soar – feel unconditional love."

"There are no conditions to love. Not money – place – space – time. They are all vanished. Five minutes of *healing is the same as forty-five. People love the energy and love to play there."*

"Why do we all feel like this is stepping off a cliff? That is not what it is. The bridge is there. Faith – you need to know you are being drawn on faith. Trust."

"Remember with Reiki? No one knew about Reiki. This work will be like that."

"What comes next? There is something great. It is a higher frequency. Notches higher. It's amazing and it's coming in months. It's a higher frequency than we are used to. We are this close. Grab it."

"Do not be afraid. He has laid the groundwork for us. Your path will be easier for the part he has played. Stop with this fear thing."

Someone asked, "What about prisoners?"

"Research has shown that part of a gene is causing violence and anger. Reconnective – DNA healing – heals DNA. Forget the National Institute of Health. Forget the Human Genome Project. Why do you need to know why anyway? It's funny. You can go in and heal DNA. Anybody can do this. The engineer is trying to share which gene is responsible. You heal DNA."

Someone asked, "Do we really need to draw the lines?"

"Healing and reconnection. It's in the information. We need to draw the lines for now. It is a sharing, a ritual. It is important in allowing the experience to unfold. It's like lighting a candle in the church. It's all the same. It is hugely important for the flow. It's your dance and your agreement to heal each other. That's why you draw the lines. You are doing them on yourself as well. You get the frequency as the lines are drawn."

One practitioner asked, "Is there a limit to the number of sessions?"

"People are attracted to that centered space. Never turn away someone who needs you for a healing. What you are concerned with is the addiction to anything. That is your culture. That is what you are watching for. People are re-centered through healing with the Divine in God."

"Working with animals... Animals are so evolved. They are our greatest teachers. Animals will save the planet through teaching us. They need energy and love, too. They get caught up in helping us and forget they are loved and connected to God. They send energy to their people and it channels back to you."

"We love animals. We cry when a species goes extinct. We feel weeping. We feel sadness. Some species are pretty big."

I asked, "What can we do now?"

"Deal with the fear first. Remember this energy. Remember how it feels to be here in Las Vegas with the practitioners. Now we are experiencing this energy in the conference. With the energy on the outside, it allowed bonding on the inside."

"Love him. Totally love him. He needs to breathe. He is afraid of where this will go. He feels as much fear now as in the beginning. Bless him. He sees the whole picture. He is such a loving soul. He has no idea how many people he has touched. He was the chosen for this work. He needs a gentle shove."

"Eric's fear. Eric's vibration. He is so frightened. We need to love him through this transition. He has intuitively found bright people to move forward. He jokes about control. He feels cold fear. Send him as much love as you can."

I asked, "Should we use 'stealth healing'?" (Stealth healing was a method used in distance healing and self-healing.)

"Yes. Obligation. Commitment. He doesn't want to let any one of us down. He wants to be what we believe he is."

"He is such a gift. It took 10 years to get here. In 10 months, he's going to be way beyond where 10 years have led him."

"It's at warp speed, through worm holes. It's spinning – go for the ride."

"Time is irrelevant. Time is now. Einstein got it. It is not rocket science. It's multi-dimensional."

"Trust your heart. Breathe, think, and live through your heart. The heart vibrates 8 feet beyond the body. Love never, never, never, never lies. Follow your heart and the feet will follow."

"Trust what comes in – not fear and judging. The high pitch tone is another way of connecting to love. For some of you here, you will use the tone. Send the tones through the hands, heart, eyes and body. All works the same. It's where you feel confident."

"You move your hands, but it doesn't come out the same. All were drawing lines in the Los Angeles seminar, but all are not the same. We work with everybody. How we work is different. How we express is in your own way. Have fun with this work!"

Someone asked, "How will we know when you are there?"

"Some sense us. Others feel serious love. As you do more work and connect, you will learn how that feels and will instantly be told."

"We know the frequency is different for each of you, just a smidge."

I asked, "Are we being entrained?"

"Yes. Yes, there's always more. We will take you as far as you will let us."

Then the practitioners began to pose their own personal questions and they received answers. One practitioner asked if she needed to focus on her mother-in-law.

"Yes. This is play. Enjoy. You are going to learn through her how to work... hospice, nursing homes."

Another practitioner asked about her adjustments to her physical body.

"You appreciate it. You know more than most where you are headed. You have underestimated your gift. Get off your butt and get busy. You're letting your fear stop you from moving forward to the next level. The body will catch up. Purity of eating is how you will keep up. Don't worry about keeping pace."

Another practitioner shared that she was experiencing different levels of vibration in her hands, feet, shoulders and head within her brain.

"We are keeping you grounded. You cannot do this work without being of the earth and being grounded. You are downloading faster than you are letting it through. You are afraid to talk about it. We will take care of you. It is like you are being strangled. Let it flow through to vent for expression. Resonating. You are strangling yourself."

Another practitioner asked about the feeling in her knees.

"Get off your knees. Stand up. Own it. Stand up with it. Suffering is optional. You are letting the energy stick in your knees and are begging for guidance in where you go next. We have never understood kneeling. Get off your knees. Stand or sit and do this work. People in wheelchairs will do reconnective."

"We feel like – why are you storing it in your knees? The DNA is changing. We see fluid. We're sending the sensation. Feel the energy move through your knees and push the energy out your toes. You do not need to know why."

"You are a conduit to move it on through. Healer group, send energy to her."

Another practitioner asked about why her legs jerked.

"The energy is moving. We are continually reconnecting you to a higher frequency. You are being moved to a higher level."

"We will not let you look like spray on the street corner. Move the energy on through."

I asked, "How will we know if...?" Before I could finish the sentence the answer was given.

"Heart. You do not have 4 eyes. You will see as you do this work. Amazing things will happen to your body. The work will heal, as it needs to heal. Detach from the outcome. We will heal in the order received. We see a higher order. God sees what needs to be healed. You heal in the order it was received."

I asked about a friend's music. "Are there tones in his music?"

"He has a special frequency. He doesn't quite get that yet. It's not in the tone he's singing. It's a harmonic that comes through. You know how... it's like a chord. He's singing that harmonic. He is reaching people to heal through music. Everybody is to heal in his or her own way. 8 – We love that number. Our business – our work. His gift is tones. That's where he heals. He could teach classes on the tones. He will."

"Tones are a way to gently bring and increase vibrations. The tones – there are more tones. There are more tones coming. You have only touched the beginning of the tonal scale. There are way more tones than people are aware of. Stand in a church and listen. You will hear them. They are in the walls. All of you have walked into churches – places of spirituality – where you could not leave. We were connecting at the time."

"All of you are experiencing download. Why does meditation scare you so? We can talk to you easier in mediation. What does your heart say? Each is a route."

"You can do this. Bring the group to that place. Group meditation. Amplify it. Expand. Lead this group. You can do it now. Time is of the essence. That's how to do it fast."

"You are all connected. When one goes into meditation, you all go into meditation. It's a Kum Bye Yah thing. Hold your own hands. Feel centered. Lift all at once. We know. Why are you whining so much? It's group energy."

Another practitioner asked, "Was it you who took me when I was 9 years old?"

"Feel the love. You were so frightened. You had not felt love like that before! We started work long ago. You were chosen – way before now. We came to take you. None of this is meant to frighten you. 'You've never been loved like this before.' It's unconditional God love."

They continued to tell us more.

"We are a group. We could work with you. Yes, we go wherever you are. We get to experience being in the physical body through you."

"We are in the position of light versus dark. We just crossed shadow into the light. In the energy, we are all One. How you use the energy will determine if we stay in the light. We need to keep the pendulum on this side of light so a large group does not have to sacrifice their lives again."

"September 11th was a wake up call – a huge wake up call. What love it took to make that sacrifice. Families, friends, jobs they loved. Very, very important."

"There is an urgency around keeping energy into the light. It is important to work in light and live in love. It's like a bungee to pull you back from anger and hate. Hold the center. Who is God? God is everywhere." [53]

It took me a couple of times to really understand the comment, *"You connect all your energies…"* from another Gift from the Heart. This statement in addition to these words about meditation helped me understand. What I learned was that if one goes into meditation, we all go into meditation. Because we are all connected, that is where we share the experience of Oneness and connectedness to God.

Gifts from the Heart, 8/25/02 — Laughter and Healing

More information was provided in a healing session the next day.

"The laughter is so healing. You – stop being so serious! We keep telling you to lighten up! It heals. The love and laughter are important. You worry about the stupid things."

"Let us take you where you need to go. Find that peaceful place and listen. You have to go in and be One. Think of the trees in the redwood forest. They clump together in threes. This is not about doing this by yourselves. You forget you are connected. A thought and you're reconnected. All it takes is a thought and breath. Why do you all resist?"

"You were afraid of today. We kept you safe. We made sure the others heard about it. He was jealous. He has his special group. He needs to honor everyone's unique gifts."

"It is launched. Are you ready? We are there. This is going to take off. We are with you always. Remember. You forget we are with you. Then you go to fear. We fear for you."

"There's something more… we know where each of you are headed. You're safe. You're guided. The road is clear. There are no shadows. Just ask for clarity. We'll send that to you."

"Candida – This issue is because of chemicals and genetic engineering. Your body needs time to clear. Vegetables and meats are easier to change their frequency because they are still somewhat living – You will get better at praying over your food. You all came to the table to heal. We had to heal all of you. We gave you what you ask for. We totally understand." [54]

Gifts from the Heart, 9/03/02 – The Journey is Underway

These words came from one client:

"It is an incredible journey. The journey is underway. We don't know the full picture. It's sort of like Oz. We started down the yellow brick road. We see the castle in the distance. We assume it is the destination. We don't know who the man is behind the curtain, but the many wonders of God will be revealed." [55]

Gifts from the Heart, 11/17/02 – You are a Survivor

One day I was experiencing some very human frustrations. I am normally a very optimistic person, but this day the pressures had built and I found myself at a really low place. I was assisting in a seminar and felt better after being in the energy all day.

I was providing the second session for a client, and we had concluded the debriefing when she said, "There are all these words coming through my head – from out to in."

I asked, "What are they?" She began to speak just as they were given to her. Here's what she communicated to me.

"We are here for you. You are a survivor. Let life challenge you. You are a survivor. The Spirit is with you. You are a survivor. Live in the Light. You are a survivor. Love. Life. Live. You are a survivor. Aspiration. Fulfillment. Contentment. You are a survivor. Love. Life. Live. You are a survivor. Peace. Love. Life. Live. Sorry. Sorry. Sorry. Love. Life. Live. Rejoice. Remember. Recall. Regain. Relive. Attitude. Healing. Constructive criticism. Rejoice. Relive. Re-life. Remember. Reborn. Restructure. Regain. Recall. Rejoice. Happy. Happy. Happy. Live. Life. Love. Maintain. Live. Life. Love. Rejoice. Renew. Restart. Remember. Recall. Rebirth. Renew. Live. Life. Love. Happy. Happy. Happy. Sorry. Sorry. Sorry. Happy. Happy. Happy..." [56]

I felt comforted. I knew that my day had started off in a really bad way, but after these words, I knew that I was a survivor and that this, too, was a lesson for me. I knew that I was also very loved and that all of these emotions that touch our humanness and words that guide us to live were another gift for all of us. I thanked her for the gift. She said, "I know these messages are for you." I agreed with her. These words spoke directly to my heart. What I also shared with her was that these messages are for all of us. She came up to me the next day and said, "You know, after I thought about it, those messages were for me, too. Thank you."

God's Gift to Us

How can we understand what all this means? I think God uses everything to remind us of Him. He gives us blue skies and fluffy white clouds, but we seem too busy to remember Him and His love. God uses beautiful music with messages of love and light, but we don't listen very well. God sends friends to us to share and enrich our lives, but we don't see God in them. God sends husbands and wives to share our blessings and pain with, but we take them for granted. We have the use of the world at our disposal. We see the beauty of the oceans, beaches, mountains and lush valleys, but we still abuse and destroy our environment rather than take responsibility for the stewardship of God's creation. We see the smile of a child, a beautiful flower, a really good book, the kiss of a lover, the hug of a friend in times of need, but we forget that God who loves us so much has sent us all these symbols of love – these heart connections. I learned that it is important to appreciate and love the gifts God has given and strive to be better stewards.

277

Next time you experience a blessing in your life, remember Who sent it. He would appreciate a Thank You, and it would be wonderful, if you would continue the flow of love by extending that blessing so that it impacts someone else in a positive way. We do things so unconsciously in our lives; recognition, acknowledgement, gratitude and a flow of love would be a miracle to share with others.

A few years ago, there was a book that touched my heart. It was all about performing *Random Acts Of Kindness*[57]. There was a lengthy list of great ideas of how to connect with others. One act of kindness I particularly remembered was paying for an additional car at the tollbooth and wishing them a great day. We have the ability to change the direction of someone's life in an instant. We can give them a smile or a warm handshake. We can treat them as someone special, because they are special. We can choose in an instant whether to do something loving or something less than loving. The choice is always ours.

Healing Through Nature's Beauty, Music and Laughter

People get so caught up in the hustle and bustle of life. We can't stop to appreciate the fragrance of flowers. We forget to have fun. We forget to enjoy life at its best. Almost every time I have been given messages, there is a comment about the beauty of the world – of God's creation. Have you ever been in an elevator filled with silence? I used to be one of the quiet ones who just wanted to be invisible. Somewhere along the way I wondered why people were not connecting. I decided that fear kept me from reaching out to others. Today, I love to ask, "Are you having fun yet?" or perhaps, "Are you having a great day?" When you accompany those questions with a smile, you are sharing your life with them. They have an opportunity to connect with you. People find it easy to talk to me. More often than not, conversation begins, people smile and laugh rather than stand and wait in silence. A moment of fear is changed miraculously to a moment of connection and love. When we connect, people feel comfortable sharing some of the most intimate details of their lives that I know they have never shared before with anyone.

One thing I have noticed lately is that people look very familiar to me. I have lived in Texas most of my life, and have traveled a great deal. I have encountered thousands of people in those travels and life experiences so it was not unusual to think that I may have met them somewhere. But I started noticing that more and more people act like they know me, too. It's not just like I've seen them, it's like I know them. Without sounding too strange, I think it has to do with knowing God. As you really get to know Him, you begin to see Him in everyone you meet. You see a familiar light, love and you remember who they are.

It keeps me going when I find things difficult in life. I know that God knows us intimately. He lives within each of us. When we do something very human and in our minds, wrong, He sees the darkness and He loves us anyway. We cannot be separated from His love. It is our greatest connection. It is more important than the air we breathe, the water we drink or the food we eat. God's love has no beginning and no end. God is love. We are love. We just forget that every now and then.

Recently I was reminded of the words of that old hymn, *In the Garden,* written by C. Austin Miles. It says, "I come to the garden alone while the dew is still on the roses. And the voice I hear falling on my ears, the Son of God discloses. And He walks with me and He talks with me. And He tells me I am His own. And the joy we share as we tarry there, none other has ever known. He speaks and the sound of His voice is so sweet the birds hush their singing. And the melody that He gave to me within my heart is ringing."[58] I realized my connection to Him is such a great gift and I know that He speaks to me because He loves me and I am open to hear Him.

When the voices and messages were shared, there were occasions where I heard music. The person on the table began to sing beautiful songs. The melody and language touched my heart. The voice was angelic and the language was something I felt I should know in my heart, but just could not remember. It was as if she sang from her heart and my heart was listening and heard her right along with my ears.

As you wander through your life, please remember to laugh. Remember that a big belly laugh is very contagious and very healing. Think about the last time you laughed hard enough to cry big tears. Remember the last time you were tickled by someone or saw a movie that kept you laughing for a really long time. Laughter is such a huge release. It makes you feel alive. It's like finding a very valuable gift that you tucked away and had forgotten that you had. One day you open a drawer and there it is! You wonder why it took you so long to remember and then you laugh...

CHAPTER 9

CHANGING OUR WORLD FROM THE HEART

"...You just weep for no known reason. You don't know why you do. You are crying for humanity. You are crying because you want to move it faster and you can't. Pray. Pray. It is important to pray. Now is the time for prayer. You are not forgotten or forsaken even though at times, you feel we have abandoned you. We have not. It is through this that you will help others."

Healers who have shared their gifts with me have enriched my life. If you ask what healing methods exist, you come up with a long list. They include allopathic medicine, naturopathic medicine, chiropractic medicine, Reconnective Healing™, Reiki, Yoga, Reflexology, Cranial Sacral Therapy, Shamanic practices, Bach Flower Essences®, Massage Therapy, Jor Rei, Qi Gong, crystal bowls, meditation and tuning forks to name only a few. Churches have ministers who practice laying on hands and intercessory prayer. People have introduced therapies that include psychology, psychiatry, and methods such as "rebirthing." For grieving families, there are mediums that receive information from people who have died. There are hundreds of other healing methods. Why are there so many different methods of healing? Which ones are valid? Are they all valid if they help even one person?

At times I have experienced and supported rigid standards and protocols. As with everything, there are benefits and deficits to a controlled approach. As I have continued to grow and experience the blessings of being in the healing equation, I have discovered that God will heal. The method doesn't really matter. If it works, that's all we need to know. I have been told the answers are in our hearts. Therefore we have the information within us that tells us if a certain method is something we should experience or not.

At times control and manipulation seem to surround the integrity of healing work. Practitioners are encouraged to hold other practitioners to a strict standard and report them when they do not operate within those guidelines. This seems at odds with what healing is truly intended to do. I have been led to understand that this work is not to be limited in any way. This work is to be extended to as many of the 6.2 Billion people on the planet that we can reach.

Although names may be trademarked or alliances formed to set guidelines, human beings do not own healing work. The reality is that like it or not, healing comes from God, not controlled by human egos or influences. This work comes like everything else as a gift from God, and is delivered straight through the heart. The heart is the vehicle that is used to communicate healing work with truth, honesty, integrity and love to everyone.

As I observed a number of people who became leaders in healing, and went on to become recognized or even famous, I saw a number of things that caused me concern. The human ego at times grows faster than the spiritual self. Occasionally, healers seemed to forget that each of us is as special as anyone else. Healing is a true democracy where everyone is truly equal. There are no means for you to increase your value beyond the value of anyone else. We are equally important. If I were to share an analogy, perhaps you could relate to and understand my perspective.

When a healer begins to recognize his particular, and perhaps unique gift and starts out on his soul's journey, it is like he is standing in the water. The stream is just a trickle. As he continues working and teaching others, the combined knowledge and experience add to the trickle until it becomes a flowing stream of water. After hundreds of people become trained in the work, it continues to grow into a fast moving stream. Now as thousands are trained, it's more like the Colorado or Mississippi Rivers. The momentum is flowing. If you try to fight it, you'll go under. If you try to dam it up, it will break through eventually. You can guide the direction, but some tributaries will form and flow in their own way. If you try to stop it, it will continue anyway. You can float and it will carry you a great distance effortlessly. You can tell people about the power. You can urge them to try it the safest way. Some will swim powerfully and some will just play in the shallow water. You can show them what you've done so far. They will make it down the river easily, effortlessly or with difficulty depending on how they approach the journey.

As the flow increases, tributaries join the river to make it stronger. They don't branch out near the mouth unless the abundance of water is greater than the banks. Together all of the experiences and all the gifts flow where everything is blended into and becomes the ocean where all is One. If only one person was doing the work, there would still be only a small trickle. The combination of all the people increases the flow. One person cannot do it alone.

You may see situations that seem familiar in another analogy. The instructor distributes "gift certificates" for all the people who read the books or attend the seminars. The "gift" is put in a box and presented to the seminar attendees. They are told, "It's a remarkable gift. You will master this work in your own unique way. You can use this gift anywhere." But there are strings attached to the gift and you might be confused with all the dos and don'ts. You may even limit the healing from the restrictions placed on you or the healing work.

One string attached says, "Don't ever take it out of the box." Another string says, "Don't change a single thing about this work." Another string says, "Be sure and report anyone who uses the gift in a way that would reflect poorly on the rest of us." Another string says, "Do it exactly this way." Another string says, "If it doesn't work exactly this way, it must be something different." Another string says, "Use your gift certificate the way I want you to or not at all."

The strings go on and on depending on the modality and the teacher of the work.

The freedom to utilize this healing gift from God is sometimes restricted in other ways. Imagine you wanted to press the limits of your gift and try new possibilities. Instead, you hesitate because you come from a place of fear and stop short of learning something new and incredible. My recommendation is trust your heart. Who knows what may happen?

Let me share one more story that helps describe how I feel about the freedom to grow in the healing arts...

A baby is born. It continues to grow. At fifteen years old, it is no longer a baby. You can dress it in very large, especially made baby clothes. You can treat it like an infant. You can restrict it from learning to speak, to count, and to walk, but it will continue to grow. You can instill fear. You can mold with love.

Other people will interact with your baby. They will visit, but may be afraid to embrace it because – there's just something wrong with this picture. One person cannot provide everything this child needs. One person cannot meet the educational needs, survival needs, govern activities and tend to the growth at the same time. Have faith that the growth and changes are in the hands of God, who gifted the child to you in the first place and let it grow to be whatever it was designed to be. It may surprise you what happens to us when we remove the restrictions of our human influences and really let the power of God work in our lives!

What was confirmed for me again and again was that healing was a gift from God. It was a gift to be shared, not controlled. It was a gift of the greatest love there was. The gift gained value from spending it freely with others. It actually renewed the gift recipient as well as the giver. Without restrictions or limitations, the gift multiplied like loaves and fishes. More people were touched. They were nourished in their lives.

My recommendation is to remove the fear and control from healing altogether. Replace the control and fear with unconditional love. If you do this work in love, you can't go wrong. You honor the work. It honors you and your client. I believe that we can learn all we can from each and every experience. I don't have all the answers, but I know if I'm open to learning, the wisdom will be provided.

A friend recently shared this piece of wisdom with me. "Everybody you meet from a bum on the street to the President has something to learn from you and you from them. So treat everyone you meet like a genius." Watch people's reaction when you treat them like a genius and honor them. See how they blossom right before your eyes, when you value them and they feel it. They may offer you great insight into the mysteries of the Universe.

We are told that we will be able to do works beyond those of our teachers. But in our hearts, we make excuses why we don't see miracles in our lives and feel we will never be "as good" as our teachers. We limit our expectations, rather than embracing our own power and gifts. When we acknowledge the truth of our direct connection and power, we will truly "own" our uniqueness and manifest miracles every day.

Impact of Organized Religion

I believe God speaks to us in the way we comprehend. If we are Christians, He speaks to us in the language we understand. If we practice Hinduism, Taoism, Buddhism, Native American, Judaism, Islamic faith or any of the other religions, He speaks to us in the language we understand. As we begin to understand the Wholeness and Oneness of God – All That Is – we can understand that we began as whole. We, humans, have fractured ourselves into splinter religions. The answer to everything is in our hearts where He has not changed. We can begin to understand as we see all citizens of the world as a part of God and also a part of ourselves. We concentrate on our differences rather than the things we have in common. I understand it may be uncomfortable to hear this. For others, this resonates with the truth which is in your heart, if you choose to listen.

I believe God is the same yesterday, today and tomorrow. I also believe that it is the human ego that limits God. It is assumed that we have nothing new to discover about God and faith. I believe that eventually we will be privileged to understand more and more about God in our lives as we allow the Oneness of God to expand our beliefs.

One thing that makes me wonder about the intentions of our religious leaders for decades and even centuries is this: why have we been led to believe that the Bible is a complete document when the Dead Sea Scrolls identified so many books that have been deleted or not included in the Bible? The Isaiah Scroll alone is reported to have 66 books that have been omitted. More modifications allegedly occurred with the King James translation. Theology courses, the Internet, historians and even the Vatican have information that points to these modifications and omissions. Copies of these translations and those in various holy places around the world are not widely distributed. I wondered why access was available only to Biblical scholars in select locations throughout the world. If there was more information included in the manuscripts and scrolls, why couldn't we all benefit from the information? Does it need to be filtered for some reason?

Did Constantine really change or delete information from the Bible in 325 A.D. as reported in theological studies?   In a subsequent meeting of the Second Council of Constantinople in 553 A.D., was information deleted from the Bible then?

New information is being discovered all the time and the gap between religion and science continues to diminish. What if the two – science and religion – are halves of a complete whole? And what if all the religions of the world together make up the religious half of that whole?

What if the amazing healing power that we accessed was described in those manuscripts that were rediscovered in the Dead Sea Scrolls? What if information in these volumes changed our healthcare and scientific approaches, as we know them today? What is really happening? Do organized religions feed us a controlled portion of information rather than trust us with the whole truth? Recently I watched a movie, *Stigmata*. In the movie, it portrays the Catholic Church as an official investigator of reported "miracles." In the investigation, the evidence of the "miracle" is packed, crated and shipped to Vatican City. What happens after that is often a mystery. Were there secrets hidden in the Vatican? How many miracles really occurred, but were denied because it would raise questions of truth, accountability and control that the Church would find difficult to answer? The Catholic Church experienced criticism recently for the handling of molestation on child victims over decades by trusted priests. Had there been other areas where decisions have been made that concealed evidence that should be made public for all of us? We might never know in this lifetime. We could only love them through whatever difficulties they faced and we could only hope that God spoke to their hearts.

What I concluded was that these questions left things unanswered for me. I believe that the information will be revealed and the process is already underway. As we grow and learn more about life, love and God, we will be given more information. The information will expand our understanding and will answer all our questions. "Now we see through a glass, darkly; but then face to face: now I know in part; but then shall I know even as I am known." [59] Perhaps this is what they were talking about. As this story and my experiences unfold, I know that I do not have all the answers. Some of the answers are not available yet and some of the questions have yet to be asked. I am continually reassured through the Gifts from the Heart that I am being assisted in this work. I am continually reminded that there is information in the Vatican that has not been made available. I have also been assured that more information is being revealed. The choice to continue on this journey is mine to make, but I have help all along the way. My team of angels, guides and souls in heaven as well as those on earth are here to help me create, learn and live these experiences while gathering new information.

At times, this path is difficult. I realize that I may be pioneering new frontiers and there will be people who have a hard time understanding or accepting my experiences as real. If I trust with my heart and encourage others to trust their hearts, we will understand more about this journey. In the meantime, I have faith that as promised, *"Everything you do, Vicki, God has already done it for you."* I see the value of these changes in my life and I am prepared to share them for those who are interested. As I love more, I find I live more in peace and serenity. Even when trials and obstacles come into my life, I am learning how to release and relinquish fear and worry.

I have every reason to believe that if I did not choose to write this account that someone else would have a similar experience and would be writing about it from their perspective. In fact, during the course of these experiences, when I began to share what was happening, I was given books to read that showed me similar experiences were occurring to other people, too. What I am sure of is that we are never alone in our work. We are all connected. This is just the beginning. This is just what has happened up to this point, but the journey is still underway, and who knows where this will lead us?

As I moved forward in faith, I was reminded of the Indiana Jones movie, *The Last Crusade*, where Indiana Jones stepped out in faith onto a bridge he could not see. He took one step at a time. He could not see where he was going until he took another step. When he placed his foot in front of him, he stepped onto something solid although he could not believe what his eyes told him. He had to trust with his heart.

I let fear keep me from moving forward to do what I was born to do. I knew once I acknowledged the fear and stepped through it, I reclaimed my power to be me. "Freedom to be" included not being concerned about what other people thought. I, like many, lived and made decisions according to the influences from my friends, co-workers, people in my community, and even the media that dictated how I was supposed to look, what I did, what kind of car I drove and where I lived without really deciding what was right for me.

When I discovered that the meaning in my life came from my relationships rather than things, I began to make real progress in the journey to grow, love and live. I recognized the Source of my guidance was heavenly, and I realized what I had to do to change how I lived. It was so simple, yet I tried to make it so complicated. I was here to connect heart to heart with each and every person I met on the planet. Yes, that was right...every single person. It was remembering and living like we were all connected.

But what about that criminal? Oh, you mean that mother's son or daughter? What about that mean man or woman down the street? Oh, you mean God's child? When we choose love rather

291

than anger, frustration, fear or hate, we love God, we love the person and we love ourselves. In I John 4:20-21, is it written, "If a man say, I love God, and hateth his brother, he is a liar; for he that loveth not his brother whom he has seen, how can he love God whom he hath not seen? And this commandment have we from Him, That he who loveth God love his brother also."

Challenges present themselves to us as we live each day. Are we able to choose love when it is easier to react and cut people who irritate us off at the knees? Are we able to love the strangers on the street that drive erratically and anger us? Are we able to love prisoners in jails around the country even if they commit horrible acts? Are we able to love the homeless families or the poor that struggle to live normal lives? Are we able to love our enemies who kill and maim our citizens? Are we able to love those who seem to have everything we deserve to have? Are we able to love those less fortunate than ourselves? Are we able to love those who are facing life crises? Or do we run from them afraid that divorce, death, or financial failure will somehow touch and taint us? The answer holds the future for our world, our churches, our country, our families, our children – everyone.

An old, old book, *At the Feet of the Master,* was written by Alcyone. It says, "In all the world, there are only two kinds of people – those who know, and those who do not know; and this knowledge is the thing which matters. What religion a man holds, to what race he belongs – these things are not important; the really important thing is this knowledge – the knowledge of God's plan for men. For God has a plan, and that plan is evolution. When once a man has seen that and really knows it, he cannot help working for it and making himself one with it, because it is so glorious, so beautiful. So, because he knows, he is on God's side, standing for good and resisting evil, working for evolution and not for selfishness."

"If he is on God's side, he is one of us, and it does not matter in the least whether he calls himself a Hindu or a Buddhist, a Christian or a Muhammadan, whether he is an Indian or an Englishman, a Chinaman or a Russian. Those who are on His side know why they are here and what they should do, and they are trying to do it; all the others do not yet know what they should do, and so they often act foolishly, and try to invent ways for themselves which they think will be pleasant for themselves, not understanding that all are one, and that therefore only what the One wills can ever be really pleasant for any one." [60]

When we try to control that which is God, we create another religion. I want a direct connection in my life. My personal belief is that as we do healing work, whatever name we give it, we continue to learn more about it each day. We continue to see miracles happen. I want the freedom to experience everything I can to witness miracles and help people heal from the inside, out. I want to have access to medical care when it is appropriate for emergency care or surgery after I have evaluated all the options. I want the freedom to operate without censure from any religion, church, medical community, special interest group or alliance.

A New Era in Healing and Healthcare Reform

We are living in a new era, where healing power and knowledge are increasing. I listened to practitioners talk about healings that were happening or were not happening. I experienced healings from the moment I began this work. I believed when you approached healing work with the innocence of a child, you might find it easier to let the healing flow from God through you and to the client and back again. I also learned when you try to remain open to the miracles of God, you witness them as a part of your life all the time. That in itself is a miracle!

Healing DNA means healing the body from the inside, out rather than from surgery or prescriptions. We are facing huge paradigm changes in medicine, as we know it today. The healthcare profession which started out as healing focused has changed as a result of economic influence and the proliferation of HMOs, insurance companies, pharmaceutical companies, advertising and the list continues... A simple solution will find great resistance because infrastructures of companies, employees, investments and research are funded by people with agendas other than healing. The incentives are built into the system for more prescriptions and more surgeries rather than healing the patient in a simple and effortless way. When we begin to really invest in our own health and well being, we will truly begin to change how we care for and heal our bodies, minds and spirits.

There are places in our societies for medical care, but there is also a definite need for a holistic approach to our health that is

294

reflected in our healthcare industry. The pharmaceutical companies bombard us with all kinds of prescription medicines that are designed to help us. If you doubt this for a moment, track the commercials you see on television and make a note of the prescription drugs that you are encouraged to request from your doctor. If you have a good friend who is also a doctor, ask where he or she gets the most up to date information about prescription medicine. What if it came from the pharmaceutical companies? How reliable can that be when the objective is to sell more pharmaceuticals? Is it an economic decision or a healing decision? What if we healed without any prescriptions at all? Are there other alternatives without prescribing another pill?

As my friend, a nurse of 30 years, says, "Let's put the heart back in healthcare." What's happening today is not working. There is a need for reform in the healthcare system to enable the healers trained as doctors, nurses, healing practitioners and other healthcare professionals to actually heal. Currently, many are frustrated with the processes that are required of them. HMOs, insurance regulations, restrictions, bureaucracy, and diagnostic techniques are sometimes in direct opposition to quality medical care and healthcare professionals get stuck in the middle.

Have you ever wondered about the role money plays in medical practice today for both allopathic and alternative health care approaches? Have you ever wondered about the control exercised by doctors, hospitals, pharmaceutical companies, and HMOs? Have you ever wondered why so many doctors and healthcare professionals are leaving their practices in huge numbers? Have you ever wondered why we have not been informed of all the options available to us rather than pushing a pill as the primary answer? Have you ever wondered why we are not encouraged to mentor and share information with each other particularly if it works for someone and is successful as a non-invasive approach? Perhaps information in the medical community is incomplete also, and as it becomes available, we will see changes in healing that will benefit all of us.

Look around. The world we have created and live in today is a direct result of the economic influence, control and doing things somebody else's way – not God's way. Worse, it's doing God's work viewed through the human ego. God needs to be outside the package or box we put Him or Her in – unrestricted in our beliefs and unrestricted in our world. Some innovative physicians are looking beyond the box and seeking to provide the best of all worlds. I support them in their journey.

Human beings are built with innate healing abilities designed uniquely by God. Are we limiting the ability to reach people? What we need is the freedom to touch as many people as possible and awaken them to the gift of healing that is inside them. It does not have to happen over a weekend. You learn a lot in a seminar, and I recommend that people go to learn as much as they can. Trust your heart which one you should investigate and go with that. It can happen in a matter of moments. Many people have read healing books and then healings occurred when they were just "playing" and working on others without benefit of a class. Is that wrong? I don't think so or the healing would not have occurred.

When and who will determine how quickly alternative and complementary solutions can be utilized in healthcare reform? How can other healthcare options help reduce costs? How do Medicare and Medicaid fit into this equation? How can research and outcome tracking help people make informed decisions about alternatives available today? How will the information be made available to help make life or death decisions in healthcare?

Measuring Outcomes with Technology

When people seek healing treatments, they often do not know much about energy medicine and alternative healing techniques. They have questions about what really happens, if anything really happens. As we learn more about the body, more about healing techniques and actually see the results of healing sessions, we can add to the knowledge that helps us understand what happens.

Imaging technology that brings us MRI — Magnetic Resonance Imaging and sonogram devices used in healthcare, is also bringing us devices that can track and measure frequencies all around us. All matter and energy have vibrational frequencies. Humans have vibrational frequencies. Plants, animals, colors, light and sound all have vibrational frequencies.

In my practice, I was introduced to a method or process known as RFI™ developed by the Institute of Technical Energy Medicine, Inc. This technology gives detailed scientific information and objective interpretations for bioenergy fields surrounding the body and in specific regions of the human brain and body. There is an instrument used to take a snapshot of the client's frequency readings before and after the treatment. In this system, there are thirty-six different areas that can be measured around the body. It is possible to see the impact of the healing in that moment of the changing energy fields surrounding the body. The software is then used to enter and translate the frequency readings to colors that have been identified through research. Each color represents a particular range of frequencies. The RFI™ system identifies and interprets fifteen different colors of bioenergy, representing all fifteen colors that can be detected in the optical spectrum of a human eye.

What I have found useful about this process is that it shows bioenergy changes in the client on both health and psychological levels. As the frequencies are entered into the system, a report is produced and then the client receives information about the reading at that moment. The information is enlightening for me as well as for the client. Each day, I take the series of thirty-six measurements on myself, track the changes and identify where there are bioenergy indications of blockages, imbalances and otherwise healthy conditions.

Living from the Heart

My heart is the ultimate barometer that tells me what is truth and what works for me. My actions and integrity decisions are made entirely by me. The consequences of making those choices are mine also. If I am living, breathing, loving and making decisions straight from my heart, the heart can never lie to me. The miracles that are happening are proof that a human blessing or lack thereof is not going to impede the healings that are available from God, Love and Life.

What I think is vitally important, is the ability to walk our talk. As healing practitioners, we are human also. I have to work really hard at walking the same path that I talk. It is extremely difficult. Striving to learn lessons and then live them on a continuing basis is important for all of us. As healers, we must introduce new ways of living to the world, but we must live it first.

For instance, we speak of living in love rather than fear. If we find ourselves reacting in fear, we just need to observe and learn the lesson. We have a tendency to judge ourselves harshly, and condemn our actions when we just need to love ourselves through the lesson and then we can begin to love others. Then we really will be living in love by choice, one decision at a time.

One other issue that has been heavy on my heart is that we truly honor those who come and go in our lives. When we honor others, we honor ourselves and we honor God. When we dishonor others, we really dishonor ourselves and God. After all, we are all connected. What you do to others, you do to yourself. Dishonor, what is that you ask? Dishonor includes behaviors described as verbal abuse, withholding feelings or information, discounting or minimizing other people's ideas and talents, misrepresenting yourself in any way. It includes changing what people say to support your ideas or making you feel more powerful at someone else's expense, by ignoring their requests and treating them with less respect than they or you deserve. When you look at your actions and words, you know whether they honor or dishonor the people in your lives.

Love and gratitude are so important in our lives. As we grow and mature, it becomes very clear how life lessons help us move forward. We would not be here without the gifts of God, the love and life lessons of our mates, friends, family, co-workers, strangers and whoever else has agreed to assist us through these difficulties and learn from them. I would encourage you to thank God for the blessings in your lives and also for the people who have loved us enough to volunteer for the hard stuff.

CHAPTER 10

HEART 2 HEART CONNECTIONS

"When I heal people, I heal them from heart to heart. I speak to people from heart to heart."

Working and traveling around the country with healing seminars enabled me to meet and connect with thousands of people. As I worked with more people, I gathered more information. With more than 3,000 practitioners who graduated from the courses, there was an abundance of information from different sources, but limited methods for sharing that information.

Occasionally, miracles happened and only later did we realize the impact on our lives. These wonderful people helped me experience more dimensions of this work. God blessed me with a good memory for remembering people I had met. They were important to me and I learned a great deal from each one who blessed my life. This provided a series of opportunities, events and sessions that enabled me to do the work I was born to do.

I had a lot of questions. The experiences in my sessions were sometimes unusual, and when I was brave enough to ask if anyone was experiencing similar things, I was told more often than not – I was alone in what was happening.

I started talking about the experiences with small groups of people. It was exciting and at the same time, a little scary. I went out on a limb, and as a friend said to me, "You've been out on a limb for about 2½ years now." That's about the time I became involved in this work. People started telling me about how the words I shared "changed their lives". People said, "You need to get these messages out on the Internet. The words, the tones and the messages need to be heard by as many people as possible."

I spoke with a friend who said, "You need to be reaching people in the government. I think there is work we are supposed to do together."

The Three Queens

Nancy Philpott is one of the most talented nurses, administrators, healers and business professionals I have ever met. She graduated from nursing school in 1972 and committed her heart and soul to "Do No Harm" like the many hundreds of thousands of practitioners who chose that path before her. She embraced the healer in her to passionately and idealistically serve the medical needs of those whose lives she touched.

Twenty years later, she completed her Masters degree from Southwest Texas State University. After practicing as a clinical nurse for twenty years, she believed that she now had both the credentials and the experience to succeed in healthcare education and administration. She watched the medical community begin to drift away from its purpose of offering "safe harbor" for those souls seeking relief from illness and injury.

In 2001, she and her family gathered around the bedside, held each other, grieved immensely and watched powerlessly as her mom's body ravaged by cancer and the ensuing medical treatments received took its final breath as her spirit escaped and moved on. The blessings and gifts Nancy received from her mom during her illness and death changed her forever both personally and professionally.

In 2002, Nancy took a soul-searching journey inward to find answers to personal and professional questions. She realized that like the healthcare delivery system that she worked in, she had become disconnected from her heart and the hearts of those she had passionately committed to serve.

Nancy, in her own words, was "deeply humbled by and grateful for the events, people, lessons, and blessings that led me to that discovery and transformation. It was in this discovery that I allowed my spirit to fully awaken, remember and embrace my true purpose in life. My purpose is simply to love, live and connect from my heart. This discovery helped me to once again become the passionate, idealistic and committed spirit who believes the world can and will change if I commit to consciously remain grounded in love and connect from my heart."

She was drawn to the healing seminars. I met her and we felt an instant friendship that if people were to see us, they would think we had known each other forever.

Nancy became excited, passionate and committed to assisting others in the implementation of a new healthcare model for healing the mind, body and spirit. These programs offered an alternative or complementary approach to health and healing. They were and still are provided by a team of like-minded practitioners and individuals dedicated to consciously live, love and connect from the heart as their lives touch others. We are dedicated to live the model as well as embrace, mentor and support those who choose this path on their healing journey.

Her vision for moving energy healing to the next level promotes a wider utilization and acceptance in the healthcare industry. Her vision is helping ease the transition from where we were to where we need to be in order to make alternative and complementary healing as well as energy medicine available to more people. By moving to the next level, more people will have access to the healing benefits provided as insurance companies and medical practitioners work together to incorporate the benefits of energy medicine and alternative healing in their companies and practices. She is not alone in her endeavor.

Part of her commitment is to create, market and implement a wellness program designed to uniquely benefit people learning to make healthy choices and eliminate suffering in all areas of their health. This program encompasses the bioenergy feedback, health assessments, nutritional needs and recommendations for people to live healthier lives. This program is about helping people own their power and make healthier choices. This program also introduces tools that help people find out where they are in the process, cope with issues and then change their lives.

Marie Schilly, an Animal Communicator, has achieved recognition and respect in the corporate world, intuitive medicine, and as a gifted intuitive healer. A mutual friend in a Los Angeles seminar introduced her to me. I believe you meet people by Divine Appointment.

Marie has given me many precious gifts. Her insights into the "Gifts from the Heart" have been so appreciated and so necessary for my understanding. She showed me what important roles our pets play in healing us, their owners. She provided great insight into the roles we play when we are in costume, and the barriers to success in business, finance and personal relationships because of these roles.

Marie is also a practicing archetypal consultant. She has been a student in a degree program over the last two years taught by Dr. Carolyn Myss and Dr. Norm Shealey. Her studies have uniquely qualified her to help us understand more about the impact of archetypes in our daily lives.

These two women changed my life. The creative birth of the Heart 2 Heart Programs has been a life changing experience for all of us. At first, It was almost as if the birth occurred without any labor pains. As we began discussions on what we could do to help change the lives of practitioners and clients, the idea was born and took on a life of its own. We greatly desire to mentor people and give them tools that really work to change the way they approached challenges in their lives. There are many things that are still being finalized, but in general terms, I wanted to share some of the exciting and the amazing things that have occurred as a result of this creative process.

As the three of us came together, we learned lessons – life lessons that we had to experience first hand before we could lead other people through the process. We developed a concept of how a life management program would benefit individuals, families and groups of people. We were so proud of the ease in which the concept was created, and then the real work began. We talked and planned how we could share this program with other practitioners who wanted more information and feedback from healing experiences. We ventured out into the world with a wonderful healing approach that was simple and effective, and yet expanded the options available in medical care today. Very quickly we realized, this was not just another dimension for healing practitioners' work. This was a way to reach millions of people who are unhappy in their current situations and want real change in their lives.

Core Values

Each and every person struggles with common issues at the core of who we are. We want to be loved and accepted. We want to experience financial success. We want to be the best we can be. We want to live and connect with other people. We want to change and enrich our lives. We want to discover what our life purpose is and how we can live it. We want to let go of baggage from our past. We want to deal with issues that keep us from succeeding at our goals and relationships. We want to escape from domestic violence and other life failures. But how are we going to accomplish that easily and effortlessly? Can it even be done, much less effortlessly and easily?

People have experienced pain and agony in their lives. These pains and injuries may be physical, emotional, mental and even spiritual in nature. How can we help people grow and release the pain and anguish they have suffered? If you listen to them, you will hear how they have tried a number of methods to deal with this pain. But why hasn't the pain gone away? Why does it still persist? Why do they continue to experience depression, hurt, anger, frustration and fear?

We felt the answers were unique to each individual. What we found during the development of this program was that we all had core values in our lives. Until we discovered what those core values were, we continued to live out of integrity. We might not have known exactly why we had a problem with an event, choice or situation. We just knew that there was something that felt wrong and was not working for us. We personally found great value in each of us determining our core values, our life purposes and the process of verifying if we were actually living that life.

We are just now learning about the long-term impacts on men who have a particularly difficult time dealing with emotional issues in their lives. In our society, men have been conditioned since around the age of 5 that it is not OK to cry. They are told, "Be tough. Don't let anyone know if you are sad or hurt. It is not acceptable for you to experience those feelings." Then they marry and we as women beg them to share their feelings with us. How confusing! The only emotions they can safely harbor according to society are success, anger, sexual pleasure and happiness. It seems to me that men cope by segregating parts of themselves. The denial of these feelings of fear and frustration contribute to domestic violence and keep men from living whole and healthy lives. Until men realize their emotions are part of their strength and their wholeness, we will never win this battle. The freedom to feel should be one of our human rights.

Costumes and Archetypes of Life

Archetypes can help us understand more about who we are, what coping skills we have acquired and developed, and how we use those coping skills to interact with others. These archetypes help us live in ways that can contribute to achieving our life purpose or keep us from achieving our goals. If your life purpose were to be a scientist and you were destined to discover a new cure for disease or to introduce new laws of physics, more than likely your list of archetypes would include a pioneer and perhaps a healer.

These archetypal responses affect how you form relationships with friends and family. These archetypal responses also help you understand how issues affect you in business and personal decisions. Perhaps your father was a doctor and four generations of your ancestors were doctors, too. The pressure to become a doctor would be great. The process may begin when you receive your very own doctor's medical kit on your fifth birthday. You are beginning to don the healer archetype. But what if you were destined to win the Pulitzer Prize in literature? Your poet archetype and healer archetype may find peace and harmony together in your life, but if you felt you had to give up your dreams as a poet, you may grow to resent the time and demands that the healer places on your life. If you became a healer to please your family or because it was expected of you, you may grow to resent that decision. These situations are neither right nor wrong. They either work or they don't work. The archetypes just help us understand more clearly what influences are involved in our life choices.

By determining the particular archetypes in your life, you can understand more about what motivates you and the coping mechanisms you use. The list of archetypes is long and includes Rulers (kings, queens, princes and princesses), Sages (critics and judges), Seekers (pioneers and explorers) and Healers (doctors, practitioners and nurses). You can recognize which character responds in certain situations. Immediately when the words leave your mouth, you observe and understand the visionary or perhaps even the teacher has just spoken. The words and phrases illustrate commanding, critical or perhaps even creative ideas that you could tie directly to an archetype. You may respond as a queen, a critic or a pioneer. What people are expecting in response from you may be straight from your archetypal role. Once you acknowledge which character is responding, you can step out of costume, observe the actions and provide a true answer that speaks from your heart. It is like you move from the stage as a leading character in the play to the director's chair. The true gift of the archetypes is that you recognize when you are responding in a manner that is inauthentic, observe the situation, consciously decide to reconsider your response, and then respond directly and powerfully from the heart.

When the three of us, Nancy, Marie and I, met together in Las Vegas, we felt an instant bond. The guides began to refer to us as "The Three Queens". We thought it was pretty cool, and then we learned on the light side, there are benevolent queens and on the dark side, there are wicked queens. On rare occasions, you would see glimpses of a wicked queen response. Although you observed the response, you didn't have to engage your feelings. There is a powerful healing opportunity to just observe and be aware in order to make choices that work better for you. It's not that it's even right or wrong. If it's working, that's great. But if what you are doing is not working for you, you have the power to choose differently. By observing your words and actions through the archetypal filters, you can realize where you want to change how you respond to people or events. By making conscious decisions, you regain your power.

The archetypes help you understand why you meet someone and know immediately that there is a connection. They may appear familiar to you. You may sense there is something you are destined to accomplish together or a lesson or gift you share. The three queens discovered common archetypes that we shared and others that provided greater dimension for us individually and for the group as a whole.

I found it fascinating that many of the questions I had about why I did certain things in my life were illuminated when I discovered my personal archetypes. For example, I was not surprised to learn my list of archetypes included a visionary, builder, pioneer, teacher, judge, politician, networker and healer among others. Suddenly it made sense why I was a Mayor and a healer. They were parts of who I was. I was relieved to know that my frustration when plans were made, modified, redrawn and then not implemented were a result of me not only being a pioneer and visionary, but also the builder that could add form and function to the vision. My builder would become testy when we spent so much time on the preparation, but we never actually finished the job.

For the visionary in me, I have always been a catalyst for change in my family, my work and even my community. I had the ability to envision a different future in vivid detail. I knew the goal. It was as if a snapshot of the future had been placed in front of me. As I studied my archetypes, it became clear that the visionary and pioneer archetypes in me was part of the reason I was comfortable forging new territories and going in new directions. On many occasions, I would press the limits and boundaries, and then go one step beyond just to see what would happen. The builder archetype would then begin creating, in order to move the vision to reality.

The teacher archetype in me felt an obligation to teach others about the lessons I learned. I had difficulty realizing that they must learn in a way that makes sense to them, or even go through the learning experience themselves to live that experience. My job to teach included finding ways to communicate the goals, lessons and visions effectively for all who needed or were willing to learn. They had to choose to learn before I could teach. Sometimes people just need to see things with an illustration that they can relate to before the light bulb clicks on. When I was a corporate trainer, it was important to me that the lights came on when students were learning new things. I had to truly embrace the fact that I cannot teach anyone anything. I can only help them to discover it within themselves. At one point, I found that I became so invested in teaching others, that I didn't have the time to live my own life.

The honorable judge was able to evaluate situations, and was not afraid to make wise decisions. It was enlightening and at the same time very sad to see how the dark side or "wicked judge" would make an appearance in my life. The "dark" side of the judge had a tendency to make snap judgments on occasion and jump to conclusions prematurely. The honorable judge could look at all sides of a situation and see it from all angles. The critical judge would offer criticism rather than suggestions for a more effective solution.

The healer in me was concerned about healing at all levels. Above all, I was here to heal – old wounds, situations, relationships and people. My archetypes fit together in a picture of a life that reflects who I have been, what I learned, and what I have to relinquish to live authentically. What amazed me about defining the archetypes was that once you knew whom and what they were, you suddenly recognized them as you would an old friend or even an antagonist. You could switch suddenly to an observer role, and that allowed you to see things from a far better vantage point. You recognized, "Oh, that was my visionary, my pioneer or even my inner child." When you lived an authentic life, you gained the ability to be true to your heart rather than living "in character."

Learning more about the archetypes helps us determine what is at the heart of the situation that tugs and pulls on the dark side of a particular archetype. Usually fear is the source of that particular emotional response to a situation.

I believe the whole world is a stage. We are given costumes – archetypes – or we decide to develop them in response to life experiences. Our families, jobs, friends and life activities are all plays within other plays within the big play that is life. In this play, or perhaps it is an improvisation, we play mothers, fathers, children, employees, villains, leaders, healers, etc. We get so caught up in our roles that we forget our true purpose in being here. We interact in the roles or archetypes. We get so engaged in the "play" and busyness that we forget we have a life to live. Once we recognize that we are wearing costumes, we can begin to look beyond the archetypes and discover who we really are.

When we look into our hearts, we can begin to live outside our parts in the play, take off our costumes and live. When we find the courage to live through the heart, we have no more need for costumes. We find out what is really important in our lives. When we live authentically, we are actively choosing our dreams, and the activities that support our dreams. We live each day with heart to heart connections among friends, families, communities, civic groups, and co-workers, and our lives reflect richer relationships.

313

As I traveled along this journey, I noticed that my life changed in amazing ways. I started looking at people with love – not romantic love, but the love that God has for all of us, His children. When we judge situations and people through our human eyes, we see only the costume. When we look at people with our hearts, we see them as children of God, authentic people, in spite of their costumes. We see them as a part of ourselves.

When people realize there is more to life than they are experiencing, they begin their search for answers. People may feel an emptiness, and although they may have achieved success in the eyes of the world, it has not brought the happiness that they expected in their own personal lives. There are many ways to understand and release the blocks they live with that keep them from living their best life. How many people do you know that are still asking, "What do I want to be when I grow up?" when they are in their forties and even fifties? How do they change their lives? How do they get out of the box? How do they know what program will work for them? There are programs that work and I am convinced that you will be drawn to the program that works for you.

Healing Anger and Changing Lives

My personal commitment is creating, marketing and implementing the Heart 2 Heart Anger Management Program™ and the Heart 2 Heart Life Management Program™. These programs have been designed with tools that help people change the way they live. Many "Gifts of the Heart" have been instrumental in creating these tools. Why not live so that every day is truly a blessing?

Instead we fly off the handle when something small adds to our mounting number of irritations. Tempers rage out of control and we say things we wish we could take back later. We hurt deep inside because of wounds or feelings of inadequacy, but that makes us feel powerless. Anger and rage make us feel like we are in control, and it's more comfortable to feel those emotions than fear, frustration or hurt. When we think back over the situations where our tempers have led us to verbal abuse or our fists physically abuse others, we realize this is just not working for us. Unless we change how we react and take time to choose differently, we will continue to do what we have been doing with the same results.

Anger and rage are escalating in alarming degrees in our society today. I know how anger affects a person. I lived it. I know how anger is really a mask to cover hurt, frustration, fear or disappointment. If we found a way that would heal the wounds that erupt in angry outbursts then wouldn't everyone benefit?

Our mission is to find ways we can share this system of healing and life management to help people change the way they live and together, change the world we live in. As you turn on the nightly news, there are often stories of fatal accidents in road rage incidents. This week there was a story of increasing incidents from air rage. Uncontrollable anger and rage are escalating and people, both victims and perpetrators, are suffering from the incidents.

In my community as with many communities, we have an alternative school disciplinary program for students who have made bad choices. These are not bad people. They have just made poor decisions. They are children, teenagers and young adults who have been influenced by the world they live in, the parental environment at home, and the situations they find themselves in at school, in the community and with their peers. Recently I heard that we are bombarded by over 2,500 negative images per minute on television. Negative thoughts, ugly words, temptations and sharp comments permeate our lives. This is the power of the media and the people who influence us. Unless we reach out to these students, and others like them, and show them better ways to deal with their issues of life, death, drugs and choices, we will be faced with continual increases of people's inability to cope with life itself. That cost is too high to suit me. Not one life can be sacrificed. ***NOT ONE***. We have to reach them all. We can't afford to ignore anyone!

People may be having a crisis in their lives. They may have had a life changing event and feel like dumping on an innocent person. They may be struggling to just survive. When someone does something to irritate us – what do we do? We get defensive. We argue. We fight. We snap at them. We react. We act as if our past dictates our future.

What other options are available to us in love? When we choose to use words that heal, we all benefit. We can smile. We can love them. We can understand their position. We can put ourselves in their shoes. We can empathize with them. We can be non-judgmental about them. We can observe their difficulty and

316

offer a helping hand without adding our two cents worth of advice. We have all kinds of other alternatives. We can bring positive energy into every situation or we can bring negative energy into every situation. Free will gives us the choice which options we choose.

A smile, a kind word, an underserved forgiveness, a blessing when things look so bad – these are the kinds of things that can change people from the inside, out. How many times have you received a hug when you deserved to be chewed out? If we were to try and add more of these positive reactions into our lives when our spouses, children, mothers, fathers, siblings and co-workers push our buttons, we could begin to make a difference in our world. It's hard, but it could be done. It just takes commitment on our part. We can create a habit in turning to love rather than anger, fear, frustration or hurt. We do this one person, one situation at a time. When we make a mistake, and we will, we learn the lesson and begin again. We choose differently the next time. It is so important that we reach every single person who is important to God. As we touch them, we touch God within them. Every person is a connection.

So, where does that take us? It places us in the position to actively create heart connections. But, how do we do that? We experienced a glimpse of this kind of generosity, compassion and love when the disasters happened in New York, Pennsylvania and Washington D.C. on September 11th, 2001. Our hearts were engaged. We gave generously. We bonded together as a nation.

We had the opportunity to look past our differences and see ourselves as united citizens of the United States.

We must go one step further and see ourselves as citizens of the world. When things happen in other parts of the world, we are not isolated. We think we are, but truly they impact us as well. In a recent *Oprah* show[61] that aired on November 4th, 2002, CNN did a report around the world that spoke to the sentiment of how we in the U.S. are perceived.

People around the world saw the United States as the rich kid who seemed spoiled rotten. Some of their impressions were based on the opulence we enjoyed as they saw it through the media. We appeared to them as generally well fed and drove nice cars while people in our country and those around the world are starving. People interviewed around the world believed us to engage in promiscuous sex and formed opinions about us based on our television programs, namely *The Jerry Springer Show*. When September 11th occurred, there was an outpouring of sympathy for our nation from all of our allies, friends and even some of our enemies. When bombs went off in that resort in Bali, the Aussies, our allies who fought side by side with us in several wars and conflicts, had casualties that we did not acknowledge. The sympathy we received was not shared when other countries experienced disasters of their own. The world began to change their sympathy to disdain, when we began to aggressively promote vengeance and war. They went on to report that our government was seen as supporting democracy at home and tyranny abroad.

There are so many people in the world who are less fortunate than we are and we turn a deaf ear and a blind eye to their suffering. When we hold ourselves separate from those who are God's children, are we not holding ourselves separate from Him, too? I recently wrote the First Lady, Laura Bush, a letter. I know she is a valued confidant of our President. I earnestly asked her to speak with him. We are a powerful nation, but our approaches make it seem like we are powerless. We can change the world we live in, through peaceful initiatives, not war. Just because we have the weapons of destruction does not mean we have to use them. Would we comply with the reciprocal requests to disarm, if asked by other countries? Fear permeates our decisions about terrorism and terrorists. Maybe we need to look deeply into the problem and see where we can understand and help them find solutions through collaborative efforts, rather than declaring war. Many of the conflicts we are engaged in are the direct result of training that the United States provided these individuals in the warfare tactics they now use against us.

Must we pay the price for these mistakes with the lives of our soldiers? I have always been very thankful and proud of the American soldiers who protect our freedoms. I know the President faced great difficulties when deciding what action was to be taken. Once the decision was made to engage in the war, I kept praying not only for our President and the soldiers, but also the enemy. I believe we are to love those that persecute us as Jesus taught us. I still believed that other leadership options were available to us that we did not act upon. I recognized that the people of Iraq would obtain freedom from their political prisons. I was also concerned that when we, as Americans, overrode the wishes of countries abroad, how could we be respected as a nation?

Recently someone told me, "War is inevitable. War is prophesied for our future in the Bible." Can we see a different vision than that? Just where do we start to change the world in which we live? When do we begin to heal and touch people from other countries who need our help? When do we begin to take care of our poor and homeless? When do we start to value the land, water and environment that God has provided for us?

Heart 2 Heart Programs™

We believe it must begin by healing ourselves first. We know we have a program that works. The Heart 2 Heart Programs have worked in our lives and we believe they will work in the lives of you, your friends, family and everybody you know. We further believe that once you go through these programs and begin living with the results, others will notice and ask, "What's different about you?" Wouldn't it be wonderful to begin to share this with them and teach them how to change their lives?

In order to know how to address the problems we face and achieve our dreams, we must know where we are right now. Where do we begin? An individual, a group or even a family can undertake this process. This evaluation includes an assessment of the physical, emotional, mental and spiritual condition of the individual or group. The process indicates ailments or injuries and identifies nutritional deficiencies or strengths, as well as energy frequency readings. Plans and solutions are recommended to address any issues identified in the assessment phase. We have implemented tools to help individuals and groups understand the effect of stressors on their bodies, minds and spirits. Techniques are shared about how people can deal with issues that have historically given them grief or caused them difficulties in relationships. If there are specific concerns over anger, money, leadership issues or people pleasing, we coach them through the appropriate program for them. These proven tools and exercises empower people to make a difference in their lives. These tools help us heal and live healthy, productive lives so we can enjoy our relationships more fully.

Healing Relationships

What would it take to learn to love yourself and in turn, develop more loving relationships with everyone in your life? How would you feel when you cultivate more loving relationships with your children, your spouse and other family members? Through this program, we learn who we are, what affects us from the past, who we have been and how by discovering ourselves, we can paint a brighter future. When we begin our inner journey, we empower our inner child, our inner teenager, our inner young adult, middle-aged and even our senior adult to be totally and completely honest with ourselves. By communicating with the different parts of who we are, we can learn the secrets behind our love, hate, disdain, pride or the myriad of other emotions that keep us from reaching our potential. We can find out what truths they have to share with us, how proud they are of us or exactly when they became so disgusted and just gave up on us. This process can be both easy and the hardest thing you have ever done. This process can be enlightening and extremely liberating. We have an opportunity to discover, learn from our experiences and embrace who we are. By accepting all of who we are, loving ourselves unconditionally, and forgiving ourselves for our shortcomings, we learn to own our own power.

One of the most important lessons I learned in this program was how to embrace and love all the parts of me that I had denied or disowned. I enjoyed getting to know me. I enjoyed remembering who I was before I became influenced by the world around me and changed who I was based on the experiences in my life. It was sad and disappointing to discover that I had dishonored the child in me as well as the adult with choices I made. It was enlightening, liberating, revealing and healing to embrace, love and forgive myself for all I had done to me. As I performed my life review, I saw how I had been supported and loved throughout my entire life – even when I did not recognize that fact.

People who undertake this life-changing program find courage to work through the difficulties and challenges that help them heal. There may be a temptation to quit before you complete the work. You have to be committed to really begin living a different way. The work may seem hard, but that's because people rarely take the time to study themselves in detail. It is definitely worth the investment of time and energy to learn more about who you are and why you are where you are today in your life. It can make a tremendous difference in the way people live their lives. I know.

Each step along the way has been lived by me and the other practitioners who share their experiences and knowledge with you.

Everyone has his or her own unique and wonderful story. Everyone has challenges. Sometimes it takes great courage to share the failures in our lives. There is great liberation in acknowledging the truth and finding ways to change how you live. We will not ask you to do anything we have not done before you. We will guide you and help you discover answers along the way, because we know the way and we have traveled down this path before you. We will coach you in a way that will support and help you reach your goals of living your life purpose with love, joy and peace. We will provide a network of mentors and trainers in your area to help you adjust and deal with issues through every step of the program. They will even support you after you have completed the work. When you see the miracles at work in your life, you can learn how to share these programs with others.

As we have proceeded along this journey, new opportunities and new programs presented themselves. I am certain that as we discover new challenges in our lives, there will be additional learning experiences and programs to share with you. Two that have been suggested take the "Gifts from the Heart" and implement them in the Heart 2 Heart Healing Program™ and the Heart 2 Heart Connections Program™. These programs help extend alternative healthcare options to more people and achieve greater impact in the energy medicine and alternative healing community. Our goal is and will continue to be focused on providing tools and approaches at an affordable cost to help people live healthier and happier lives. We are committed to the freedom of observing and measuring outcomes. This will help us make continual improvements to the process along the way.

We fully expect that as we have experienced things outside the box, our clients will also experience things we did not anticipate that add new dimensions to the work. As we see how this work manifests itself in people without restrictions or limitations, we want to embrace the differences and learn from them. And as uncomfortable as it makes us sometimes from a human ego perspective, we want to relinquish the need to control the outcomes and results. As we embrace the freedom and look outside the box for expectations, who knows what we will discover!

What if you could learn to speak your truth more lovingly? What if you could take control of your health every day for the rest of your life? What if you allowed the flow of abundance to affect all areas of your life? What if you could choose to own and use your power rather than feel powerless in situations? These programs empower us in the ways we communicate to our families, our spouses, our friends, our co-workers and even strangers. We practice ways to live differently, choosing innovative and intuitive solutions that are straight from the heart.

Would you like to learn how to increase the joy in your life and make your dreams come true? Would you like to learn how to be... just be? Many people find themselves in the frenzied world and fight to keep up with all the activities they feel compelled to accomplish.

In work, there is competition to do more, complete more activities, work on more projects, and participate in more groups. We find fewer moments to enjoy life. We have difficulty setting limits and boundaries. We go on vacations with cell phones and e-mail communications, because we do not honor ourselves or our families by saying, "This is my time to be with my family. I won't be available for communication during my vacation." We find few opportunities to enjoy nature at its best. We can prioritize time spent with family as opposed to working long hours. As we remember how important it is to be... just be, we can choose actively to live more simply, make healthier choices for ourselves, and experience life as a human being rather than a human doing.

I have been able to create and enjoy true heart to heart connections with people that I have just met and also with people who have been in my life from the very beginning. The quality of my life has increased tremendously. Even through the ups and downs, I have been blessed with joy, serenity, compassion and a new exciting heart connection to the Divine. I encourage you to find a quiet place and ask your heart, "Am I enjoying everything I deserve to in my life? Do I know what my dreams are and am I achieving them? Are there things I can do to heal and become a better father, mother, daughter, son, etc? Where do I need to go from here?" Listen very carefully to that still, small voice inside.

CHAPTER 11

RECONNECTING BACK TO GOD

"When God reconnects with people, He doesn't just reconnect with hands. He reconnects with spirit, mind and heart. When He speaks, He reconnects. When He looks, He reconnects. When He embraces, He reconnects."

Many people who have had extraordinary experiences with this healing shared how they have had a near-death experience. Two of my clients said they had experienced this energy when they were children. Each of them had had a near-death experience. They both told me how they would take the energy and play with it in their hands. One client said, she stopped playing when she realized other people couldn't play with the energy and she became frightened of the unknown. In Dr. Pearl's book, *The Reconnection: Heal Others, Heal Yourself* [62], he related how his mother experienced death and then life again as he was being born. When we die, we become One again with God and a part of the Oneness that brings us back into wholeness.

When my second marriage ended in 1995, I was traveling back from Minneapolis and had purchased Betty Eadie's book,

Embraced by the Light[63]. I read the book on the flight back to Dallas. I was so enthralled, I couldn't put the book down, and I resonated with her story. I felt the love in Chapter 4 as she and Jesus stood together with their lights merging together. I felt the love. I recommended this book to others facing their own deaths, the death of a loved one or other crises in their lives. I knew the love experienced by the author in this book would help them. I bought copies of the book and distributed it to people I knew who were struggling with life and death issues. It touched me in a miraculous way, and I know it made the divorce I was experiencing a little easier to accept. The divorce brought my life, as I had known it, to an end. Because of the circumstances surrounding the divorce, I changed jobs, homes, family relationships and life, as I had known it for over ten years.

When I arrived at the courthouse for the divorce proceedings, it was a time of great personal failure for me. Not once, but twice had I ventured into divorce court and down this path. I thought I had chosen more wisely the second time around. I read my daily Bible reading that morning. It was Ezra 10:1-14. The passage was all about divorce. What a surprise, but I figured it was meant just for me. I knew that somehow this was exactly what was supposed to happen and although painful, I would get through it.

Hitting the Wall

This life after death experience intrigued me. Once or twice I remembered an incident in late 1980 or early 1981. I went to softball practice and we were rained out. Some of my teammates and I went to a restaurant and bar, and we proceeded to drink for most of the day. I had my first drink when I was the legal age of 18 and I was never much of a drinker. This day was different for some reason. I kept up with everyone drink for drink. I have no idea why I decided to do that. It was probably for some stupid reason, perhaps to show how "cool" I was. Who knows? I was not sober when I left the restaurant. I drove home – thankfully without incident. I lay on my couch. At some point, I became thirsty and went into the kitchen for some water. The next thing I knew was that I was lying on the floor with the remains of the water in the glass on top of me. I thought to myself, "I better go sleep this off." Then I went to bed.

The next day, I awoke with a headache or what I thought was a hangover at the top of my head. It was the strangest thing. If I were wearing a beanie on the top of the head, it would be that area that hurt. I thought that it was a strange place to experience a hangover, but I didn't really know how a hangover felt and dismissed it. I went into the kitchen and was surprised to see a hole in the kitchen wall. Just an inch above the baseboard was an indention the exact size of the top of my head. I couldn't quite believe that my head created that hole. It was ½ inch deep. It looked as if someone had taken a bowling ball and slammed it into the wall. I crawled over on my hands and knees to get a better look. Much to my amazement, hairs from my head were actually stuck to the hole. I considered myself very lucky to have lived through the experience without incident and didn't think much about it until 20 years later.

During December 1985, my cousin was killed in a hit and run accident. He was jogging beside the road and was struck and killed by a car. The driver was identified by an eyewitness, but was never convicted of the crime. My cousin had just turned twenty-one three short days before he died. In dealing with the grief, I came across a number of books about death and near-death experiences. I read about them in *Life After Life* by Raymond Moody and *Beyond Death's Door* by Maurice Rawlins. I was unable to put them down. The people who had experienced death and returned were forever changed by the experience.

I kept wondering if there was more to the falling incident. In April 2002, I was visiting another healing practitioner. During our discussion and feedback session, she said, "Tell me about hitting the wall." At first, I did not recall the incident and then the light bulb came on. I told her about hitting the wall and asked, "Did I die that day?" Her answer was, "Yes, you did."

What I found incredulous about the whole thing was that everything I had read about everyone who shared his or her near-death experience was very similar. The person went into the tunnel, saw the light, stood with Jesus and felt this incredible love. I remembered nothing about my experience. All I recalled was that I resonated with Betty Eadie's story. I was curious why I had no recollection of the event.

Gifts from the Heart, 9/12/02 – No Near-Death About It!

During a session with another client, this comment was shared.

"Vicki, you have had a near-death experience. You died. There was nothing near about it." [64]

God is omnipresent. That means He is everywhere all the time. He envelops us with His love all the time. We perceive Him as distant, but He can never leave us. He is with us in times of great joy and great sorrow and everything in between. He embraces us when we die and welcomes us into His presence. His presence surrounds us and 1 John 4:8 NIV tells us that, "Whoever does not love does not know God, because God is love."

Review of Gifts from the Heart, 6/21/02 – You Died

In the Gifts from the Heart message from June 21, 2002, I was reminded of my strange behavior the day I hit the wall.

"We were so taken aback by your actions that day – the nature of your actions! You really hit the wall! Not to truly – boy, did you hit the wall!"

"This experience allowed us to come to you – stronger, more visible. When people die or come close to death, they take energy from the other side and bring it back. It's like if you throw a tennis ball into a pool of water and bring some water back with the tennis ball. Molecules from the water are still in the tennis ball. It's the same with people. It's the same with you." [65]

How amazing! When we get near to death or have a near-death experience, we are forever changed because God's love and energy from heaven touches us and comes back with us. Have you ever encountered someone who has had a near-death experience? I have been privileged to know several. There is a special, soft quality about them that honors who they are and who you are. They exude a loving, gentleness about them.

"You hit the wall. You were out. You went there. We were there. Lola was there. Francis was there. Jeanine was there. Erica was there. Cathy was there. They all were there."

"When you went there, we were able to work with you – bring you up to speed. You wanted to stay. You begged. You cried. God said, 'Go. You're not ready yet. It's not your time. Go.' It's OK. We know it's hard. This life is not meant to be easy. Those who have a purpose must live that purpose."

"The thing about death – when death occurs, people think this is the only time God envelops you with His love. God envelops us all the time. Most people see premonitions of life as it comes to an end. They bring themselves to be ready." [66]

What I really learned is that I could have stayed there, but I would not have lived my life purpose had I stayed. My purpose would be unfulfilled. It must have been a very difficult choice for me at that time. I can imagine how hard it was to leave that loving place in God's presence and come back into this body to continue my journey.

Review of Gifts from the Heart, 5/11/02 – Death and the Divine Connection

"It [doing this work] is not about the length of time. It is about love. You are about love. The more love you put into this work, the more healing occurs."

"Reconnection is so scientific…It is not indicative of the love. It is beyond DNA Reconnection. This is about Divine love, embracing your Divine Purpose. When you embrace this love, you are embracing your Divine Purpose. This allows you to connect with God. People are afraid of that. God is love. We see God as punishing. Only a few of you have seen God as loving. That's why we brought you to the other side. You need to connect with love. People are afraid of God – even more now. The books are meant to help people recognize and understand."

"Just be in connection with this energy. Talk to God. Talk with God? They think they must be Mother Teresa. If you could have people understand, they will talk to God."

"All that is – is your fear. You are keeping yourself from moving forward. Trust and know everything is in Divine order." [67]

Talking to God means communicating in whatever way works for you. It's not about how good you are or if you do everything exactly right. It's about beginning wherever you are right this minute and realize that God is omnipresent within you.

We pray and talk to God. Sometimes we get caught up in the words and forget to feel the love behind the words. We feel emotions and our hearts communicate with God where there are no words at all. This is also a form of prayer. People experience this connection in times of great difficulty where words cannot describe how we feel. We can speak to God through our hearts. We can sing praises to God. We can love others, and ourselves and in doing so, we are communicating and loving God. When we get to that quiet place in our hearts, we hear God talk back to us.

I have understood the truth of this so far and know I will need to be reminded during the turbulent times that I am loved, cared for and protected as I do my work. How awesome is the thought that we can help change our world by the desire and willingness to serve and tell people how very much they are loved by God.

God accepts us wherever we are. If we are not in a place in our lives where we can accept this work and this knowledge, we will be embraced. If we do accept this work and understand that it is working in our lives, we will be embraced. There is no difference. We are all embraced wherever we are in our lives. We are loved, truly loved unconditionally.

Review of Gifts from the Heart, 6/21/02 – Death and the Divine Connection

"We listened to your conversation today – all the misfortunes – the experiences through life – the relationships – men – people. These things profoundly affected your life. You could not grow or be at this point in your life without them."

"The question is… What is the next step? What is the next step?" [68]

When I heard this, I felt like a whiner. What they said to me helped me look at the experience from a different perspective. I was able to embrace the truth that I had learned great lessons through the difficult times of my life. I knew it was time to quit whining and accept the lessons that helped me grow into the person I am today. I am grateful to those who worked with me throughout my life to learn. It was oh, so painful at times, but the person I am today is a happier, healthier and more peaceful person than I used to be and I am still growing and learning.

Review of the Gifts of the Heart, 6/21/02 – The Next Step

"This is what we will not do. We cannot choose your life for you. We can guide and help you. The gifts – you can choose to use them. You can ignore them. You can leave them. Gifts are there. These gifts lay dormant. They will come. When you are ready, they will be ready for you to use… Jesus, our Lord and Savior,

335

as you say, was betrayed, put down, shunned, crucified, but He still showed love for humanity. With gifts, come great power, strength and humility. Love first and foremost mankind. When others turn their back, snarl and turn on you, love them. These gifts work with love..."

"You must learn a true healer heals from the inside, out. This is very important – the inside, out." [69]

We have to choose the direction for our lives. We receive guidance, but the choice is ours alone. We also choose if and when to use the gifts we have been given. When we love others and suffer through the pain of betrayal, we will follow and live the example that Jesus showed us. That is what we are to do with our lives and our gifts. As we love unconditionally, we love God.

Review of the Gifts of the Heart, 6/21/02 – Baby Hannah

They continued to share this story about death, birth and life.

"Hannah battled with these hands, thinking she was crazy. She is beautiful. We work with her. When she came to be, when her mother was pregnant, she had a mission far beyond imagination: 'To bring life, healing and love to this world.'"

"Upon birth, she died, and was as God said, and Jesus was 'resurrected.' Her mother was unaware – she was drugged. The doctor knew, but because baby Hannah

was revived, nothing was said. But the truth is there and it's always been there." [70]

This was another confirmation that we are changed when we come near to death. Baby Hannah came back from heaven with molecules of energy.

Review of the Gifts of the Heart, 8/16/02 – When God Reconnects

"Reconnective is every being of your self and spirit... When God reconnects with people, He doesn't just reconnect with hands. He reconnects with spirit, mind and heart. When He speaks, He reconnects. When He looks, He reconnects. When He embraces, He reconnects." [71]

In the Bible, we are told in Matthew 22:37-40, KJV, ..."Love the Lord, thy God, with all thy heart, with all thy soul, and with all thy mind. This is the first and great commandment. And the second is like unto it, Thou shalt love thy neighbor as thyself. On these two commandments, hang all the law and the prophets."

We forget how God envelops us with His love all the time. We forget how loved we feel when we crawl up into the safe place He offers us and just loves us wherever we are. If we love God, and we love each and every person we know or even strangers on the street, as we love ourselves, we will have little time for judgment, strife or war. If we truly love them, we see them as God sees them – His children who are busy learning the lessons they need to become whole or "holy". My friends get really tired of hearing from me when someone irritates them or makes them angry. I repeatedly say to them, "Love them through it." I know it's hard, because I try to do that and I am often unsuccessful. One of these days, when we take off our costumes, we will see that all of us are a part of God's creation – filled with light, love, truth and peace. We may regret how we treated others when we are faced with the choices we made and the ways we withheld love from God's children and even ourselves. When it is time for our life review, will we be rejoicing or regretful? Now is the time to decide. The messages have reminded me that if we listen, they will talk to us.

I'm listening as fast as I can. There are so many miracles with this work. I am learning new things everyday. You, too, can listen and learn. You can begin your inward journey. You can feel the love God has for you. You can feel how special you are to Him. You can be assured that God is Love. You can feel Him all around you.

Gifts from the Heart, 9/12/02 – Every Soul is Important

During a session with another client, this information was shared. The topics vary, but contain vital information for our future and our world.

"Your gift is because you have been there and back. People want what you have."

"...There are times to reach you. We like to talk to you through water. Use the bath. We love water – cleansing, purifying. Water is going to purify the world."

338

"...Every soul is so important to us that it matters. Every soul is important. Every role is important. To lose 1 to this work dramatically impacts the outcome. We cannot afford one lost soul."

"There is currently the struggle between light and dark. The outcome is still uncertain. That is why our work is still so urgent."

"You are a gift. The time will come when you understand how much."

"Remember the mustard seed? The mustard seed moved mountains. A drop of water can move the world. Water contains all life – all healing. Some day your science will see that, but not today. They have enough trouble with prayer over water."

"You are so blessed. You are so loved. We will move you when the time is right. There are still people to be healed in your area. You are still learning the lesson of loving through the pain. Learn the lesson on a small scale. You will learn the lessons well now so you will be prepared."

"You will know who to trust. You will know who lives in the light and who doesn't. You already know. You just don't trust it. You will know. You will look. You will ask light? Not light? Love? Not love?"

"Mother Teresa lived in light. She was doing God's work. Was she uncertain? Was she frightened? Yes, but she didn't let it show. How would she make ends meet? By the time she passed, she really knew about Divine love and support."

"Two small boys using the world as a toy. We have to let it run its course. We cannot intervene. One ego is larger than the other. They are going to be so disappointed and saddened to come to the other side and realize they have not lived their life purpose."

"… His advisors want war. One is a military man. Do not forget that. He is also seeking glory. Each person who seeks glory is willing to sacrifice many. Others have sought notoriety – they sold their souls to have it."

I asked, "Is the Kabbalah truth?"

"Is the Kabbalah truth? Yes and no. There is a fine line. It's only a part of the picture. There's so much more you don't know about yet. It was written for people to understand then. There's more for now – knowledge for larger consequences. The basic truths of the Kabbalah are truth – important truths. There is more beyond that. There are more advanced truths you will be given. You, the scribe, will come to know them."

"Kabbalah is important for culture to give them their due. It is no different than the Koran, no different than the Torah, no different than the Bible. With all of these, they are the same. It's in volumes that are in the Vatican. Other volumes are there. Only a part of them have been released. It is no different than government and all are about to fall. Systems that control, harm and limit will fall."

"Missy[72] spoke and was genuine. She blocked us after that. We do not understand how we frighten you all… Yes, she needs to channel us. She is afraid. When more people come forward, it will be more accepted. She is afraid of being ostracized – seen as odd."

"You need to be 'Madonna' where being odd is part of the program." [73]

Gifts from the Heart, 9/14/02 – Loving The Dark Side Into Light

During a session with another client, this comment was shared.

"The dark side is like a noisy fan. It's a distraction. If you listen to it, you will only be diverted from your goal. Love, but don't let them distract you from doing your work. This work is vitally important. Love them, no matter what! We can't afford to lose one to the dark side. We need everyone to work together – to hold each other and love each other as One. The dark side is all about ego and humanness. They have forgotten how to love and think they are powerful because of their intellect. The heart is way more powerful than the mind. Remember that! There's NO ONE [individual] and then there's ONE [all]."

Love today. Love him. Help him see the light. After all, it is his choice, but we need him, too. We need him to learn to trust, learn to love, see the hope. We need him to lead the dark side to the light. We love him. This is a triumph of light and dark. It's an old battle."

"You have the same ability to connect in your heart as this one. You know you need to use them more. She will open up to more healing. You will open up to more communication with us. We are working on that with you." [74]

Gifts from the Heart, 9/30/02 – The Fate of the World

During a session with another client, this information was shared.

"...You just weep for no known reason. You don't know why you do. You are crying for humanity. You are crying because you want to move it faster and you can't. Pray. Pray. It is important to pray. Now is the time for prayer. You are not forgotten or forsaken even though at times, you feel we have abandoned you. We have not. It is through this that you will help others."

"They will never see what you see. They will never feel what you feel because you all are chosen. Your gift is to help them find peace. It is time."

"We do not understand the push for war when the country is asking for peace. This does not make sense to us. Can you explain? We cannot understand why when the majority of the country is shifting. We will do what we can, but you have free choice and free will... The battle between good and evil is being fought on all planes."

"...Shadow energy is about power – control – the individual – not love, giving and the One. Manipulation. Manipulation... We stop it with love. Protect yourself with love. Love vanquishes all. Love heals all. Love is

343

*light. Mother Teresa came to no harm. The Dali Llama
comes to no harm. Live in the love. Live in the light."* [75]

Recently, I received an e-mail from a fellow practitioner. She
shared a list of things that young children had to say when asked,
"What is Love?" This is my favorite response:

"Love is what's in the room with you at Christmas if you stop
opening presents and listen." Bobby - age 5

Maybe we will hear something miraculous when we stop and
listen with our hearts. Maybe we will remember Who We Are and
what we came here to do. Maybe we will remember how very much
we are loved.

How do you connect to God? Live your life. Love each person
you meet or encounter in the world. Then you will know and
experience the Power of Lovingness. Then you will know and
experience the Power of Oneness. Then you will know the Power of
Prayer. Then you will know the Power of I AM. Then you will know
intimately that you are One with the Father. You will know without a
doubt that all of us, every single person on the planet, fit together
along with the Father as One. We are connected heart to heart.

Gifts from the Heart, 2/01/03 – Connecting to the Divine

When I thought the book was finished, God showed me yet
another facet of His Magnificence. Hannah came over for a session.
It was a little different than the other sessions, but the message was

still the same. God wants to be real in our lives in His Magnificence. This is what happened during her session.

When she was lying quietly on the message table, her hand began to move in the now familiar ballet. Then her hand caressed her growing baby. Her hand moved to caress her face. What I saw reminded me of someone caressing the face of someone very dear. Her hand brushed each cheek and then her eyes, which were closed. Then her hand lay on her left cheek. Then she began to speak, "I hear a voice that says Chakala, Homina and Usepha."

Her hands moved into two different symbols and then she blew and breathed into the palm of first her right and then her left hand. Then her hands lay quietly on her chest.

She said, "I see angels in here. There's one here." She pointed above her head. Then her hand formed another symbol. "There's another one here." She pointed to her right side. "This one's stronger – a man – much stronger. The other one's a woman."

She pointed to another one on her left side. "This one feels like silk."

Her hands rose over her heart. "There's one here – it's a woman. They call her Mother." Her arms extended as I have seen her do before and then moved slowly.

She began to describe the angels to me. "OK, the first angel above my head seems like a woman. She has gold tips at the bottom of these wings. It seems like wings – feathered wings interchanged with light and gold at the bottom. Her eyes are hazel-colored, but there's so much light in them – they shine in and out."

"The next one – the one to the right. He's strong. Every time I touch him, he shows me his strength. There's so much power."

I asked, "Is he always here?"

She responded, "Yes. His wings extend beyond this room, although I can't see his face. I feel his presence. I see his body."

I asked, "Is he an archangel?"

She responded, "He likes to think of himself as a warrior angel. The archangels are in some kind of different class."

I asked, "Was he in Portland?"

She said, "He said he's always here."

She continued, "The angel on the left – I can't tell the sex on this one. It's more like – now I'm rubbing up and down the wings. It feels like silk – soft – something. It's almost like liquid – something really, really soft. As you run up and down, you could lose your hands in it. It's white, pure white. Very affectionate, very loving, almost childlike."

I asked, "Are they your angels?"

She went on to explain, "They exist differently for different people. They are here for all of us."

She said, "The one above me – Mother. She's very, very nice. She has more colors – blue, gold, white, red, orange, yellow – all the colors. Mother says:

> " *'Not to worry.' She wants me to tell you this: 'She is going to take me in 2 ½ months. But she will bring me back stronger, with more wisdom and more insight. Don't be alarmed.' She tells me to give her your right hand.*"

I walked over to Hannah and placed my right hand in hers. She moved my hands to where she could see the angels. I felt them one by one. I felt the strength of the warrior angel. I felt the angel at her head. I felt "Mother," but I could not feel the angel on the left, the silky angel.

She said, "There's somebody walking around in a sheet. It's a flowing sheet, but I can see His feet moving. When He walks, He changes into different colors, different skin colors. His feet change to white, black, red, blue, and gold feet. He's walking above – more like flowing – like there's wind around Him and behind Him. When He walks, His image changes just like His feet. His robe – His sheet – stays the same. He asked me:"

> *"Do you see Me in your mind?"*

Hannah answered, "Yes." He asked her:

"Why are you here today?"

Hannah answered, "I am here to know You." He responded:

"You have always known Me."

I asked, "Who is He?" She responded, "He says:

'The words are written in the sky – God, Jehovah (He pronounced it – Jahovah), Akrazuel, Elohim...'

He just goes on and on – different languages, different names. He just walks around showing different feet colors and different eye colors. He's beautiful. He has so many different images."

I replied intuitively from what I felt, "He is all of us."

She said, "The more I look at Him, the more He adds to Himself. Now He has wings that I didn't see before now. He keeps changing – even the shape of His wings. His height changes. He says:

'I AM WHO I AM. MAKE NO MISTAKE ABOUT IT. I AM THE LAW. I AM THE WAY. I AM THE TRUTH. I AM YOUR SALVATION. HEAR ME.' "

"He continued:

'Ponder not on a moment's notice or a moment's thought. Don't wonder WHO I AM. **KNOW** *WHO I AM. I*

*AM THE WAY. I AM YOUR SALVATION. Seek Me and
I will seek you.' "*

Hannah went on to say, "Many, many people are behind Him
– He shows me. You can't see how far they go. It's like looking at a
river that never ends. It just doesn't end! Neither do the angels on
both sides of Him. Neither do the children that extend before Him.
They go on and on."

She continued, "There's like a big ball of light on top of Him
that circles around. It doesn't move, because He is in control of it.
When He extends His hands, I see different levels of hands,
different colors – different hands – like a fan almost. He has stars
on His shoulders – big bright stars – big stars. They go on and on –
on both sides like a general. He is the Prince of Peace and
Principalities."

"Now it's just Him again. He does this to show He is real. He
says:

*'Look to Me for answers. Look to Me for Truth. I will
give you rest. I will give you peace.' "*

She continued, "He has a little girl with Him. She has what
looks like a baby doll dress on – It looks blue. First it looked white.
She has long hair – like a brown color with light sun highlights in it.
She has like those little black shoes that girls wear and a light blue
dress. She has long, straight hair, but she's young. Maybe she's...
she's three. She puts up three fingers."

She continued, "She comes to me. She tells me she loves me. She says she'll see me soon. He says:

'He loves you very, very much. He tells me to go now. He'll see me soon.' "

I asked more questions and I received answers. He said,

"Learn. I will give you the tools to learn. I'm more concerned with the Book of Life. The Book of Journeys."

I was a little confused because the "Book of Life" meant something different for me and asked, "My book?" He replied,

"My book. Your book."

Then Hannah said He gave me the "thumbs up" and made imprints with the thumb. He made five imprints.

The remaining moments of this session were spent reviewing scenes and people. I asked a couple of questions for a direction on my path and the people who interacted with me along the way. I asked about my future and was told:

"That is for you to decide. Lead your heart and your feet will follow."

Hannah said, "Today seemed different. I am here, but today, I can still see and hear." [76]

Hannah normally does not remember the words or the information until I share with her what was said. Then she recognizes the words, but it is more like she heard them rather than spoke the words herself. It did seem different, but it was vitally important to share.

God is everyone and everything – all races – all people everywhere in the world. All of us together as One form All That Is. Every single person is special. Every single person is necessary. Every single person is loved beyond our wildest imagination! Together, we are all One.

Vicki L. High

BIBLIOGRAPHY AND READING LIST

Alcyone. *At the Feet of the Master.* Los Angeles, CA: Yogi Publication Society.

Braden, Gregg. *The Isaiah Effect.* New York, NY: Three Rivers Publishing, 2000.

Eadie, Betty J. *Embraced by the Light.* Placerville, CA: Gold Leaf Press, 1992.

Hawkins, David R., M.D. Ph.D. *Power vs. Force.* Carlsbad, CA: Hay House, 2002.

Hurtak, J. J. *The Book of Knowledge: The Keys of Enoch.* Los Gatos, CA: The Academy for Future Science, 1977.

Markova, Darina. *Random Acts of Kindness.* PR: Conari, 2002.

McTaggart, Lynne. *The Field.* New York, NY: Harper Collins, 2002.

Moody, Raymond. *Life After Life.* New York, NY: Bemis, R. Publishing Unlimited, 1981.

Mother Teresa. *No Greater Love.* New York, NY: MJF Books, 1997.

Pearl, Eric S. *The Reconnection: Heal Others, Heal Yourself.* Carlsbad, CA: Hay House, 2001.

Rawlins, Dr. Maurice S. *Beyond Death's Door.* New York, NY: Bantum Books, 1979.

Zukav, Gary and Linda Francis. *Heart of the Soul.* New York, NY: Gale Group, 2002.

Scripture texts used in this work, unless otherwise indicated are taken from *The Holy Bible, King James Version.*

Index

ABOUT THE AUTHOR

Vicki L. High is the former Mayor of Crandall, Texas as well as a healing practitioner. Although an unusual combination, her abilities have enabled her to change the lives of people in her work and community. She has touched people across the nation and shared extraordinary healing experiences that changed her life and others as she received "Gifts from the Heart." She is a domestic violence survivor as well as an accomplished corporate trainer and developer of over 50 courses in healing, professional development and corporate computer application programs. Everything she has experienced has led her to perform this work. As an author, she finds a way to share these experiences with the world.

Heart 2 Heart Connections
www.heart2heartconnections.com
Mailing address: P.O. Box 160, Crandall Texas 75114
Phone #: 972-427-3546

Endnotes

[1] Gifts from the Heart. 6.01.95

[2] The Oprah Winfrey Show. March, 2000, Hidden Faces of Anger.

[3] The Oprah Winfrey Show. June 29, 2000, Hidden Faces of Anger.

[4] Eric Pearl. The Reconnection: Heal Others, Heal Yourself. Hay House. 2001.

[5] Eric Pearl. The Essence of Healing Seminar.

[6] Gifts from the Heart. Dallas, Texas. 7.28.00.

[7] Eric Pearl. The Reconnection: Heal Others, Heal Yourself. Hay House. 2001.

[8] J.J. Hurtak. The Book of Knowledge, The Keys of Enoch. The Academy for Future Science. 1977. Key 314:59 and Key 317:22

[9] Eric Pearl. The Reconnection: Heal Others, Heal Yourself. Hay House. 2001.

[10] Eric Pearl. The Reconnection: Heal Others, Heal Yourself. Hay House. 2001.

[11] Braden, Gregg. The Isaiah Effect. Random House. 2000.

[12] Emoto, Dr. Masaru. Messages from Water. HADO Kyoikusha. 2001.

[13] The Holy Bible. 1 John 4:18.

[14] Eric Pearl. The Reconnection: Heal Others, Heal Yourself. Hay House. 2001.

[15] J.J. Hurtak. The Book of Knowledge, The Keys of Enoch. The Academy for Future Science. 1977. Key 113:44

[16] The Holy Bible. Psalms 51:10.

[17] Eric Pearl. The Reconnection: Heal Others, Heal Yourself. Hay House. 2001.

[18] Name has been changed.

[19] Gifts from the Heart. 11.17.00.

[20] Gifts from the Heart. 11.18.00.

[21] Gifts from the Heart. 9.15.01.

[22] Gifts from the Heart. 11.28.01.

[23] Name has been changed.

[24] Name has been changed.

[25] Gifts from the Heart. 11.29.01.

[26] Gifts from the Heart. 2.01.02.

[27] Gifts from the Heart. 2.02.02.

[28] Gifts from the Heart. 2.10.02.

[29] Gifts from the Heart. 3.29.02.

[30] Gifts from the Heart. 3.29.02.

[31] The Holy Bible. John 4:10.

[32] Gifts from the Heart. 3.29.02.

[33] Gifts from the Heart. 4.21.02.

[34] Gifts from the Heart. 4.27.02.

[35] Lynne McTaggart. "The Field." HarperCollins. New York, NY. 2002.

[36] Gifts from the Heart. 5.04.02.

[37] Gifts from the Heart. 5.10.02.

[38] Gifts from the Heart. 5.11.02.

[39] Gifts from the Heart. 5.22.02.

[40] Name has been changed.

[41] Gifts from the Heart. 6.21.02.

[42] Gifts from the Heart.7.19.02.

[43] Gifts from the Heart. 9.20.02.

[44] Gifts from the Heart. 9.20.02.

[45] Gifts from the Heart. 9.20.02.

[46] Gifts from the Heart. 12.14.02.

[47] Gifts from the Heart. 12.14.02.

[48] Gifts from the Heart. 8.07.02.

[49] Gifts from the Heart. 8.12.02.

[50] Gifts from the Heart. 8.16.02.

[51] Gifts from the Heart. 8.16.02.

[52] Gifts from the Heart. 8.16.02.

[53] Gifts from the Heart. 8.24.02.

[54] Gifts from the Heart. 8.25.02.

[55] Gifts from the Heart. 9.03.02.

[56] Gifts from the Heart. 11.17.02.

[57] Darina Markova. Random Acts of Kindness. Conari. 2002.

[58] In the Garden. Written by C. Austin Miles. The Rodeheaver Co. 1940.

[59] The Holy Bible. I Corinthians 13:12.

[60] At the Feet of the Master.

[61] The Oprah Winfrey Show. November 4, 2002, CNN Report.

[62] Eric Pearl. The Reconnection: Heal Others, Heal Yourself. Hay House. 2001.

[63] Betty Eadie. Embraced by the Light. Gold Leaf Press. 1992.

[64] Gifts from the Heart. 9.12.02.

[65] Gifts from the Heart. 6.21.02.

[66] Gifts from the Heart. 6.21.02.

[67] Gifts from the Heart. 5.11.02.

[68] Gifts from the Heart. 6.21.02.

[69] Gifts from the Heart. 6.21.02.

[70] Gifts from the Heart. 6.21.02.

[71] Gifts from the Heart. 8.16.02.

[72] Name has been changed.

[73] Gifts from the Heart. 9.12.02.

[74] Gifts from the Heart. 9.14.02.

[75] Gifts from the Heart. 9.30.02.

[76] Gifts from the Heart. 12.14.02.

Printed in the United States
1389800001B/28-45